STORMY BEN BUTLER

THE MACMILLAN COMPANY
NEW YORK · CHICAGO
DALLAS · ATLANTA · SAN FRANCISCO
LONDON · MANILA

THE MACMILLAN COMPANY
OF CANADA, LIMITED
TORONTO

(*Mathew Brady Photograph*)

Benjamin F. Butler

Stormy
BEN BUTLER

by Robert S. Holzman, Ph.D.

New York - 1954

THE MACMILLAN COMPANY

ACKNOWLEDGMENTS

PERMISSION to make use of quotations has been graciously extended by the following publishers and authors:

APPLETON-CENTURY-CROFTS, INC., New York City: Mary Boykin Chesnut, *A Diary from Dixie* (copyright 1905, D. Appleton and Company); J. B. Mc-Master, *A History of the People of the United States During Lincoln's Administration* (copyright 1927, John Bach McMaster).

THE BOBBS-MERRILL COMPANY, INC., Indianapolis: Robert S. Henry, *The Story of Reconstruction* (copyright 1938, The Bobbs-Merrill Company, Inc.); Richard S. West, Jr., *Gideon Welles* (copyright 1943, The Bobbs-Merrill Company, Inc.).

UNIVERSITY OF CHICAGO PRESS, Chicago: Frank Lawrence Owsley, *King Cotton Diplomacy* (copyright 1931, University of Chicago Press).

TRUSTEES OF COLBY COLLEGE, Waterville, Maine: Edwin Carey Whittemore, *Colby College* (copyright 1927, Edwin Carey Whittemore).

COLUMBIA UNIVERSITY PRESS, New York City: Harrison Cook Thomas, *The Return of the Democratic Party to Power in 1884* (copyright 1919, Harrison Cook Thomas).

CROWN PUBLISHERS, INC., New York City: Lamont Buchanan, *A Pictorial History of the Confederacy* (copyright 1951, Lamont Buchanan).

THE DIAL PRESS, INC., New York City: Georges Clemenceau, *American Reconstruction* (copyright 1928, The Dial Press, Inc.).

DODD, MEAD & COMPANY, New York City: James G. Randall, *Lincoln The President* (copyright 1945, Dodd, Mead & Company, Inc.); David S. Muzzey, *James G. Blaine* (copyright 1934, Dodd, Mead & Company, Inc.); Allan Nevins, *Hamilton Fish* (copyright 1936, Allan Nevins).

DORRANCE & COMPANY, INC., Philadelphia: Clarence Edward Macartney, *Lincoln and His Generals* (copyright 1925, Dorrance & Company, Inc.).

DOUBLEDAY & COMPANY, INC., New York City: Carl Schurz, *Reminiscences* (copyright 1906, 1907, Carl Schurz).

v

DUKE UNIVERSITY PRESS, Durham, N.C.: Milton E. Flower, *James Parton* (copyright 1951, Duke University Press).

E. P. DUTTON & Co., INC., New York City: Samuel Gompers, *Seventy Years of Life and Labor* (copyright 1925, E. P. Dutton & Co., Inc., and copyright 1952, Mrs. Gertrude Cleaves Gompers).

OTTO EISENSCHIML, Chicago: *Why Was Lincoln Murdered?* (copyright 1937, Otto Eisenschiml).

GEORGETOWN UNIVERSITY PRESS, Washington, D.C.: *John Dooley, Confederate Soldier* (copyright 1945, Georgetown University Press).

HARCOURT, BRACE AND COMPANY, INC., New York City: Lloyd Lewis, *Sherman, Fighting Prophet* (copyright 1932, Harcourt, Brace and Company, Inc.); Carl Sandburg, *Abraham Lincoln: The War Years* (copyright 1936, 1937, Carl Sandburg, and copyright 1939, Harcourt, Brace and Company, Inc.).

HARPER & BROTHERS, New York City: Emanie Sachs, *The Terrible Siren* (copyright 1928, Emanie Sachs); Gamaliel Bradford, *Wives* (copyright 1925, Harper & Brothers); James Harrison Wilson, *The Life of Charles A. Dana* (copyright 1907, Harper & Brothers); Frederick Trevor Hill, *Decisive Battles of the Law* (copyright 1907, Harper & Brothers); Lew Wallace, *Autobiography* (copyright 1906, Harper & Brothers).

CAPTAIN B. H. LIDDELL HART, Buckinghamshire: *Sherman* (copyright 1929, Dodd, Mead and Company, Inc.).

WILLIAM B. HESSELTINE, University of Wisconsin: *U. S. Grant, Politician* (copyright 1935, Dodd, Mead and Company, Inc.).

HOUGHTON MIFFLIN COMPANY, Boston: Gideon Welles, *Diary* (copyright 1911, Edgar T. Welles and Houghton Mifflin Co.); Henry Adams, *The Education of Henry Adams* (copyright 1918, Massachusetts Historical Society); Charles Francis Adams, *An Autobiography* (copyright 1916, Massachusetts Historical Society); Samuel McCall, *Thaddeus Stevens* (copyright 1909, Samuel McCall); Helen Todd, *A Man Named Grant* (copyright 1940, Helen Todd); Allan Nevins (ed.), *Letters of Grover Cleveland* (copyright 1933, Allan Nevins and Frances Folsom Cleveland Preston); Gamaliel Bradford, *Damaged Souls* (copyright 1922, 1923, Harper & Brothers); John Fiske, *The Mississippi Valley in the Civil War* (copyright 1900, John Fiske); Claude G. Bowers, *The Tragic Era* (copyright 1929. Claude G. Bowers).

ILLINOIS STATE HISTORICAL LIBRARY, Springfield: Orville Browning, *Diaries* (copyright 1933, Illinois State Historical Library).

ALFRED A. KNOPF, New York City: Herbert Asbury, *The French Quarter* (copyright 1936, Alfred A. Knopf, Inc.); William B. Hesseltine, *Lincoln and the War Governors* (copyright 1948, Alfred A. Knopf, Inc.).

J. B. LIPPINCOTT COMPANY, Philadelphia: William McFee, *The Law of the Sea* (copyright 1950, William McFee).

LITTLE, BROWN & COMPANY, Boston: Atlantic Monthly Press: Catherine

Drinker Bowen, *Yankee from Olympus* (copyright 1944, Catherine Drinker Bowen); Burton J. Hendrick, *Lincoln's War Cabinet* (copyright 1946, Burton J. Hendrick).

LOUISIANA STATE UNIVERSITY PRESS, Baton Rouge: Willie Caskey, *Secession and Restoration* (copyright 1938, Louisiana State University Press); E. Merton Coulter, *The Confederate States of America* (copyright 1950, Louisiana State University Press and the Littlefield Fund for Southern History —The University of Texas); E. Merton Coulter, *The South During Reconstruction* (copyright 1947, Louisiana State University Press and the Littlefield Fund for Southern History—The University of Texas).

MACRAE SMITH COMPANY, Philadelphia: Ellis Paxson Oberholtzer, *Jay Cooke* (copyright 1907, G. W. Jacobs & Co.).

GEORGE FORT MILTON, Arlington, Virginia: *The Age of Hate* (copyright 1930, Coward-McCann, Inc.); *Conflict* (copyright 1941, George Fort Milton).

JOHN MURRAY, London: J. F. C. Fuller, *Generalship of Ulysses S. Grant* (copyright 1929, Dodd, Mead & Company).

RALPH G. NEWMAN, Chicago: Otto Eisenschiml, co-ed., *The American Iliad* (copyright, 1947, Bobbs-Merrill Company).

UNIVERSITY OF NORTH CAROLINA PRESS, Chapel Hill: Charles H. Ambler, *Francis H. Pierpont* (copyright 1937, University of North Carolina Press); George Townsend, *Rustics In Rebellion* (copyright 1950, University of North Carolina Press).

UNIVERSITY OF PENNSYLVANIA PRESS, Philadelphia: Fred Harvey Harrington, *Fighting Politician* (copyright 1948, American Historical Association).

RINEHART & COMPANY, INC., New York City: Charles E. Russell, *Blaine of Maine* (copyright 1931, Charles E. Russell).

CHARLES SCRIBNER'S SONS, New York City: *Dictionary of American Biography* (copyright 1928, American Council of Learned Societies); George Meade, *Life and Letters* (copyright 1913, Charles Scribner's Sons); Douglas Southall Freeman, *R. E. Lee* (copyright 1935, Charles Scribner's Sons); Douglas Southall Freeman, *Lee's Lieutenants* (copyright 1942–4, Charles Scribner's Sons); E. S. Martin, *Life of Joseph Choate* (copyright 1917, Caroline Sterling Choate and copyright 1920, Charles Scribner's Sons); Charles Minor Blackford (ed.), *Letters from Lee's Army* (copyright 1947, Charles Scribner's Sons); Edward Mitchell, *Memoirs of an Editor* (copyright 1924, Charles Scribner's Sons).

WILLIAM SLOANE ASSOCIATES, INC., New York City: Fletcher Pratt, *Ordeal by Fire* (copyright 1935, Harrison Smith and Robert Haas, Inc., rev. ed., copyright 1948, Fletcher Pratt).

Permission to make use of photographs has been kindly given by the following:

Roy A. Meredith, Philadelphia, has supplied the frontispiece portrait of Butler, from the original Mathew Brady negative that Mr. Meredith now owns.

Dr. Frederick Hill Meserve, New York City, has furnished three Butler photographs "From The Meserve Collection." Mr. Meredith, Dr. Meserve, and the author are fellow charter members of The Civil War Round Table of New York.

Mrs. Joseph Knowles, Wellesley, Massachusetts, has provided the photograph of the Butler home in Lowell.

Of the many libraries used, particular thanks are offered to the Manuscript Division of the Library of Congress, the American History Room of the New York Public Library, and the Rare Book Department of the Boston Public Library.

A very special acknowledgement of appreciation is made to Dr. Ralph B. Flanders of the History Department of New York University for his substantial contributions to the preparation of this work.

TO MY MOTHER

Quod spiro et placeo, si placeo, tuum est.
HORACE, *Odes,* iv, III, 24.

FOREWORD

MANY generations of Americans would have wondered that a writer should have to explain *why* he was presenting a book about Ben Butler. In *his* time the idea of an explanation would have been rather ridiculous. The New York *Tribune* called him "one of the most picturesque characters that ever figured in American history. . . . [H]e was seldom out of sight for any length of time." [1] A New York *Herald* editorial referred to "the remarkable career of a remarkable character." [2] "[H]e was for many years," said the New York *Post*, "one of the most prominent figures in the public eye." [3] Butler, observed the Boston *Globe*, "will assuredly rank among the famous and commanding figures of the nineteenth century. . . . He was, in truth, not merely part of the career of the nation, but in a peculiar sense a real maker of our history." [4]

"It is too bad," wrote a present-day historian, "that Butler has been biographically neglected, for in war as in peace he was a P. T. Barnum character. Gross in body, he was unscrupulously clever in mind and incorrigibly political in purpose." [5] This neglect is history's loss, and literature's; for in the words of the Boston *Globe*, "Soldier, statesman, lawyer, patriot, the career of General Butler reads like a romance." [6]

Butler's peculiar star rose long before the Civil War, but at what was literally the first bloodshed "began one of the most astounding careers of the war. Butler was," continued the *Dictionary of American Biography*, "until Grant took control, as much a news item as any man except Lincoln. He did many things so clever as to be almost brilliant. He moved in a continual atmosphere of con-troversy which gradually widened from local quarrels with Gov. Andrew of Massachusetts until it included most of the governments of the world; in which controversies he was sometimes right. He expected the war to advance his political fortunes and the financial fortunes of his family and friends." [7]

"[I]t is doubtful," noted the New York *Post,* "if he rendered any real military service to the nation, although he managed to keep him-self in evidence more than the generals . . . who took up his bad jobs and carried them to triumphant success." [8] Yet Salmon P. Chase declared of Butler, "There is the fittest man in the United States to be Secretary of War!" [9] A modern historian referred to "Benjamin Butler, a problem on two legs—a classic example of the bartender politician, with one eye and that bleary, two left feet and a genius for getting them into every plate, too important to snub." [10]

"The moralist," declared the New York *Times,* "can find little to commend in the career of Gen. BUTLER, but to the unscrupulous seeker after entertainment his death would be a considerable loss. . . . [H]e was about the most 'picturesque' figure in our public life. He was always bobbing up in the most unexpected places and appear-ing in the most surprising characters, always fighting somebody with great vigor and vindictiveness, and neither giving nor expecting quarter, while his fighting seemed for the most part to be undertaken for its own sake, and without any ulterior intention whatsoever." [11] "His career," thought the New York *Post,* "was one of great restless-ness coupled with considerable smartness and an entire lack of moral sense. He has a place in history, but to the American youth it teaches the not unpleasant lesson of what should be avoided." [12]

Butler was a difficult man to appraise. "His whole career was filled with bitter controversy. He has been the object of more abuse than any other great figure in the war." [13] Yet "every denunciation of Butler can be matched with just as vigorous praise." [14] "Butler is a man it is fashionable to abuse," declared President Grant, "but he is a man who has done the country great service, and who is worthy of its gratitude." [15] The Boston *Weekly Journal* wrote, "He was al-ways arrayed against an army of enemies and was always supported by an army of friends." [16] This military analogy was an apt one, for he was constantly alerted for combat; life was an unceasing battle-ground for him.

That the American scene would have been *duller* without Butler, the following pages will show; whether it would have been *better* without him, the reader must decide for himself.

CONTENTS

ILLUSTRATIONS

STORMY BEN BUTLER

CHAPTER I

THE WAY UP

NO one ever would have suspected that Ben Butler could be so colorful or bizarre a figure as his father, John. After all, Butler *père* not only had been an officer in the War of 1812, but subsequently he had donned the mantle of piracy: he engaged in what might have been called trading in the West Indies, although actually he held a privateer's commission from the great Central American hero Bolívar. It was a great pity (in one sense) that John did not live to see his son Ben's ringing achievements: counsel for both labor and capital, West Point rejectee who became the senior major general in the army,* a Democrat who was the most powerful politico in Republican Massachusetts, a New Englander who was offered a high Confederate post, military administrator who caused simultaneous protests from the world's greatest nations without his leaving the country, poor boy who raised trading with the enemy (and Congressmen) to big business proportions, soldier that the Confederate President proclaimed "an outlaw and common enemy of mankind" while the Federal President was in "abject fear" of him, the man who would have succeeded the assassinated Lincoln but who declined, a sinister figure that Grant feared as a soldier but trusted as a politician. . . .

The Butlers settled on the American scene at an early date. Nicholas Butler arrived from Eastwell, Kent, England, with his wife, Joyce, in 1637.[1] Later Malachi Butler and his wife, Jemima, sailed from England and settled in Windham, Connecticut, about 1720.[2] The first Benjamin Butler in this country was Malachi's son, who was graduated from Harvard College in 1752.[3]

* See footnote, page 251.

The future General Butler could trace his ancestry on both sides to martial characters. His mother was a descendant of Colonel Cilley who at the Battle of Bennington in 1777 commanded a company that never had seen artillery; to allay their fears he sat on a cannon while it was being discharged.[4] His maternal grandfather, Richard Ellison, had fought at the Battle of the Boyne for King William, and his reward enabled him to come to America, where he settled in Londonderry, New Hampshire.[5] His paternal grandfather, Zephaniah Butler, was born in Woodbury, Connecticut, of "a most strictly Irish Presbyterian family"; [6] he was subsequently to participate in Wolfe's attack on Quebec in 1758 as well as in the Revolutionary War.[7] Ben's father, John, was born in Nottingham, New Hampshire, on May 17, 1782. His first wife, Sarah Batchelder, died after bearing him three daughters; two years later he married Charlotte Ellison, who also bore him three children, of whom the third, Benjamin Franklin Butler, was born in Deerfield, Massachusetts, "about four o'clock in the afternoon," as he later recalled. The date was November 5, 1818,[8] celebrated in England as Guy Fawkes Day. It was a symbolic date, this anniversary of what might have been one of history's greatest explosions.

Ben never was acquainted with his father. John Butler had achieved some local prominence in the War of 1812, when he had recruited a company of light dragoons among his neighbors; but an injury sustained while on frontier duty necessitated his discharge. John then went to sea as a privateer, a not unlucrative profession that was punctuated occasionally by government service. On one such occasion he was sent to New Orleans with dispatches for General Jackson; and the much impressed privateer named his first son Andrew Jackson Butler when he was born on February 13, 1815.[9]

After that war, John entered upon trading in the West Indies; and it appears that it was on one of his visits home that Ben was conceived. But John found the Indies more alluring, and it was there that he spent most of his remaining few days. In March, 1819, when Ben was four months old, his father died of yellow fever on the Island of St. Christopher.[10]

Ben was to be touchy on the subject of his father's profession

("... the difference between a pirate and a privateer was academic").[11] "A few evil disposed persons, I have heard, have denounced my father's acts as piracy. The man has never lived who suggested that to me." [12] That was not entirely true, for one "Brick" Pomeroy (whose attacks Butler's literary masterpiece was to admit) had written how John had been "hung in irons from the yard-arm of a vessel off Cadiz, for piracy and murder on the high seas." [13] Even less of a basis of truth was discernible in the New Orleans *Picayune* in May, 1861: "Our readers may recollect old Ben, the barber, who kept a shop in Poydras-street, and emigrated to Liberia with a small competence. Gen. Butler is his son." [14]

Throughout his life Ben was to be sensitive on this subject. In his fifty-fourth year he was still seeking to get the record in order, and his sister compiled a family genealogy for him. "I have wrote it from there old family Bible and some other dates he sent me," she informed him. "I wrote more particulars about father, for the reason that there had been so much said, I thought I would let them know that we knew when he died and where." [15]

In any event, Charlotte Ellison Butler was left "in a state of comparative poverty" [16] upon her husband's death; letters of marque are not transferable, nor did Captain Butler's "business" pay dividends or royalties after his demise. Accordingly, her three children were "farmed out" to relatives for long periods. This presented some problems as to education, and Ben's first schooling was at home, using whatever books were available. A shoemaker lent him *Robinson Crusoe,* but his mother thought that a four-year-old boy had better read the Bible. This situation was resolved when Ben made a deal —the first of many that he was to make: for as many verses as he would learn in the New Testament she would help him to read a stipulated number of pages from Defoe, with whatever explanations were necessary.[17]

As a small boy, Ben saw few other lads. "My reading, thereupon, was almost continuous, scarcely anything but eating and sleeping intervening." His relatives had to conjure up imaginary errands just to get him out of the house.[18] His puny size and delicate health were only logical under the circumstances.

At five, Ben was sent to school at Deerfield Parade, New Hampshire; this community had been named in honor of the slaying of a deer that one Mr. Batchelder thoughtfully had sent to Governor Wentworth at the time when the township's organization petition was under review.[19] Young Butler felt that he had not been a troublesome scholar to his teacher, "except in the way of asking very many questions, and of seeking explanations about matters which I was not infrequently told did not concern me." [20] This was to be a lifetime characteristic.

But school was not so much fun as home reading. He read anything he could get his hands—and eyes—upon. Almanacs and astronomy were early subjects before his seventh birthday, as was history of all periods: Assyrian, Greek, Persian, Roman. American history became his favorite subject, and here his education was generously spiked with the personal recollections of Revolutionary War pensioners of the neighborhood. Ben here acquired his lifelong hatred of the British, and he was taught that the highest achievement to which one could aspire was to get behind a stone wall and shoot down a Redcoat.[21]

His memory was always fabulous. In addition to what he remembered for himself, he flattered his gentle mother by memorizing the Four Gospels, including the opening eighteen verses of the first chapter of Matthew, "where everybody begat everybody else." [22] His religious education was very helpful when, at eight, he was sent to Exeter Academy.[23] To President Benjamin Abbott of the forty-four-year-old school [24] the lad presented a letter of recommendation: "I find him to be a promising youth, and forward scholar for his age, and his age is short of ten years. His talents bid fair for distinguished usefulness could he be favored with the means of obtaining an education. I am informed that he is remarkably steady in his habits, and of a studious turn of mind, and of a fair moral character." [25]

Despite his frail physique and undeveloped body, Ben quickly became a seasoned fighter, with some success.[26] He hit Jo Brindlet with a stick when Jo called him a little cockeyed devil.[27] He perforce was a member of a pugnacious minority, for his father had been a Jef-

fersonian Democrat at a time when this was considered highly un-
fashionable in New Hampshire.[28] There was family honor to be
maintained, as well as one's own face. Thus Ben would reply to
taunts about his family's lack of a crest: " 'Tis true my family had
no coat of arms, but we have the arms." [29] The dogged Pomeroy wrote
that Ben "was known as the dirtiest, sauciest, lyingest child on the
road. . . . He was tricky and wanton, serving in youth as a warning
to other boys. No boy in the country could lie like Ben Butler." [30] But the New York *World* was to report that "There is no
record of any especial display of belligerency during his infancy." [31]

If Ben's religiously inclined mother shuddered at fighting, the
lad got better moral support elsewhere. He was considerably in-
fluenced by his paternal grandmother, with whom he spent much of
his plastic youth. She told him of her Revolutionary War father, of
Indian scalpings not so far distant. She was a robust five-feet-eleven
herself, although not quite so sturdy as her own sister, who at ninety-
nine could still mount a horse unassisted and ride for miles.[32]

By the time Ben was ten, his mother decided to move to a different
community. She was then engaged in running a boardinghouse, but
business could have been much better, perhaps in a growing town.
The persistent Pomeroy declared that this move was necessary because of the son's larcenous career. "His mother was called on at
last to settle for articles taken from the trunks and wagons of her
guests, and thus lost the profits of her business, and removed to
Lowell, Mass., where she opened a respectable boarding house." [33] The
authorized version, however, is that a clergyman-friend built a house
for her in Lowell, thinking that she could grow up with this new
manufacturing community.[34] In 1828 she and her children moved to
the seven-year-old town.[35]

"The origin and growth of Lowell constitute the first instance in
America of the development of a city of the primarily industrial
type, a city which owes its existence to its mills." [36] The community
is at the confluence of the Merrimac and Concord rivers, a region
of numerous waterfalls, some twenty-five miles northwest of Boston.[37] The first cotton mill on the Merrimac River, the Merrimac
Manufacturing Company, began operations on the present site of

the city in 1823,[38] with a capital subscription of $600,000, to be called for as required.[39] Soon other mills were erected by the Hamilton Manufacturing Company, the Lowell Manufacturing Company, and the Middlesex Company.[40] From a manufacturing point of view, Lowell quickly became one of the show places of America.[41] The mills were laid out neatly in rows along riverbanks or canals, but each factory had only one entrance, which was next to the office window of the superintendent. That official watched carefully not only the working conditions of his employees but also their living conditions, especially the boardinghouses.[42]

That Mrs. Butler was permitted to conduct a boardinghouse in Lowell was a proof of her good character and respectability. The mill-owners kept close supervision over such establishments, and no person could be boarded without a superintendent's permission unless the applicant were a millworker. Doors of the house were locked at ten o'clock each evening. Frequent reports had to be rendered to the proper mill superintendent as to the general conduct of each boarder "and whether they are in the habit of attending public worship." One of many rules provided that no boarder "will be allowed to keep swine." [43] A boardinghouse close to Mrs. Butler's was maintained by the mother of Gustavus Vasa Fox, who was to become Lincoln's Assistant Secretary of the Navy.[44]

One occupant of Mrs. Butler's boardinghouse was the Reverend Enoch W. Freeman, and it was generally believed at that time that Ben was intended for the Baptist ministry. But it was not to be. "As Pope sighed, 'How sweet an Ovid was in Murray lost,' so many others lament that a Boanerges of the pulpit was spoiled in Butler." [45]

After the move to Lowell, Ben did not return to Exeter. Instead, he was sent to what was to become the Edson School, under the tutelage of Joshua Merwith, a renowned "knight of the birch." [46] The lad got a job of sorts at Meecham and Mathewson's bookstore,[47] but it was necessary to think of a better job, for which some more advanced schooling was required. To Ben, that meant West Point, which not only provided a fine education without cost, but which could lead to an exciting military career, in the manner of his martial forebears.

Mrs. Butler earnestly tried to get her younger son a West Point appointment; after all, was she not a soldier's widow? Congressman Isaac Hill of New Hampshire replied to her letter that he would gladly render any possible assistance, except that she now lived in the district of Congressman Caleb Cushing of Massachusetts, who doubtless would help her.[48] She wrote to Cushing, but without awaiting his reply she rounded up some character references for West Point. A teacher in the Lowell school said of Ben that "his rank as a scholar, the evidence given of good native talents, and his moral character are such as to entitle him, in my opinion, to the confidence of an enlightened community." [49] His physician wrote:

This may certify that I was present at the birth of Benjamin F. Butler, and that he is eighteen years of age. I am well acquainted with the young man. He is an excellent scholar, a young man of industrious habits and would make, in my opinion, an excellent scholar at West Point Academy. His moral character is good and he is highly respected in this town.[50]

The rector of St. Anne's Church wrote:

This may certify that Mr. Benj. F. Butler is a young gentleman of good moral character so far as I know and believe and that during a residence of several years in this town he has been esteemed as a person of interesting and promising talents.[51]

But Congressman Cushing's eventual reply to Mrs. Butler informed her that there were no vacancies for appointments from his district; in fact, there were other applications already on the waiting list.[52] Ben was horribly disappointed, but this setback taught him something he was never to forget: political influence is the key to many desirable things. He also acquired at this moment a lasting contempt for all those who *had* been to West Point, a reaction that psychologists could easily explain.

Mrs. Butler's spiritual adviser counseled her that this circumstance was all for the best, for West Point was full of freethinkers, and Ben, after all, was to be a clergyman. Should not, rather, a good Baptist college be selected, such as the one at Waterville, Maine? [53] Ben was not so certain, but meanwhile he dutifully went to Waterville College, subsequently to be renamed Colby. He was a smallish youth, infirm in health, fair of complexion, with reddish brown hair. His upper forehead retreated almost like that of a flathead Indian.[54]

Waterville College had been chartered on February 27, 1813, as the Maine Literary and Theological Institution,[55] although it was not formally opened until May, 1818. Three years later the name of Waterville College was adopted.[56] The college population consisted of 175 students when Ben was matriculated.[57] The youths, he found, were disputatious; and as most of them were studying for the clergy the unceasing debates were chiefly on religious subjects. It took Ben only the first year to decide that the church was not for him; he preferred chemistry, particularly alchemy; [58] in his entire adult life, it so happened, he had the ability to turn things to gold. His mother could give him little financial aid, although an uncle helped some, and Ben worked three hours a day at chairmaking,[59] for which the industrial department of the institution paid him thirty cents a day. "In the workshop he made chairs, for which furniture he never had much use, with astonishing rapidity and financial profit." [60] He also had time to become president of the Literary Society.[61]

Ben did not get along too well with the faculty. In geometry class his instructor vouchsafed that Butler did not know anything, which elicited the reply: "Not about that demonstration; but I can tell you a good many things that you don't know." Later Butler added that this "was as true as it was impudent." [62] Ben also argued on the evidences of Christianity with the college president, the Reverend Robert B. Paterson.[63] But it was compulsory chapel that really brought the lad into difficulties. Daily prayer attendance was required, in addition to two Sunday church services; and although absences only cost ten cents, a reduction in scholastic grades was a concomitant of excessive cuts. Ben thereupon drew up a formal petition to Dr. Paterson, asking for relief from chapel. The students were taught, said the petition, that heathen had a better chance of salvation than inhabitants of Christian colleges who neglected their opportunities; [64] hence a religious education seemed only to increase his possibility of damnation. How could his attendance at chapel change the unchangeable that the Calvinistic doctrine described? Furthermore, since not more than one in a hundred Christians could be saved, that meant six for the college population; and as there were nine doctors of divinity there what chance would there be for him, admittedly a graceless soul? [65] Butler was rebuked for irreverence before the entire student body, and apparently his dismissal was seriously considered.[66]

Philosophy was more to Ben's liking, and he literally devoured Wayland's *Moral Philosophy*; in his final examination on the book he recited thirteen pages verbatim.[67]

Toward the close of his junior year, Ben heard the celebrated attorney Jeremiah Mason argue a case in a neighboring county. The lad's mind instantly was made up: he would be a lawyer.[68] But he kept up his interest in physics and chemistry, thinking that they might help him in poison cases.[69]

During Ben's senior year he first felt the shock of the slavery question. On November 9, 1837, Elijah Lovejoy, of the Waterville College Class of 1826, was brutally mobbed in his newspaper office in Alton, Illinois, and his college associates were tremendously affected.[70] An antislavery society had been set up at Waterville four years earlier, after William Lloyd Garrison had lectured there.[71]

The four-year course ended for Ben in 1838, when he was twenty.[72] His final contact with the faculty was as strained as before. In his examination before the trustees by an instructor whom he did not like, he was asked about a speech of Demosthenes: "What is this part of the oration called?" "The peroration, sir." "How do you know it is the peroration?" "Because you told me so, sir." Butler later recalled that this instructor had hoped to be made a professor; and he added gleefully, "Suffice it to say that he did not get the professorship." [73]

When he was graduated, Ben weighed only ninety-seven pounds. An uncle invited him for a sea voyage to recuperate, and the lad eagerly accepted. He brought along a crate of books for the trip, but his skipper scornfully sent the unopened box into the hold.[74] That was more than symbolic; Ben's days of book learning were over. Now he had to work with his own brain and skill.

From his underprivileged childhood and youth, a psychiatrist could have noted certain characteristics that were to shape his adult life: to fight, to hate England, to despise West Point, to appreciate the potentialities of politics, to make money.

When Ben Butler returned to Lowell after his four months' "toughening" voyage, he at once began the study of law. In the manner of that day, he read law in the office of an established attorney, William Smith. Smith also had an office in Boston, where much of his time was spent; and most of his efforts were actually devoted to real-estate work there. As a result, Ben was left pretty much to his own devices. But he threw himself into this assignment with amazing vigor and persistence. He commenced reading law at seven every morning, stopping at noon to eat. Before one o'clock he was back at his books for another five-hour stint, after which he would take time off to eat again. At seven o'clock in the evening he was back in the office, where he would remain until ten. Then he would rent a horse and ride for a few hours, reciting poetry aloud. For two years this schedule was not varied, unless Butler was so engrossed in a problem that he could not leave the office at ten; on occasion he did not call for his horse until midnight. But he made quite a dent in Blackstone's *Commentaries,* Kent's *Commentaries on American Law, Stephens on Pleading,* and the like.[75]

In the September, 1840, term, Ben felt ready to apply for admission to the bar. He applied to Judge Charles Henry Warren of the Court of Common Pleas, who was frankly skeptical: after all, there was a three-year reading time prescribed, and Butler had read for only two years. Furthermore, His Honor felt that Butler's reading list had been woefully small. Then the judge turned to his applicant and observed that he had seen him in court that day. What were the facts of that case? Butler outlined what had taken place; and the judge replied that that was correct and that he had so ruled. To his amazement Butler interrupted, "I thought Your Honor ruled incorrectly." Before Warren could recover, the young man declared that after the verdict he had gone back to his office, studied the point, and found an authority for his thinking in the *English Common Law Reports.* The judge asked him to get the volume. The next day, in open court, Judge Warren recalled the parties of the preceding day, reversed his decision, and directed the jury to bring in a verdict accordingly. On appeal, his corrected verdict was sustained by the Massachusetts Supreme Court.[76]

As a young attorney, Butler worked the eighteen-hour day that he had pursued as a clerk. But he was not too busy to keep the most meticulous records. Apparently he never threw a scrap of paper away. The first of the 277 manuscript boxes of the Benjamin F. Butler papers in the Library of Congress contains a tremendous assortment of leases, quitclaims, assignments, bills of sale, and applications in bankruptcy, most of the documents being in Butler's own handwriting. For several years his only diversion was military exercises with the City Guard, which later became a part of the state militia.[77] He joined as a private, but in time he was to serve in every rank up to the top. The young lawyer apparently enjoyed the military pageantry, and upon one occasion he sent a note calling for his full-dress uniform: "Gauntlet Gloves . . . Full Dress Sword Sash Spurs Cap belt Pompon and *all*." [78]

Butler as a lawyer "almost from the first acquired a marked reputation as a bold, astute and not too scrupulous practitioner." [79] His first clients were factory girls, who felt that they had been wronged by the big manufacturing corporations of Lowell. No one else would handle their petty cases, for two- and three-dollar fees, but Butler accepted all comers.[80] There was plenty of work to be done. No one who worked for a corporation in Lowell could get a job with another without a release (or "pass") from the first one, and an ex-employee who left with an unsettled grievance might find she was blacklisted.[81] The mills worked long hours: thirteen and a half hours a day for six days a week; actually, a fourteen-hour day, with thirty minutes for eating purposes.[82]

After a time the factory girls were so confident of his abilities in their behalf that his good offices were sought in a strike. He advised against such action, pointing out that the girls could be easily replaced; [83] instead, he advised an appeal for relief to the state legislature. He always favored the orderly processes of the law; they were easier to manipulate than was force.[84] Butler's first political action was the result; he sought a ten-hour day for all manufacturing establishments in the state. The indignant mill operators asked how they could function on such a short day, when the Rhode Island and Connecticut mills ran fourteen or fifteen hours daily. "Let Massa-

chusetts set the example of short hours," declared Butler; "her manufacturers are strong enough to do it, and the others will soon be
brought in." He argued that with a shorter day, Massachusetts mills
would get the best employees and could thus produce more per man
hour. But when he spoke of the manufacturers' duty to their fellow
creatures, the operators replied that "our duty is to give the people
as cheap calico as can be made." [85]

By the time that Butler was beginning his law career, the nine
major textile companies in Lowell had about 8,000 employees, who
produced a million yards of fabric weekly.[86] There were about thirty
mills.[87] But these workers took no part in the activities of the New
England Association of Farmers, Mechanics and Other Workingmen, which already had started the general agitation for a ten-hour
work day.[88] By 1842, petitioners from Lowell asked the state legislature for a law that would prevent all manufacturing companies
from employing workers more than ten hours a day, and organizations were formed to work to this end.[89] Working conditions had
changed; no longer were the employees a group of persons who did
not have to work.[90] For the first time foreigners had become a noticeable element in the factory population.[91] Furthermore, the second
generation of millowners had now taken over the mills; and when they
saw how their earnings and capital were jeopardized by competition
they became very hard on their workers.[92]

Butler stumped the state for his ten-hour-day legislation. Although
he was a Democrat, he made a coalition with the Free-Soil party to
present a slate of ten-hour men as candidates for the legislatures.[93]
Nine representatives were elected from Lowell on Election Day
(November 10, 1851), giving the coalition a majority in the House.[94]
But a recount was ordered when 8,000 votes were polled in Butler's
district of 800 voters. Feeling ran very high, and the Hamilton Corporation posted the following sign:

NOTICE.

Whoever, employed by this corporation,
votes the Ben Butler ten-hour ticket
on Monday next, will be discharged.[95]

Butler called a workers' meeting; but when, on his arrival, he found that the hall was so crowded that he could not get to the rostrum, he was picked up and rolled over the heads of the audience, with the result that he landed on the platform in disheveled condition. Though even his political co-workers apparently had deserted him at this juncture,[96] Butler heatedly told the crowd that the Revolutionary War had been a failure if workingmen could be deprived of their freedom and rights by threats of starvation.[97] He cried:

I am no revolutionist. I do not counsel revolution or violent measures; for I do not, *I can not,* believe that the notice posted in the mills was authorized. . . . For tyranny less odious than this, men of Massachusetts, our fathers, cast off their allegiance to the king and plunged into the bloody chaos of revolution; and the directors must know that the sons stand ready to do as their sires have done before them. But if it should prove that this infamous notice *was* authorized, if men are to be deprived even of the enjoyment of the primeval curse, "By the sweat of thy face shalt thou eat thy bread," for exercising the right of an American citizen to vote as their consciences dictate, than WOE TO LOWELL! The place that knows it now shall know it no more forever! To my own house, I, with this hand, will first apply the torch. All I have I consecrate to the flames.[98]

The situation was tense. Many workers thought that the politically potent millowners would contrive to have the militia called out to apply force at once. But Butler knew that was impossible. *He* was now the colonel of the Lowell regiment.[99]

The next day the corporation repudiated its notice; [100] Butler carefully had left a face-saving opening for the company by his hint that the notice must have been unauthorized. And in the recount most of the ten-hour men were elected to the legislature.[101] The legislature passed a compromise 11¼-hour working day.[102] Nevertheless, Butler had made some enemies. The Lowell *Courier* of November 19, 1851, suggested that Butler's inflammatory purpose was to depreciate the stocks of the city's corporations so that the shares could be bought up at bargain prices.[103] One paper declared:

BEN BUTLER. This notorious demagogue and political scoundrel, having swilled three or four extra glasses of liquor, spread himself at whole length in the City Hall last night. . . . The only wonder is that a character so foolish, so grovelling and obscene, can for a moment be admitted into decent society anywhere out of the pale of prostitutes and débauchés.[104]

Butler at once sought an indictment against the publisher, but Judge Hoar, a Whig, said there was no proof that the Ben Butler reference was to Benjamin F. Butler. Yet Butler always settled his accounts. Many years later, when Hoar had become Attorney General under Grant and was nominated for Justice of the Supreme Court, Butler was able to get the Senate to reject him; [105] and when Hoar's brother ran against Butler for the House of Representatives in 1876 the latter won.[106]

Yet Butler was decidedly the winner in *this* contest. Now he was known as a friend of labor, and workingmen would have no other lawyer. He also got important legal work from the major corporations of Lowell. "If I am not for you," he told the millowners, "I shall be against you; and you can take your choice." [107] The choice was not a hard one to make; the corporations found that it was cheaper for them to engage Butler than to let the workers do so.

Butler rose rapidly in the law. He "was a lawyer by profession, but possessed in an eminent degree the peculiarly American quality of ability to adapt himself to any circumstance or duty, with a quick perception to discover and a ready courage to seize opportunities." [108] "He liked audacious surprises," noted one of his most bitter enemies. "He was seldom content to try a simple case in a simple way." [109]

He followed the letter of the law—when it was to his interest. Thus when a pompous city marshal learned that Butler was to defend a man caught in the very act of stealing a key, the official said he would relinquish his commission if Butler could get an acquittal in this larceny case. "Mr. Adams," said the attorney, "I did not expect so large fees for trying this case, but for it I will do my best." Turning to the Court, he declared: "Larceny is the taking of personal property furtively and devoting it to one's own use. . . . The evidence is that the prisoner at the bar took the key out of its proper place in the door, and that is taking real estate, and taking real estate is not larceny." The indictment being faulty, Butler won an acquittal.[110] But at the very next session of the legislature, an act was passed which made the severing of portions of real estate larceny, if there was a felonious intent.[111]

Butler's service to the letter of the law was also evidenced when Lowell passed an ordinance to the effect that all dogs on the street had to be muzzled. His dog was seen thereafter with a muzzle, not on the mouth, but on the tail;[112] yet as the statute had been complied with nothing further could be done.

When the captain of the City Guard brought his third-lieutenant to trial for perjury, the evidence was overwhelming; but Butler won an acquittal by discovering a flaw in the record.[113] On another occasion Butler's defendant-client privately asked his lawyer what he should do after his confession, and Butler merely looked pointedly at an open window, which technical form of escape was quickly utilized.[114]

He was not impressed with "experts"; in fact, Butler was usually the senior expert present. Thus when he was asked by opposing counsel to be more respectful to a witness because he was a Harvard professor, Butler replied: "I am well aware of that. We hung one of them the other day."[115] In challenging expert hostile witnesses, he would confuse them with such questions as, in examining a physician: "State the origin and insertion of all the muscles of the forearm and hand from the elbow to the tips of the fingers," or "Give a list of the names and the positions of all the bones in the body."[116]

Even judges did not awe him. But when, in his early days, Butler spoke of the harsh treatment of Chief Justice Shaw of Massachusetts with counsel, another lawyer observed: "While we have jackals and hyenas at the bar, we want the old lion upon the bench, with one blow of his huge paw to bring their scalps over their eyes."[117] Yet Butler was less easy to put in his place as he gained experience. In one case opposing counsel referred to precedents which Butler declared were erroneous. The judge announced that *he* preferred to err with the ancients rather than to be right with the new notions which were being pressed upon the court. When Butler got a reversal by the Supreme Court, he sent the trial-court judge a copy of the decision, with a

note to the effect that he hoped His Honor would have the pleasure
of knowing that he had "erred with the ancients." [118] Butler must
have known when he wrote this sarcasm that he would practice before
this judge again; but doubtless he felt he could handle the next situation as well.

Butler did not want it to be thought that he won his cases solely by
questionable practices. "I do not mean it should be understood that
I won in all the sharp points I took; far from it, but I took them all
the same and not infrequently won." [119] Apocryphal is the story that
a factory girl had a suit against a corporation for a small sum and
Butler, looking for a piece of property to attach of about equal value
to the claim, attached the water wheel of the mill, with the result that
the machinery could not operate without a court order.[120] The story
proved to be helpful to the reputation of Butler's resourcefulness;
thus he "let" it be told so frequently that, in his later life, he declared
he had a proprietary right to the story.[121]

No one ever denied that Butler was entirely conversant with his
law. "I held that a good point of law in his favor was as much the
property of my client as was a good point of fact, and that I had no
more right to waive one of them than to give up the other." [122] Judge
J. G. Abbott declared that "in one faculty Butler was never excelled,
that was the keeping out and getting in of evidence." [123]

His legal work was characterized by the most laborious thorough-
ness. On August 19, 1841, Congress passed a bankruptcy law. "There
had been no bankrupt law since that of 1800, and I saw that I should,
by studying it, know as much about the new law as anybody and
more, if I examined the decisions under the English bankrupt laws
with more diligence than anybody else. I also reasoned that there
would be a large number of private cases arising under that law. I
therefore gave it most painstaking and exhaustive study, devoting to
it all the time I had and what I could rob from my sleep, in order to
prepare myself in this branch of professional work." [124]

Typical of his exhaustive and thorough work was the case of a
seaman who had contracted scurvy on an East Indiaman. The defendant corporation was represented by Rufus Choate, one of the most
brilliant lawyers of the century; but Butler was never overly im-

pressed by the reputation of others. "The whole of sanitary science and the whole of sanitary law, the narratives of navigators and the usages of navies, reports of parliamentary commissions and diaries of philanthropical investigators, ancient log-books and new treatises of maritime law, the testimony of mariners and the opinions of physicians, all were made tributary to the case. I exhibited to the jury a large map of the world, and taking the log of the ship in my hand, read its daily entries, and as I did so, I marked on the map the ship's course, showing plainly to the eyes of the jury that on four different occasions, while the crew was rolling with scurvy, the ship passed within a few hours' sail of islands, renowned in all those seas for the abundance, the excellence, and the cheapness of their vegetables." He studied gazetteers, atlases, treatises (including one in Latin) on scurvy; and the net result was a verdict for his client.[125]

In connection with insanity cases Butler studied medicine profoundly, and in order to learn the capabilities of iron to resist pressure for an accident case he worked in a machine shop. In connection with a railroad negligence case he learned how to run a locomotive. He often said that an attorney who tried cases on the basis of what his clients told him would be beaten.[126]

Butler's legal work was not only in the lower brackets; his amazing practice included some of the major legal plums. He drew up the specifications for Elias Howe's patent of the sewing machine.[127] At twenty-seven he was admitted to practice before the United States Supreme Court, perhaps the youngest man to have attained that distinction.[128] He argued before that Court in the celebrated case of *United States* v. *John A. Sutter,* representing the defendant, on whose property in California there was first discovered the yellow metal that precipitated the gold rush; Butler was largely successful in a title-validity suit that involved such complexities as the Mexican Law of 1828, the legal requisites of a Mexican grant, and the effect of the Treaty of Guadalupe Hidalgo.[129] He successfully handled personal litigation for President Pierce.[130]

In 1853 he was engaged to try to prevent the proposed annexation of Charlestown by Boston, and he successfully postponed this inevitable event for twenty years.[131] He there argued that the annexa-

tion bill was unconstitutional, as notice of the contemplated action
had not been sufficient. Charlestown's mayor, who had favored the
bill, objected to Butler's course of action and said that it was regular
practice in his town to hold meetings on short notice; "We only gave
a week's notice for our election of Mayor." "I should think," replied
Butler, "they got up their Mayor on short notice." [132] But Butler's
clients had been genuinely worried when they heard that during the
trial he had publicly stated that he was going to bring his dog into
the courtroom, for "I thought that I would show him the chief justice
so as to teach him to growl." The Chief Justice also heard, but ignored, the remark.[133]

After ten years' practice in Lowell, Butler opened an office in
Boston, with a partner in each city. His work schedule then called
for his leaving the Lowell depot at seven in the morning, reaching
Boston shortly after eight, functioning in a Boston court from nine-
thirty till close at five o'clock, dining in Lowell at six-thirty, and
then going to his Lowell office until midnight.[134]

"His professional brethren," said a contemporary account, "and
the public of his own State certainly had no reason to doubt his ability. They say they had every reason to doubt the delicacy of his
moral fibre." [135] As a lawyer, he held his own with such super-
luminaries as Webster, Choate, Curtis, Evarts, and Cushing.[136] A
fellow practitioner declared that Butler tried at least four times as
many cases as any other Massachusetts lawyer.[137] At the start of the
Civil War, he had the most lucrative law practice in New England,
worth at least $18,000 per year,[138] a very respectable figure in those
days.

J. Q. A. Griffen has left this portrait of Butler the Advocate in the
days before the Civil War:

He is earnest and zealous. He compromises nothing. If he feels anger,
he doesn't smother it. . . . And, on the whole, it cannot be doubted that
he is the most skillful lawyer, in many respects, now living in New England, even though Mr. Choate be among that number.

We look down the line and find hardly one whom this young athlete
has not conquered in open forensic encounter. The scalps of Choate, the
distinguished head of the American bar, of Lord, who leads the Essex cir-

cuit without a rival, and Judge Abbott,—among the living,—and of Far-
ley, the sturdiest advocate that Middlesex county has yielded from loins
prolific of lawyers, we have seen dangling from his belt. It detracts
nothing from this eulogy that we are reminded that his triumphs were
from legerdemain rather than from the exercise of the highest faculties
of the intellect. The mind's highest powers find but limited scope for
development in any profession in America,—scarcely any in a large part
of the efforts of a lawyer's life.[139]

But Butler had time to get married. In 1839 he first met the sister
of one of his friends, Sarah Hildreth, a cultured and intellectual
actress.[140] She had been born on August 17, 1816, in Dracut, Massachusetts, the daughter of a physician.[141] In the spring of 1843 Butler
journeyed to Cincinnati, where Miss Hildreth was being starred, and
they became engaged. But she refused to leave the stage until he
"won his spurs" and could make a home for both of them. He *had*
purchased his first land, in Lowell, the preceding year,[142] and in a very
short time he was able to persuade her that he had won his spurs. So
on May 16, 1844, they were married in St. Anne's Church in Lowell
by the Reverend Dr. Edson, the rector,[143] and she retired from her
theatrical career. Thereafter "the one thing that counts in her existence is the love for Benjamin F. Butler, and the longing to have him
love her in return." [144] The Butlers soon were able to live lavishly, as
shrewd investments helped his professional fees,[145] and a stately
house was built in Lowell "on the lofty banks of the tumbling Merrimac." [146] The house, commenced in 1843, derived its form from
Regency models.[147] "Belvidere" they called their home, which was
their headquarters until her death. Here were raised their children:
Paul, born in 1845, who died five years later; Blanche, who was born
in 1847; a second Paul, who was born in 1854; and Ben Israel, who
followed two years later.[148]

Butler felt that no lawyer should go into politics until he had
made some money, so that he would not have to live on politics.[149]
He began work as a Democratic politician at the exact moment he
appeared for the first time in the Lowell Police Court in 1840,[150] and
that autumn he vainly spoke for Van Buren against Harrison.[151] Most
of his early political activities were in vain, as Lowell was a Whig

community, its industry being promised protection by a tariff; and the Whigs made the most of their pre-Hoover slogan of "Two dollars a day and roast beef." [152] Butler none the less maintained his allegiance to Van Buren, and was given the party designation of "Barnburner" in the 1848 campaign.[153] From that year until 1860, he attended every Democratic National Convention as a delegate.[154] Butler began a fruitless series of campaigns for election to the United States Congress, and he followed in the train of an important Massachusetts attorney, Caleb Cushing,[155] who was no more successful in Butler's behalf than he had been in young Ben's efforts to enter West Point.

But Butler was gaining political recognition on his own. At the 1850 Worcester Convention it was noted that he was coming into prominence as a politician. There he supported the Compromise of 1850, including the Fugitive Slave Law.[156] In 1851 he helped to form a coalition of Democrats and Free-Soilers that finally defeated the Whigs, as a result of which he was elected to the Massachusetts legislature the following year.[157] One of his first acts there was to seek financial redress for the Ursuline Convent in Charleston, which had been burned down by an anti-Catholic mob.[158] His efforts were not very successful, but they endeared him to the increasingly large Catholic population of Massachusetts.

In that year, 1852, Butler also was engaged in a bitter political quarrel with John H. Warland, editor of the Lowell *Courier*. The quarrel began when Butler called attention to the editor's facial disfigurements, which he said were attributable to "illicit dealings with the fair, frail, black-eyed Creoles whom he had met while with Gen. Scott in Mexico." Warland replied with invectives of the same type in his newspaper. That did not disturb Butler, but when the editor engaged Benjamin W. Ball to write insults about the new legislator *in verse,* that was too much for Butler, and he appealed to the courts. In February, 1852, the Court of Common Pleas found the defendant guilty of libel.[159] Thereafter Butler endeavored to find means of punishing his detractors without recourse to the law.

As a legislator, Butler's tongue was as biting as in the courtroom; and in displeasure at a ruling of the Speaker, George Bliss, he said audibly, "I should like to knife that old cuss." The remark was widely quoted as a proof of the licentiousness of popular government.[160]

In addition to his Ursuline Convent bill, Butler endeared himself to the large Catholic population by opposing the Native American Know-Nothing party,[161] which was concerned with immigration, naturalization, and the Catholic Church. "Americans," cried the Nativists, "must rule America." [162] The election of Franklin Pierce, a Democrat, in 1852 had led the Whigs and Nativists to think that the foreign-born vote was responsible for the political upset.[163] The Know-Nothing party was especially strong in Massachusetts, where it controlled the state government.[164] Considerable pressure was put on Butler to disband an Irish company in his militia regiment; and when he refused to do so the governor disbanded the entire regiment.[165]

On March 7, 1853, Butler was elected a delegate to the Constitutional Convention on the coalition ticket.[166]

His legal and political work not unnaturally brought him into contact with many of the same persons. By the time that Butler had been practicing law for five years, he was corresponding with the great attorney Rufus Choate,[167] and a few years later he was working with Caleb Cushing on legal matters.[168] Nathaniel Banks wrote him from Washington about Massachusetts patronage,[169] and Senator Charles Sumner discussed Massachusetts nominations with him.[170] Butler's aid was sought in obtaining a senatorial nomination for a candidate, "If it is at all consistent . . ." [171]

At the Democratic National Convention at Cincinnati in 1856, Butler was noted as "a smart Lowell lawyer," [172] and two years later he was elected to the Massachusetts Senate, the only Democrat to be elected.[173] He took a prominent part in the Massachusetts Constitutional Convention, at which twenty-seven different schemes for a system of representation were offered, which were referred to a committee of the twenty-seven sponsors. Observed Butler, "As well refer twenty-seven babies to their twenty-seven mothers to decide which is the prettiest." [174]

In 1859 Butler was a dominating figure in the joint special committee of the Massachusetts legislature that was appointed to consider the judicial system.[175] He was the father of the Act of April 5, 1859, which abolished the Court of Common Pleas and established the Superior Court, and he engineered the bill through the legislature for motives that, said Senator Davis, could not be estimated or fathomed.[176]

In 1859 was the first of Butler's seven campaigns for the governorship of Massachusetts. His acceptance of the Democratic nomination on September 26th declared that the issues most important to the country were the tariff and slavery. Slavery, he declared, existed nowhere by natural right but only because of positive enactment. Yet home matters should be regarded first.

It is ours to awake our fellow citizens to the needs of their own community, now neglected in dreams of false philanthropy or the wrongs of the slave and in futile efforts of interference with the concerns of our neighbors, to rouse the spirit of patriotism, so that we may frown upon all attempts at sectional agitation, from whatever quarter, and thus speedily to bring our beloved Commonwealth in conjunction with the Democratic States of the Union—the proud position which she has not held since she voted for Jefferson.[177]

Yet despite his sudden switch to a protective tariff, Butler could not attract sufficient votes to carry the election. Massachusetts had been foremost in the fight against slavery, and appeasement scarcely had a pleasant sound. The various humanitarian and reform groups that had produced the Abolitionists were largely of Massachusetts origin, and they would not compromise with what they regarded as evil. Butler had not taken a strong enough stand against slavery. And the politically conscious people of the state felt that the best way to woo the Western sections was to present the moral aspect of the issue forthrightly.

CHAPTER II

WAR APPROACHES

IN June, 1860, the Democratic National Convention was held in Charleston, South Carolina. Secession already was a real danger. Erasmus Beach was the delegate of the Douglas Democrats in Massachusetts, and Butler was the delegate of the Breckinridge branch of the party,[1] although there is some reason for believing that Butler's personal choice was Horatio Seymour.[2] But by the time the convention was called to order on April 23, 1860, the Northern Democrats felt that they had to unite on Douglas as their candidate, for no other man could possibly capture the North's support.[3]

Butler thus had instructions to vote for Stephen A. Douglas, but he had his own misgivings: Would the Union stick together under Douglas? As usual, Butler was free with his advice to the other delegates as to how they should vote, and finally Reverdy Johnson of Maryland taunted him as being a Massachusetts man who gave the Democrats advice, even though that state had not supplied a Democratic vote since Jefferson's time. "Comparisons are odious," replied Butler, "but I say that any man in Massachusetts can walk up to the polls and vote as he pleases, without danger of having his head broken by a club." [4] Less than a year later came the first bloodshed of the war, when Massachusetts troops (one of Butler's own regiments, in fact) were mobbed in Baltimore.

Douglas's essential platform was this: Let the people of each territory decide whether they would come into the Union as a free or a slave territory; in case of dispute let the Supreme Court be the arbiter.[5] But Butler, who knew something about how even judges

could change (or be changed) in their thinking, felt that this was un-
realistic,[6] so after seven futile votes for Douglas he decided on his
own initiative to ignore his state's instructions and to switch his vote.
His choice was Jefferson Davis of Mississippi, who, Butler felt, was
sufficiently well regarded both in the North and in the South to serve
as a fine appeasement candidate. In the next fifty ballotings, Butler
firmly voted for Davis as the party candidate for President of the
United States.[7]

The convention broke up heatedly when delegates from seven
Southern states refused to accept a popular-sovereignty plank in its
party platform. After this walkout the remaining delegates adjourned
to Baltimore, where they reconvened on June 18th.[8] It now appeared
certain that Douglas would gain the nomination, and Butler was
completely off the band wagon. He tried to read a statement from
the Massachusetts delegation about its vacillating position, but the
convention chairman repeatedly ruled him out of order. Butler was
not the man to be discouraged by formalisms, so he got up and loudly
read his communication despite the chairman's angry calls to order.[9]
The convention was rapidly disintegrating; some of the Southern
delegates already had walked out, although not in the dramatic manner of the Charleston convention.[10] Butler took this moment to stage
a walkout with the Massachusetts delegation, "upon the ground
that I would not sit in a convention where the African slave trade,
which is piracy by the laws of my country, is approximately advocated." [11] He definitely had changed his position since his advocacy
of the Compromise of 1850, for he now felt that a candidate who
favored letting the people decide on the issue thereby approved of
piracy.

Butler returned to Boston with the unenviable task of explaining
to his party why he had failed to follow its instructions as to espousal
of Douglas; Massachusetts would now be deprived of all Federal
patronage. He had betrayed a definite trust that his state party had
given him.[12] But first he had a case in court, and during both the
morning and afternoon sessions of the trial he wrote out his speech
of explanation for the party, at the same time cross-examining witnesses and conducting his case.[13] That night he went to Huntington

Hall in Lowell, where the Democrats had met to ratify the action of their delegates to the national convention. Butler stepped on the platform, but he was hissed and groaned at. One man got up to move that Butler be declared "not a Democrat." The hoots and jeers were so strong that Butler had to retire. An effigy labeled "Gen. Butler the Traitor" was found suspended upon a tree in the South Common.[14]

On May 15, 1860, Butler did get an opportunity to justify his actions to a Lowell audience, and he declared:

I am quite aware that I am addressing a constituency whose first choice was Judge Douglas. . . . [But] any man, however gifted, however wise, however able, must give way in our hearts when he hinders those principles on which we believe that the future well-being of our country depends.[15]

"The manoeuvres of Benjamin F. Butler . . . served to strengthen the Southern extremists," noted Professor Randall.[16] Butler, in an entirely unofficial capacity but with known political power, talked with Southern leaders and tried to dissuade them from secession. They in turn tried to win him with inducements of office, honors, and even cash.[17]

That branch of the Democratic party that could not accept Douglas then nominated Breckinridge as their candidate for the Presidency. The Massachusetts "Breckinridge Democrats" named Butler as their gubernatorial choice in that state, and he campaigned for governor on a platform condemning the Republican party as "the growth of all ULTRAISMS of recent times."[18] But he polled only 6,000 of the 169,534 votes cast, whereas he had gotten 35,326 of 108,495 votes in the 1859 election as an unqualified Democrat.[19] "You had better come down and live with us," the Southern Breckinridge contingent told Butler; "we will take care of you; we want such men as you are."[20]

After Lincoln's election South Carolina promptly seceded from the Union and sent "commissioners" to represent the state in Washington. Butler visited these commissioners, who told him: "The union is dead. . . . We shall have room for our friends. Come with us." When they assured him that the North would not fight, Butler replied: "The North *will* fight."[21] The Attorney General of the United

States, Jeremiah S. Black, felt that Federal troops could not be used in South Carolina, as secession was legally defensible as a riot, but Butler insisted that it was treason for the President of the United States passively to surrender part of the domain to a foreign nation.[22] He demanded that the Southern commissioners be turned over to a United States marshal, to be indicted by a grand jury, and he offered, as an experienced criminal lawyer, to help the district attorney— without fee.[23] President Buchanan declined. Then the South Carolinians (Barnwell, Adams, and Orr) exclaimed to Butler in horror, "Why, you would not have hanged us, would you?" "No," he replied, "not unless you had been convicted." [24]

Butler then went to see Senator Jefferson Davis of Mississippi, for whose presidential candidacy he had labored so long. Davis declared that his first duty was to his state. "I never afterwards saw him," Butler later wrote, "which was a piece of good fortune to him; for if we had met while I was in command in the United States army, he would have been saved a great deal of the discomfort which he suffered by being confined in prison." [25]

Butler's conversations with the Southern leaders were more intimate than the talks with other Northerners, as the discordant element thought that he was one of them. In consequence, he knew better than most that general secession was coming, and probably war. He went straight to Governor Andrew of Massachusetts and informed him that the state troops might have to enter upon service in the wintertime, whereas drills always had been held in the confines of an armory. "I stated to him, then, that our militia . . . required overcoats." [26] That in itself seemed an innocuous enough statement, but by one of those curious coincidences that were to be found in Butler's career the cloth for these overcoats was furnished by the Middlesex Company of Lowell, in which Butler was one of the largest stockholders.[27] It so happened that Butler's corporation was to profit handsomely from its overcoat contracts. Thus in 1862 the company paid dividends to the extent of 31 per cent; 1863, 45 per cent; 1864, 37½ per cent (plus a 50 per cent stock dividend) ; and 1865, when the war ended in springtime, 27½ per cent.[28]

On April 15, 1861, Secretary of War Cameron sent Governor Andrew a telegram requisitioning 1,500 militiamen. Butler was trying a case when he received word that the Sixth Regiment of his brigade was to report at Faneuil Hall the following day. Butler immediately left court; he had much work to do before Massachusetts' first troops could go forward. He had known Simon Cameron when they were both Democrats; now he wired to this leader of the Pennsylvania Republicans: "You have called for a brigade of Massachusetts troops; why not call for a brigadier-general and staff? I have some hope of being detailed." That night the desired requisition came through.[29] Butler's strategy had been simple: if the troops had been ordered by the regiment, each unit would be commanded by a colonel; but a *brigade* obviously would require a brigadier general to be commander. Of course, there were several seniors to be by-passed, but details did not worry Butler.

Early on the morning of April 16th, Butler went to see James G. Carney, president of the Bank of Mutual Redemption of Boston. Butler realized what had occurred to no one else in those hectic hours: it would take money to get the Massachusetts troops to Washington. And the state had no ready funds at hand. He spoke to the banker with great persuasiveness; after all, Butler's mills were good customers. It was quickly arranged that the bank would advance the state the necessary funds for transporting the troops, without awaiting the necessary legislation; furthermore, the bank would put a condition in its patriotic offer that Butler should command the contingent. No Butler, no loan: it was that easy.[30] Butler then went to see the governor to ask for the command of the troops. Andrew pointed out that there were two other generals greatly senior to Butler; one of them, Edward Pierce, was a veteran political ally of the governor.[31] Pierce, in fact, was pacing in the anteroom at that moment. At that propitious juncture the treasurer of the Commonwealth, Henry K. Oliver, burst into the governor's room to announce that he had just discovered there were no funds available for transportation; the troop movement would have to await action from the legislature. "Governor," exclaimed Butler happily, "I am aware of this condition of things, and I can remedy it." He said that the banks might be persuaded to honor the state's drafts, if the matter were approached properly. For instance, President Carney . . . "Here is his letter." The governor got the idea immediately, but he did not have the luxury of an option. Butler was given the assignment,[32] and Andrew had the job of making explanations to Pierce. Pierce need not have felt that this was a slap at his military prestige, for Butler himself announced that he had gotten this designation because he had caused the Boston banks to bring pressure on Andrew.[33]

Butler did not deem it odd that he should go to the front as a general. Had he not spent many peaceful days in the state militia, which unquestionably was a soldierly body? His logical mind even showed that he was better equipped for command than General in Chief Winfield S. Scott himself, for in the summer of 1860 Butler was the senior officer present at the state militia encampment at Concord, where 6,000 men were present. Scott never had commanded so many men as 6,000. Therefore Butler could regard himself as a more experienced commander.[34]

Massachusetts's new general was widely noted. A regular army lieutenant spoke for all his confrères when he stated that Butler had no military experience at all, never having been at West Point. "He forgot," said the lawyer-general acidly, "that putting an animal into a stable does not make him a horse; that point being better determined by the length of his ears." [35] The constitutional commander in chief of the army, Lincoln, was not dissatisfied with the appointment, for he enjoyed converts for their zeal.[36] As the Abolitionist Wendell Phillips declared, "Butler . . . and a score of such Democrats, by accepting commissions, and flinging their fortunes in with the flag, settled the doubt [as to a war of one party], and saved the Union." [37]

On April 16th, the day of Butler's appointment, governor and general jointly addressed the Massachusetts troops in front of the state house. "While we were speaking to the soldiers," their commander recalled, "the tailors busied themselves in the rear of the regiment, sewing the buttons on the backs of the overcoats of the men." [38] The Third and Sixth regiments were sent by steamer to Fortress Monroe, Virginia; the Eighth, with Butler in immediate command, entrained for Washington by way of New York and Philadelphia.[39] Butler quickly commissioned as a staff officer his brother, Andrew Jackson Butler, who "happened" to be there on a visit from California; brother Andrew also seemed to have had the coincidental advantages that befell Ben.[40] Andrew had spent eleven years in California after the gold rush,[41] and he was a handsome addition to this expedition, with his six-foot-two frame. Admittedly he was not a military man, and when danger threatened he would seize a convenient ax handle.[42]

In New York, Butler's troops were well received, and they checked in at the Astor House and the Metropolitan Hotel.[43] Senator Baker of Oregon was with Butler when his troops cheered their commander; the latter was to remember Baker's words: "All very well, General; for them to cheer you when they go out, but take care of them so that they will cheer you on their return."[44] As Butler's farewell speech to his soldiers was to show, he took care.

The next stop on the advance was Philadelphia, where the citizens "encamped" Butler's troops at the Girard.[45] It was there that the bad news from Baltimore was learned: Butler's advance regiment, the Sixth Massachusetts, had been attacked by a hostile mob in Baltimore. The troops had fired into the crowd. There had been much bloodshed, the first of the war. The journey to Washington could not be made through Baltimore, as the bridges had been fired. Some other route had to be taken.[46]

Butler did not hesitate in his duty to bring his troops to Washington. He set out by ship for Annapolis, which would by-pass Baltimore and land him not too far from the capital. He wired to Governor Andrew of his changed plans, concluding: "If I succeed, success will justify me. If I fail, purity of intention will excuse want of judgment or rashness."[47]

CHAPTER III

BALTIMORE

AFTER various false alarms Butler's little naval expedition finally arrived at Annapolis. Governor Hicks of Maryland sent an envoy with a message begging Butler not to land; tension was so great that the presence of soldiers could only lead to trouble. Butler none the less landed at the Naval Academy, where he saw the old hero of so many naval battles in the War of 1812, the U.S.S. *Constitution*. He immediately ordered the ship to be towed to safety, lest the Confederates capture it; and back home his increasingly large number of enemies gibed, "Butler saves the Constitution." [1]

Commodore Blake, the commandant of the United States Naval Academy, asked Butler what he proposed to do next. "I have no orders," replied the general. "I am carrying on war now on my own hook; I cut loose from my orders when I left Philadelphia." [2] His words were grimly prophetic.

His troops were now landed, but their reception by the Annapolis townsfolk was not friendly. Maryland was officially a still neutral border state, but its sympathies at that time appeared to be pro-South. When shopkeepers refused to sell food to the troops, Butler let it be known that if ordinary means did not serve to procure it there were other measures known to soldiers that would not fail. [3] The shopkeepers quickly decided to *sell* their supplies. But Butler tried to be a friend from the North. When he heard that a Negro insurrection was threatening in Baltimore, he offered Maryland's Governor Hicks his own Massachusetts troops in putting down the revolt. Naturally the Massachusetts governor was furious when he learned how his troops were being offered without his knowledge, but the general calmly noted only that "an unfortunate variance of opinion occurred between Governor Andrew and myself." [4] Andrew had more to say: "I can perceive no reason of military policy why a force summoned to the defence of the Federal Government, at this moment of all others, should be offered or diverted from its immediate duty to help rebels, who stand with arms in their hands, in obstructing its progress toward the city of Washington." [5]

And there was other friction. The Seventh New York Regiment arrived in Annapolis while Butler was planning his expedition to Washington, but Colonel Lefferts showed no eagerness to put his troops under Butler's command. "The trouble with Lefferts appeared to be that he had picked up somewhere a man who had once been at West Point, to accompany him and cosset him in his command." Butler solved that difficulty by assigning companies of Lefferts's regiment to his own commanders, despite the protests of that colonel's military adviser. "That was the first time in carrying on war, that West Point had ever interfered to render my movements abortive, but not the last time by a good deal, as we shall see hereafter. It stirred me then, as it always has stirred me since." [6]

The railroad tracks to Washington had been breached by the Confederates in several places, and the locomotives had been sabotaged. "But Gen. Butler," noted an admiring journalist, "was not a man to be stopped by such impediments." [7] His men repaired the damaged trackage and equipment and with howitzers mounted on flat cars to overawe Southern sympathizers, Butler's men made the trip to the capital.[8] This brigade was the first to "break the siege" of Washington.[9]

On April 27th a new military command, the Department of Annapolis, was created, comprising the country twenty miles on each side of the railroad from Annapolis to Washington. Butler was placed in command.[10] The following day he wrote to his wife: "I am ordered by the War Department to take command of this department of Maryland. A high honor never yet conferred upon a Militia Genl. who had seen no service. *We have won.*" [11] But a military figure he was not, and a British journalist left this contemporary portrait: "He is a stout, middle-aged man, strongly built, with coarse limbs, his features indicative of great shrewdness and craft, his forehead high, the elevation being in some degree due perhaps to the want of hair; with a strong obliquity of vision, which may perhaps have been caused by an injury, as the eyelid hangs with a pendulous droop over the organ." [12]

Maryland was causing the Union leaders considerable concern. Both Lincoln and Scott were convinced that the state could only be drawn into the Northern ranks by moderation and consideration. If the North did not seem too eager to have Maryland, if all possible assurances could be given that Maryland's institutions would not be violated by the Federal army, if no hints of threat or intimidation were made, perhaps Maryland's support could be won. But no more troops were to be sent to Baltimore until such a large army could be assembled that "incidents" would not occur. [13]

"I think no man has won more in ten days than I have," Butler wrote to his wife. [14] He was kept very busy at his desk; his correspondence was tremendous. There were letters about youths who had enlisted without their mothers' approval, about those who were disappointed with their assignments and who delicately hinted at sabotage "unless," about hoped-for commissions, about would-be army purveyors, about laundry services for the troops, about alleged damage by his men, about music that was being dedicated to him. [15] But he thought that his wife would make things more pleasant for him, and he telegraphed her from Annapolis: "I am stationed here. All well. How would you like to come on here and live with me." Lest there be difficulties with prudish censors, he added, *"Your husband,* BUTLER." [16]

From Lowell, his wife wrote to him: "And how do you like this life? Will the glorious excitement more than balance the labour and anxiety? I hope so. One who strives as you do ought to meet his reward somewhere. I do not much like these last lines but I must leave them." [17]

A general who was assigned to Butler later observed:

I saw plainly that he possessed phenomenal activity and persistence of brain-power, and that he considered himself fit to be the leader in all pursuits, callings, professions and occupations of men whether he had studied them or not.[18]

But Butler found too little at Annapolis to satisfy his military ardor. First he obtained permission to change his base of operations to Relay House, which commanded a strategic railroad nine miles west of Baltimore.[19] Arriving there on May 4th, he immediately cast a covetous eye upon Baltimore. In the best cloak-and-dagger tradition he had one of his officers purchase a hand organ and accompanying monkey, thus to stroll through the streets of that city in disguise and learn of the complexion of things.[20] Then, on May 13th, he loaded 1,000 troops into a train, which left Relay House *away* from Baltimore to confuse spies, after which the telegraph wires were cut and the train was reversed for a fast trip to the city. In a driving rainstorm Butler arrived in Baltimore, rushed his troops to a commanding position on Federal Hill,[21] and issued a proclamation that declared: "A detachment of the forces of the Federal government, under my command, have occupied the city of Baltimore for the purpose, among other things, of enforcing respect and obedience to the laws, as well of the state, if requested thereto by the civil authorities, as of the United States laws, which are being violated within its limits by some malignant and traitorous men; and in order to testify the acceptance by the Federal government, of the fact that the city and all the well-intentioned portion of its inhabitants are loyal to the Union and the Constitution, and are to be so regarded and treated by all." [22]

When Butler was notified that Federal Hill might have been mined, he declared: "Well, Captain, there will be one comfort in that; we shall at least get dry." [23] But he did not linger to find out; instead, with three of his staff, Butler rode around the city, "desiring to show the secessionists of Baltimore that I had them fully in hand." [24]

But the general might have got into serious trouble that night. As his scribe wrote:

General Butler does not mount a horse quite in the style of a London guardsman. In mounting before the Gilmore house, across a wide gutter, he had some little difficulty in bestriding his horse, which, a passing traitor observing, gave rise to the report, promptly conveyed to Washington, that the general was drunk that day, in the streets of Baltimore.

Such a misfortune it is to have short legs, with a gutter and a horse to get over.[25]

A journalist-general left this picture of Butler at the time:

I found him clothed in a gorgeous military uniform adorned with rich gold embroidery. His rotund form, his squinting eye, and the peculiar puff of his cheeks made him look a little grotesque. Only a person much more devoid of a sense of humor than I was, would have failed to notice that General Butler thoroughly enjoyed his position of power, which, of course, was new to him, and that he keenly appreciated its theatrical possibilities. . . . While we were conversing, officers entered from time to time to make reports or to ask for orders. Nothing could have been more striking than the air of authority with which the General received them, and the tone of curt peremptoriousness peculiar to the military commander on the stage, with which he expressed his satisfaction, or discontent, and with which he gave his instructions. And, after every such scene, he looked around with a sort of triumphant gaze, as if to assure himself that the bystanders were duly impressed.[26]

Butler's sway over Maryland was now complete and autocratic. When the state legislature was about to meet in Fredericksburg, he declared that if it passed an ordinance of secession he would arrest every last man present. He seized the Annapolis and Elk Ridge Railroad, allegedly to prevent its use for hostile purposes.[27] He took possession of the Great Seal of the state so that no action of the legislature could be legal unless he approved it. He issued passports, arrested suspicious characters,[28] removed the mayor and police chief of Baltimore.[29] He arrested Ross Winans, a member of the Maryland legislature who was a successful and wealthy inventor but who was also a strong pro-secessionist. It was Winans who had armed the Baltimore mob that had mauled Butler's advance regiment.[30] He was the perfect man to cite as an example, Butler decided. "I . . . thought that if such a man, worth $15,000,000, were hanged for treason, it would convince the people of Maryland, at least, that the expedition we were upon was no picnic."[31] To Washington rushed Reverdy Johnson, Maryland's outstanding lawyer and an old political foe of Butler's, and Winans's release was ordered by Lincoln. Butler impotently raged at Johnson, "the rank and bitter secessionist, and worse than the others because he concealed it. . . . How much of Winans's $15,000,000 it cost him, I do not know, but it should have been a very large sum." [32] Later Butler told the Secretary of the Navy that if he, Butler, had not been removed from Baltimore, in forty-eight hours he would have hanged Winans in Union Square to show that he was in earnest.[33]

One of Lincoln's secretaries noted in his diary on April 25th that "General Butler has sent an imploring request to the President to be allowed to bag the whole nest of traitorous Maryland legislators and bring them in triumph here. This the Tycoon, wishing to observe every comity even with a recusant State, forbade." [34]

Only the women of Baltimore successfully defied Butler. They would wear Confederate flags on their bosoms, and assiduously sweep aside shawls or cloaks to reveal their defiance to Federal troops. Some of the Union soldiers learned a form of rebuttal, however: when such a scene took place, they would ceremoniously raise the tails of their coats to reveal small Confederate flags fastened to the seats of their trousers.[35] Butler pondered carefully on the problem of coping with female defiance, and when next he met it, at New Orleans, he knew exactly what to do about it.

To his wife Butler wrote: "You will hear of me before long. 'Either this or upon it,' the Spartan Mother said to her son as she gave him his shield. So say I—I will either bring back my shield as a proud trophy to you, dearest, my own heart's home, or come back upon it with a name which you will not be ashamed to bear and teach our children to love and reverence." [36]

Yet a third alternative seemed about to be realized: that Butler would have his shield taken away by his superiors. His seizure of Baltimore was greeted with consternation in Washington. The aged General Scott feared that the occupation indicated that the United States was overly eager for war.[37] He immediately wired to Butler: "Your hazardous occupation of Baltimore was made without my knowledge, and, of course, without my approbation. It is a godsend that it was without a conflict of arms." [38] At 2:17 the next morning came a message from Scott: "Issue no more proclamations." [39] Butler said that Scott had been angered because *he* wanted to capture

Baltimore himself "by moving great bodies of troops as soon as he thought he had enough to make a sufficient display for a lieutenant-general." [40] The Massachusetts general did not admire Scott; he sadly recalled one order that he had obeyed "with my usual folly in bowing down to 'Fuss and Feathers' . . . with whom I desired to remain on good terms." [41]

On May 16th Butler received Scott's rebuke and strong indication that he was to be superseded. That same evening he was notified by Lincoln that he would be appointed a major general. The commission was signed on May 16th, which made Butler the first major general in the new army, outranked only by some ancient figures from the Mexican War who would shortly be retired. [42]

On the evening of Butler's recall to Washington, he was serenaded by a cheering mob; he was the first Union general to have shown his teeth. Butler happily told the crowd: "Many things in a man's life may be worse than death. So, to a government there may be many things, such as dishonor and disintegration, worse than the shedding of blood." [43]

CHAPTER IV

FORTRESS MONROE

WHEN Butler was offered a major general's commission by Lincoln, the acceptance should have been a simple, straightforward, routine matter. But nothing about Butler was thus constituted. He wanted to be coaxed by the President of the United States.

Indeed, Butler had every reason to anticipate this very thing. General in Chief Scott's removal of Butler from Baltimore might have been a wise military step, but it was bad politics. Both Lincoln and Butler knew better. If Butler took the removal for a rebuff (which it was) and went home to sulk, that would have been very dangerous for Lincoln. He could not afford to spurn the services of such a Democrat [1] and man as Butler. Yet unless Lieutenant General Scott were to be over-ridden, the rebuff stood—unless, of course, Lincoln could offer Butler a better (that is, higher-ranking) post.

Two days after the offer Butler called upon Lincoln. "Mr. President," began Butler, "I doubt whether I ought to accept this commission; the withdrawal of myself and troops from Baltimore is a reproach upon me for what I have done. I have a wife and children largely dependent upon me for their future happiness and station in life. I came here in the hope of doing some good for the country; I have tried my best and have been successful, and yet I am brought to see the army is no place for me."

Lincoln was soothing. "Certainly, General, the administration has done everything to remove any thought of reproach upon you; and I wish very much that you would accept the commission."

"Well, Mr. President, will you allow me to go to my room and consult with the mother of my children before I finally decide?"

"Certainly," replied the President; "you cannot do a better thing." [2]

Mrs. Butler advised acceptance, as otherwise her husband might be unhappy and discontented. He returned to Lincoln with these words: "I will accept the commission, with many thanks to you for your personal kindness. But there is one thing I must say to you, as we don't know each other; That as a Democrat I opposed your election, and did all I could for your opponent; but I shall do no political act, and loyally support your administration so long as I hold your commission; and when I find any act that I cannot support I shall bring your commission back at once, and return it to you."

"That is frank, that is fair," Lincoln replied. "But I want to add one thing: When you see me doing anything that for the good of the country ought not to be done, come and tell me so, and why you think so, and then perhaps you won't have any chance to resign your commission." [3]

The astute Lincoln must have seen through Butler's consummate cleverness: the general offered his loyalty "as long as I hold your commission." Clearly he could never be removed without cost. But the deed was done; and in conclusion Lincoln said, "I guess we both wish we were home trying cases." [4]

Now that his relations with the constitutional commander in chief of the army were settled, Butler doubtless felt he could afford to be generous with the general in chief of the army, Winfield Scott. Scott was then seventy-five years of age, partially disabled from an old wound, and not unnaturally this general who could not take to the field was easily irritable. Butler called upon Scott in a friendly manner, and the old man reacted in the same vein. When he turned over to the younger man his orders to take over his new command, Scott declared: "General, you are very fortunate to be assigned to duty at Fortress Monroe."

The bellicose Butler pricked up his ears in savage expectancy, while Scott slowly continued: "It is just the season for soft-shelled crabs, and hog fish have just come in, and they are the most delicious pan fish you ever ate." [5]

Butler immediately took over his new command. Scott followed his orders with some advice born of experience; the major general was told that "great circumspection is a virtue. In important cases, where time clearly permits, be sure to submit your plans and ask instructions from higher authority. Communicate with me often and fully on all matters important to the service." [6]

Fortress Monroe was a sixty-five-acre field with a low but substantial wall around it, mounting cannon. Within the walls were long barracks, hospitals, a chapel, parade grounds, gardens, and a mansion for the post commander. It was of great strategic importance, commanding the navigable river approaches to Virginia and North Carolina.[7] The commander, now junior to Butler, was the aged Colonel Dimmick, whom Butler found puzzling over a letter: If the ladies of Hampton threw up a battery on the shore of Hampton Creek, opposite the fort, would he fire upon them? He thought he would.[8]

Butler immediately grappled with his more realistic problems. What good was an army without cavalry? The uninhibited commander wrote that "the only four-footed animal I found there, besides the cats, was a small mule which dragged the sling cart, into which were regularly emptied certain necessary vessels in order that their contents might be carried to the seashore." [9] Therefore Butler delegated Andrew, his brother, to go out and purchase some horses. Almost immediately they were commandeered by a high-ranking officer, for Andrew "was not an old campaigner," his brother noted sorrowfully, "and did not know that there were as many horse thieves in the army as there were out of it." [10] But he was to learn—fast.

"Colonel Butler, his [the general's] brother, is a jolly, fat fellow, but very stern when occasion requires," observed one soldier. With remarkable vision, he added, "I think he would be an excellent business man." [11]

And there were always business matters to be discussed. J. F. Whipple, a hat manufacturer of 37 Broadway, New York, offered Butler some caps for his army. "Can you let us have six thousand at your price," asked the general, "giving my quartermaster ten per cent to divide around?" The indignant hatter replied that Butler had mistaken his man, that Whipple's factory could be kept occupied without resorting to that sort of thing. A manufacturer of stoves and kettles reported to Whipple that Butler's quartermaster selected what he wanted and then had the articles billed to Fisher A. Hildreth, the general's brother-in-law, who invoiced them to the army at *his* price.[12]

Toward Scott, Butler remained diplomatic. In requisitioning landing craft, he asked for fifty surf boats "of such construction as the lieutenant-general caused to be prepared for the landing at Vera Cruz [in the distant Mexican War]."[13] But toward everyone else he was properly pugnacious. Secretary of War Cameron, despite past favors, was an especial target, for the Pennsylvania political leader did not stand up well under this savage cross-examination.[14] As to his assignment to Fortress Monroe, Butler demanded of his civilian superior: "What does this mean? Is it a censure upon my action? . . . I am not disposed to be troublesome to you, but I wish this matter might be laid before the President. . . . I desire a personal interview with you and with the President before I accept further service."[15] Actually, Lincoln was thoroughly familiar with Butler's views by this time.

Butler jumped into the details of his command with similar impetuosity. "He had hardly arrived at Fortress Monroe . . . when he began to disorganize the medical service of the hospitals by his favoritism, until the Sanitary Commission had to apply to the President to put a stop to it."[16]

There was no denying that Butler had his favorites. His brother Andrew was a colonel; as aide-de-camp there was a nephew, Lieutenant Butler.[17] On one occasion the general sent his aide to the colonel of a regiment accused of vandalism. "Colonel, Uncle Ben wants you and is going to give you hell," began the lieutenant without preamble. "Who is Uncle Ben?" demanded the colonel. "Why, General Butler!" The colonel refused to be impressed. "Very well, I will attend, but not to 'get hell,' young man. I did not come here for that purpose." Now it was the lieutenant's time to be impressed. "That's right, I like to see men who are not afraid of Uncle Ben."[18]

Other officers who were unimpressed took pains that their commander should not learn of this disrespect. After Butler had intervened in a dispute about rank, one officer said: "I'm d——d if I submit to such treatment if all the lawyers in Massachusetts with stars on their colors [*sic*] were to order me tomorrow."[19] Butler was strict in all matters, and a visiting English journalist observed in the mess hall that "I am not sure the General would not have liked to place a young doctor in close arrest, who suddenly made a dash at the liver wing of a fowl on which the General was bent with eye and fork, and carried it off to his plate." [20]

All army camps of the day were plagued with some drunkenness, and Butler tried to stop the liquor traffic with these appealingly simple words: "In view of the alarming increase in the use of this deleterious article, the general earnestly exhorts all officers and soldiers to use their utmost exertions, both of influence and example, to prevent the wasting effects of this scourge of all armies." [21] But he resented criticism of his soldiers' habits from others. When a clergyman wrote from Astoria, New York, that he had heard one of Butler's soldiers had been drunk for a week, a sign of a demoralized army, the general replied: "No spirituous liquors are permitted to be sold within the lines in my department. . . . I have assumed that the officers chosen and commissioned by the State of New York could be trusted to receive unopened packages from their friends. If in your judgment they can not be so trusted, please apply to the governor, and upon his suggestion I will have the stores and boxes sent to New York officers seized and searched." [22]

But not all the general's correspondence was of such formal type. From the daughter of his arch political foe came a package with this note: "Will you accept this pocket hancckerchief [sic] from a little girl eight years old. You know my father very well. He is Governor Andrew of Massachusetts. With much respect, Bessie L. Andrew." [23]

Soon after Butler's succession to the command, serious military questions awaited his decision. Major Carey of the Confederate army asked whether families of Virginia citizens could have free access to safety through the lines. Butler refused, saying, "The presence of the families of the belligerents is always the best hostage for their good behavior." [24]

A more serious question was the status of runaway Negro slaves who sought refuge in the Federal lines. On the evening of May 24, 1861, Butler was again visited by Major Carey, who asked what was going to be done with Colonel Mallory's three Negro slaves who had surrendered to a Northern picket. Butler replied that he had put the Negroes to work on his fortifications. The major expressed surprise at this, demanding to know how this could be reconciled with Butler's obligation to return fugitive slaves. He should have known better than to try to beat Butler on a point of law. The general replied: "I mean to abide by the decision of Virginia, as expressed in her ordinance of secession passed day before yesterday. I am under no constitutional obligations to a foreign country, which Virginia now claims to be."

"But you say we can't secede, and so you can't consistently detain the Negroes," protested Carey.

"But you say you have seceded: hence you can't consistently claim them. I shall hold them as contraband of war. You were using them against the Government: I propose to use them in favor of it. If, however, Colonel Mallory will come in and take the oath of allegiance to the United States, he shall have his Negroes." [25]

"An epigram abolished slavery in the United States," exclaimed one of Butler's officers in approval.[26] One of the country's greatest parliamentarians was to declare that "General Butler's judgment is justified by the rules of modern warfare, and its application solved a question of policy which otherwise might have been fraught with serious difficulty. In the presence of arms the Fugitive-slave Law became null and void, and the Dred Scott decision was trampled under the iron hoof of war." [27]

A large segment of the Republican party immediately espoused Butler because of his Negro-emancipation policy; here was a Democrat who was the first to effectuate what many Republicans impatiently had been demanding that Lincoln proclaim as a war objective.[28] From Paris, the United States consul wrote that the Democrats long had regarded slavery as a sacred bird, like the Egyptian ibis, not to be attacked. "But I think that delusion has been nearly cured and I shall be surprised if General Butler wastes more time in writing letters to Washington to know what to do with Run-away negroes." [29]

The Postmaster General wrote to Butler that "the question is to come up in the Cabinet to-morrow, and whilst your brother says that old Scott said he intended ordering you to change your actions, the President told me this morning that he has not seen old Lundy [30] as merry since he had known him, as he was this morning at your decision on the fugitive slave question. He called it Butler's fugitive slave law." [31] And the Secretary of War wrote to Butler, "Your action in respect to the negroes who came within your lines from the service of the rebels is approved." [32] There followed the Act of August 6, 1861, which confiscated any slave who had been used for a military purpose against the United States; one of the purposes of this act was to legalize Butler's "contraband" order.[33]

Not all of Butler's acts were on such a grand scale. When his Confederate adversary General Magruder sent a letter to Butler, "Comm'd'g Federal Forces at Fortress Monroe," the Massachusetts general testily replied: "I have the honor to call your attention to my address, 'Benj. F. Butler, Maj. Gen. Commanding the Dept. of Virginia.' You will remember, that my countryman, Gen. George Washington, was a little particular on the subject, and I am sure the omission of a proper address was a mere matter of inadvertence." [34]

But Butler was able to indulge in the militaristic as well as the legalistic side of war. A correspondent of the London *Times* recorded how he was invited to share the general's hospitality: "I own I felt rather uneasy on seeing that he wore a pair of large brass spurs, strapped over white jean brodequens. . . . [Later] the General broke his stirrup leather, and the ponderous brass stirrup fell to the ground; but, albeit a lawyer, he neither lost his seat nor his *sang froid*, and calling out to his orderly 'to pick up his toe plate,' the jean slippers were closely pressed, spurs and all, to the side of his steed, and away we went once more through dust and heat so great I was by no means sorry when we pulled up outside a pretty villa." [35]

The excitement of it all was keenly felt by Mrs. Butler, who was visiting her husband; and to her sister she wrote: "Of course, it was my duty to play the courtier to the people who have it in their power to send troops here and everything else that is wanted! . . . We kept the carriages and horses running, guns firing. . . . A review in the

Fort, into the carriages and away to the boats, to go on board the 'Minnesota,' a vessel of War. Back from there and out to Hampton, two miles outside the Fort for another review." [36]

But the general's sense of modesty was not lost, and he wrote to Brigadier General Pierce that the camp known as Butler should be known henceforth as Camp Hamilton.[37]

Meanwhile Butler was aspiring to conduct war on a higher plane. John La Mountain of Troy, New York, had offered his services as a balloonist to the Federal War Department, and by May 1, 1861, he had submitted a long petition to that Department. Nothing was done.[38] On June 5th Butler, who had heard of the offer, wrote to La Mountain and offered him the position of balloonist. La Mountain jumped at the opportunity and replied that he would leave for Fortress Monroe shortly with two of his balloons.[39] On June 21st he reached New York, but he could find no one willing to give him authority to procure materials for making the necessary gas.[40] Therefore the balloonist went to Washington and managed to see the Secretary of War; but Cameron refused to take any action on the ground that his generals had full authority. "It is for them to say what they think they need." Accordingly, La Mountain listed his needs, amounting to $490. "The Gas Tanks and Pipes would last as long as the war continues." [41] Butler advised Cameron that he was quite willing to procure the necessary materials without Washington red tape. "For myself, I neither love nor fear these Gentlemen drones who loll in the easy chairs of the Ordnance Bureau—and I am quite willing to take issue with them at any time." [42] He notified La Mountain to come to Fortress Monroe.

The balloonist hastened to answer, "Your order is received. I will come on immediately." [43] But another thirteen days elapsed before he packed his equipment aboard the schooner *Arctic*.[44] On the evening of July 25th, La Mountain made some flights from Hampton Roads, but the wind prevented his aircraft from gaining much altitude.[45] The Confederates witnessed the attempt, and Colonel Robert Johnston wrote to Major G. B. Cosby on July 27th, "I forgot to report, in mentioning yesterday's proceedings, that the enemy made two attempts to inspect us in balloons." [46] On July 31st two more successful ascensions were made, one of 400 feet and one of 1,400. La Mountain then made to Butler the first report of aerial reconnaissance ever recorded:

In the rear of the Battery on Sewalls Point—obscured from the water side by trees is a cleared tract úpon which I counted fifty Two tents beside Six bush tents in their rear—I could distinctly see "Tanners Creek" but could not observe any appearance of works progressing in that vicinity— For twenty miles I could trace distinctly the James River but could not discover any movements thereon. From "Pig's Point" I could count about Forty tents I should judge about half a mile in the rear of the Battery—and about opposite from Newport News—And like the tents at Sewalls Point behind a cluster of trees—I could not discover any encampment beyond Newport News or in the direction of Yorktown except about half way from the Bethel Church and Yorktown I could see a small cluster of tents—In Back River I could see nothing but the one sloop I saw in my ascent last week.[47]

On August 10th La Mountain made two flights and attained an altitude of 3,500 feet. He could see not only a number of encampments but also two large warships at Norfolk, preparing to go to sea; and the balloonist sent his commander a diagram.[48]

Butler was delighted with these reports, and he notified Assistant Secretary of War Thomas A. Scott of the intelligence he had gleaned. "La Mountain is a daring and apparently reliable man," he declared, "and thus far I have taken the liberty to encourage his effort." [49]

Butler's active mind also turned to ordnance, and he acquired twelve of the brand-new Gatling guns that had just been produced in Indianapolis.[50] But when he had to go through official channels, his innovations were not so successful. Thus he conceived the idea of a free postal service for his officers, but the Postmaster General would not approve of this "patriotic measure." [51]

The Massachusetts general yearned for a fighting war, which Fortress Monroe apparently could not supply. He obtained plans of Richmond through private sources, and not through Washington, so that the War Department could not know what his intentions were; [52] then he advised that Department that the Southern capital could be captured by way of the James River.[53] Nothing was done, so he decided to launch an attack that he could mount without assistance from Washington.[54] Big Bethel was his target. Thirteen miles below Yorktown, a bend in the Back River was fortified by 1,400 Confederate troops, with a howitzer in battery.[55] It was rumored that the commander of the Southern contingent, Colonel Magruder, had challenged Butler to mortal combat, singly, in the approved manner of chivalry; [56] but the Massachusetts general preferred to make his attack according to the rules of modern warfare, as he understood them. To command his assault column, Butler selected Brigadier General E. W. Pierce, who *should* have commanded the Massachusetts militia at the start of the war; the assignment was "by way of atonement to General Pierce for having taken the place which belonged by seniority to him." [57] At dawn on June 10th, the regiments of Colonels Bendix and Townsend set out on separate roads.[58] "When the troops got out four or five miles to the junction where the regiments were to meet, it being early dawn and the officers being very much scared," Butler reported, "Colonel Bendix mistook the colonels and staff of the other regiment for a body of cavalry, and fired upon them. The fire was returned; and by that performance were . . . lost more men than were lost in the battle." [59] But that was not all. No skirmishers were sent out to look for masked batteries, which opened fire at point-blank range.[60] Butler's men were literally stampeded back to their fortress base,[61] to the chagrin of the major general, who said that "if Pierce had given the order to sit down and take lunch, the enemy would have run away (as is now known they did so) because they would have supposed we had come to stay." [62] Later the Confederates sent word that they had buried with honors the body of the Northern Major Winthrop, the only Union soldier who had displayed "even an approximation to courage," and his watch and other personal effects were returned.[63] Such were the amenities of war in the first stage.

To Major Winthrop's mother, Butler wrote his condolences about her son's "unfortunate expedition." Then he corrected himself. "Nay not so! Too fortunate thus to die doing his duty, his whole duty to his country as a hero and as a patriot. Unfortunate to us only who are left to mourn the loss to ourselves and to our Country." [64]

Big Bethel witnessed the first field-battery shot of the war at a hostile field target.[65] "It was the first step towards emancipation," observed one newspaper, "and the first warning that the soothing system of warfare towards rebellious States so far pursued would be pursued no further." [66] But the setback had been nearly catastrophic: reports of mismanagement at Big Bethel almost cost Butler the confirmation of the Senate upon his commission, and he got through by but two votes.[67] Furthermore, the quartermaster general of the army wrote to Butler:

In the notice of the assault at Big Bethel I see it stated that there was little artillery with the troops on account of the want of horses.

A general commanding an army in the field has a large discretionary power and I think would be able to procure horses for his guns of which I am told there were plenty at Fortress Monroe.[68]

So the Massachusetts general turned savagely upon Brigadier General Pierce, whom he had selected to lead the assault:

Suppose I had told the story as I might have done, where would you have been? . . . An attack in overcoats, a fusillade of small arms upon an unseen enemy with cannon, for some minutes, two Howitzers not brought into action. . . . And then you sign your name to a letter, written by a thief, wherein you are made to say that you retreated for want of ammunition, when two Regiments with 20 Rounds each had not fired a shot, and you brought away 12 Rounds of Artillery Projectiles in your Caissons. How could you do so? and then write to me, claiming to be an honest man, when you admit yourself an imbecile? [69]

The Southerners were delighted with the result of this engagement, and poetry appeared in the Confederate press:

Butler and I went out from camp,
    At Bethel to make Battle,
And then the Southrons whift us back,
    Just like a drove of cattle.
Come throw your swords and muskets down,
    You do not find them handy,
Although the Yankees cannot fight,
    At running they're the dandy. . . .

> To say that Butler will not fight
> Is certainly no scandal,
> For not a trophy he has gained,
> Except an old pump-handle.
> Come throw your swords, etc.[70]

But Butler's spirits were not dampened by adversity. "A vivacious, prying man, this Butler," wrote the London *Times*'s correspondent, "full of bustling life, self-esteem, revelling in the exercise of power." [71] The word "prying" was used advisedly. Butler always had his own secret service. Thus he knew, long before orders, that he would receive no reinforcements. "I had ascertained before, from a private source, that I was not to have any aid before the battle of Bull Run, and that some of my troops were to be withdrawn." [72] After the Federal defeat at Bull Run, four regiments were taken from Butler's army. But that was not all. After two months and twenty-seven days in command, Butler was superseded by the venerable General Wool, a Mexican War hero who had long been living in retirement. The New York *Times*, among others, approved of the change: "The nation was deeply dissatisfied, not to say indignant, at the fact that one of the bravest, as well as one of the most skillful and experienced of American generals, was persistently kept in quiet retreat at Troy, N.Y., while political brigadiers were fretting away the spirit of the army by awkward blunderings upon masked batteries." [73]

"What does it mean?" the Massachusetts general wrote to Postmaster General Blair. "Why this? . . . Is this because General Scott has got over his quarrel with Wool, or is it a move on the part of the President, or is it because my views on the Negro question are not acceptable to the government?" [74] To his wife he wrote:

I have received no word of explanation from the Administration for this move, and I have taken yet no step about it. They have not relieved me, but I suppose expect me to resign. I think there will be a fight at Washington, perhaps ere this reaches you, and its result one way or the other will determine much. . . . I grieve for my country and am sorry to leave her in her extremity, for extremity it is. She may have many a better but no truer soldier than I am.[75]

When Butler was relieved of his command at Fortress Monroe, he was given no other assignments; but as he was not recalled to Washington he stayed at the fortress, with what reactions from Wool no one can imagine.[76] Ultimately Wool gave him the strange assignment of command of whatever troops were outside the fortress.[77] That was too small a contingent to satisfy Butler; but as he suspected he would get no reinforcements through the regular channels he wrote to Senator Wilson to use his influence with the Secretary of War to get men.[78] Butler's friends jumped into action. "I cannot understand why Butler is kept with such reduced forces," the Postmaster General wrote to the Secretary of War.[79]

Butler's friends helped him think he was purposely being kept from the chance to gain victories. The rather sinister Adam Gurowski [80] wrote: "A lightning-like blow dealt from Fortress Monroe on Richmond, putting you in possession of the nest of the Rebellion, transforms you into an irresistible favorite, and a candidate for the presidency. Of course Lincoln . . . will never put you in possession of sufficient means for such a *coup.*" [81] Montgomery Blair, one of Lincoln's own brain trust, suggested a complete Cabinet reorganization (except for the Secretary of the Navy), with Butler to be considered for Secretary of War.[82] Prominent Republicans, like Simon Cameron and Ben Wade, thought that Butler was the ideal standard bearer of the cause.[83]

Butler remained for the time at Fortress Monroe. On July 4th he led a patriotic observance of the day, which was somewhat marred by the unfortunate circumstance that no one could find a copy of the Declaration of Independence when it was most needed for the ceremonies.[84]

The general's troubles were not lessened by the letters he was receiving from his wife at this point. "I know you are too busy to have much thought for us," she wrote, "but yet, sometimes *remember.*" [85] The following day, August 8th, she wrote:

Oh, dearest, have half an hour at night, when you are alone, and let it be sacred to me, to home, and the children. I feel, I know, that you will never fathom all the deep emotion, the yearning sympathy that holds me to you. Beside the fond devotion of a wife, there is still the same responsibility felt by me when you laid your head on my lap, and prayed me to look kindly and lovingly into your face. I saw then what I have since seen in Paul, but not in the other children, peculiarities easily wrought upon, and dangerous from their very simplicity.

Do not disdain this, it is the finest attribute you possess, though it may sometimes leave you open to the designing.[86]

In apparent exasperation he replied: "Why do you write me so much grief and despondency? Our home is not to be broken up or our lives embittered. We are as fortunate as the lot of humanity will admit." [87] Yet he too was homesick, and he wrote, "I would give up my commission to see you if I should not disgrace myself by losing it." [88]

At this time the possibility of an attack upon Fort Hatteras was considered. Wool was too old a man to lead the attack himself, so Butler easily talked himself into the command. Wool, he said, "was an officer in the regular army and I knew would never attempt such an expedition without a great many men with him; it must be a great expedition." [89] To his wife he confided, "Wool is completely taken by me, I think." [90]

On August 26th a joint army-navy expedition set out from Fortress Monroe to attack Forts Hatteras and Clark, which commanded the Hatteras Inlet, on the coast of North Carolina, a place of some importance to the Federal fleet that was attempting to blockade the Atlantic coast.[91] Five warships and two transports comprised the armada, with 800 troops.[92] Butler commanded the army contingent; Flag Officer Stringham, the naval. To his wife the general wrote en route to Fort Hatteras aboard the *Minnesota:* "You see, my dearest wife, that I give you a detailed account of this expedition with my hopes and fears because before this is sent you the affair will be over for 'better or worse.' May it prove so much better as was my fortune when we met on an expedition to the Church together, of which I have never repented, have you?" [93]

The following day, August 28th, the bombardment of the forts began,[94] and after a time 300 Federal troops were landed on an island

north of Fort Hatteras. But the surf boats were damaged in the landing, and the troops were marooned there. Though no provisions had
been provided, and ammunition was wet and useless, resourceful and
hungry officers attacked wild sheep with their swords, and soon meat
was being toasted on bayonets.[95]

Meanwhile the attack on the forts was being pursued by the remaining forces. Butler demanded unconditional surrender of the forts,
while the Confederates offered instead to evacuate; so Butler, to show
his formidable array, "demonstrated" with his transports, and while
so doing both transports went aground. A lesser man might have reduced his terms of surrender; but from his grounded "flagship" Butler insisted upon complete surrender—and got it.[96] On August 29th
the surrender was effected, and 670 prisoners were taken.[97] When
Butler arrived at Fort Hatteras, his first act was to seize the keys to
the powder magazine, to "have a major general's salute fired in honor
of the victory." [98]

In Washington the Assistant Secretary of the Navy declared: "We
have a joke down here on the two late commanders of the 'Hatteras'
expedition, That after the fight they had a foot race North to see
who should get there first and get the most credit." [99] But Butler
had a reason for getting there first; he had been ordered to block up
Hatteras Inlet with two sand-laden schooners that should have been
sunk there. "I had positive orders from Washington," he said, "to
sink the sand vessels. With my usual 'hazardous bravado' I came to
the conclusion to disobey orders and not to sink the vessels. I could
do that with some safety, I thought, provided I got to Washington
and carried the news of the capture myself." [100] He got to Washington first by bribing a locomotive engineer to make the journey without his train of cars; stopping only to pick up the Assistant Secretary
of the Navy, he dashed to the White House. It took fifteen minutes
to arouse a watchman to open the door, which prompted Butler to
exclaim that "if I were on the other side I could have come here
and captured the President and carried him off." [101]

Finally Lincoln arrived in his nightshirt, and a jolly scene ensued.
Butler was to recall this with relish:

Everybody knows how tall Lincoln was, and he seemed very much taller in that garment; and Fox was about five feet nothing. In a few hurried words, without waiting for any forms or ceremonies, Fox communicated the news, and then he and Lincoln fell into each other's arms. That is, Fox put his arms around Lincoln about as high as his hips, and Lincoln reached down over him so that his arms were pretty near the floor apparently, and thus holding each other they flew around the room once or twice, and the night-shirt was considerably agitated. The commanding general [Butler] was entirely overcome by the scene, and lying back on the sofa roared with the most irresistible merriment.

It was the first considerable success that the navy had anything to do with up to that time, or, indeed, the army either, except at Baltimore and Annapolis.[102]

With becoming modesty, Butler forebore to mention who had been the ranking officer at the Baltimore and Annapolis operations.

It is superfluous to add that after that scene nobody censured Butler for deliberately disobeying an order on the battlefield.

CHAPTER V

THE DEPARTMENT OF NEW ENGLAND

BUTLER was now in a quandary militarily: What should he do next? After his ringing victory at Fort Hatteras (two small forts of sand and pine logs surrendered, with a commodore [1]), how could he return to a secondary role at Fortress Monroe? Furthermore, how would he be received by Scott's old confrère General Wool after his deliberate disobedience of orders while under fire? He could not return to Baltimore in the face of the high command's lack of approbation of what he had done there; besides, the Department of Annapolis had passed to the hands of General Nathaniel P. Banks, whose qualifications were unassailable; he was a Republican stalwart who once had been the Speaker of the House of Representatives.[2]

Butler thought about the problem, and finally asked Lincoln for relief to go home. "You have a right to go home, General, for a little rest," spoke the war President hopefully; "but study out another job for yourself." [3]

So the general returned to Lowell for many ovations, accompanied, as he said, "with an enormous quantity of stuffing and feasting." [4] His reception was most flattering. People, he found, "would get in my way to examine me and look me over (and this refers to both sexes). . . . I think I at last came to know what hero worship meant." [5] The government's financier, Jay Cooke, sent an agent up to visit Butler, to see what could be done about "touching the money in stockings and chests in the city of Lowell." [6] The agent reported that "But-

53

ler is a great power in Massachusetts and is a good man to set on fire." [7]

But bond rallies were not enough for Butler. A warrior who once has tasted gunpowder and adulation must have more; and yet, here was a commander who had left his army at Fort Hatteras. A general must have troops. But there were no troops available for Butler. All possible man power was being diverted to the Army of the Potomac, under its new commander George B. McClellan.[8] Therefore the Massachusetts general went to Washington for another of his friendly chats with Lincoln. "Mr. President, when I accepted the commission with which you were kind enough to honor me, I told you that we had disagreed on politics, but that so long as I held the commission I should fully and faithfully sustain all the acts of your administration, and when I felt that I could not do that, I would return the commission. But you asked me to promise to lay before you any matter upon which I disagreed with you, before I took that step. Accordingly I have come here to lay before you your method of carrying on the war as it strikes me, and to put before you what I think must be the result if some change is not made. I can speak freely, because the thing to which I wish to call attention is not your fault but your misfortune, and were it not for that fact it would be deadly to your administration and your cause."

"To what do you refer?" asked Lincoln.

"To the method in which your armies are being raised. I, as you know, had nothing to do with recruiting a single soldier, but I have lately been at home looking into the matter. I find all the good men of your army are Republicans as a rule, or are all scallawags, State prison birds, and other vagabonds, picked up to fill out enlistments. As I told you, I am a Democrat. Now there are no Democrats as privates or subordinate officers going into the war. . . . The Democrats in their localities, not having any confidence in their politics and looking substantially upon the war as a Republican war, are taking no part in it.

"This seems to me to be bad statesmanship. . . . Furthermore, if the present methods of recruiting go on until the election, which is next year, and then you have a million of men or so in the field, you will be short that number of Republican votes because your voters will be in the field. . . ."

"There is meat in that," Lincoln vouchsafed; "but what would you advise me to do?"

"Well, I will begin with myself; I am out of a job. . . . Give me the authority and the money to organize and pay the troops with, and I will go to New England and enlist six to ten thousand men. I will make every officer a Democrat. . . . I won't reject any Republicans that want to be enlisted, but I will have four-fifths of every regiment good, true Democrats. . . . And if I succeed, you had better try it in a good many other States."

"I think you had better do it," the President decided; "draw such an order as you want." So Butler drew up an order, had the Secretary of War sign it, and then had Lincoln countersign.[9]

So Butler went back to Boston to create an army; obviously he could not serve in McClellan's Army of the Potomac, for he out-ranked that commander. But immediately he ran into a snag. Governor Andrew insisted that *he* had the sole right to commission officers in his state, and said he would sign no commissions for men recruited other than by the state. This strained relationship was worsened when Butler wrote a letter to Andrew, referring several times to the governor as "His Excellency"—in quotation marks. Andrew furiously regarded this as sarcasm, and "Butler officers" were refused commissions.[10] "But," wrote one of Butler's persistent admirers, "his indefatigable energy and activity at length triumphed over all impediments."[11] First he got his officers commissioned in other regiments; then he had them transferred to his command.[12] But that was slow work, so Butler went back to Washington and had a new "Department of New England" created, under his command. The six New England states were under his jurisdiction, for recruiting purposes only.[13] But Governor Andrew could no longer over-rule Butler on enlistments, for he now had official War Department status for recruiting.[14]

Andrew then declared that troops raised by Butler in Massachusetts would not be entitled to the aid granted by the legislature to the families of volunteers.[15] Therefore Butler let it be known that families of his enlistees *would* get such aid: if necessary, "I will personally, and from my private means, guarantee to the family of each soldier the aid which ought to be furnished him by his town, to the same extent and amount that the State would be bound to afford other enlisted men." [16] Furthermore, the indomitable Butler even got an order from the War Department that all troops enlisted under his command would get a bounty for joining the colors [17] or else they would get a month's pay in advance, "and," added the general triumphantly, "the governor could not get any such inducement." [18]

When higher authority was needed, Butler did not overlook the Secretary of State, and to William H. Seward he wrote: "Shall I rely upon your friendly intervention if necessary to prevent any orders which shall embarrass me?" [19]

Butler had no difficulty about finding men to fill certain positions. It was very convenient, for one thing, to have his personal physician present amidst war's ardors, and hence he commissioned Dr. Gilman Kimball as Department surgeon. [20] In writing in considerable detail of his staff, Butler limited one paragraph to the terse notation, "My commissary was my brother, of whom I see no occasion to speak further." [21] In one letter he referred to his brother as "Comm. of Subsistence." [22] But this dream never reached fruition; brother Andrew "as chief commissary lent a powerful and dexterous hand to the equipment of the expedition till he . . . was rejected by the senate." [23]

Another dream that was not acted upon was Butler's desire to become commissioned in the regular army rather than in the volunteers. He wrote to Lincoln on November 9, 1861:

Gen. Wool has resigned. Gen. Fremont must. Gen. Scott has retired.

I have an ambition, and I trust a laudable one, to be Major General of the United States Army. Has any body done more to deserve it? No one will do more. May I rely upon you as you have confidence in me to take this matter into consideration?

I will not disgrace the position. I may fail in its duties.

The general then added a sly postscript, "I have made the same suggestion to other of my friends." [24] But Lincoln took no action at that time.

Meanwhile the long-suffering governor writhed; here, at least, his apologist erred in writing that "Governor Andrew never allowed himself to be drawn into a quarrel." [25] On December 21, 1861, he wrote to the two Massachusetts Senators in Washington, Sumner and Wilson, "I am compelled to declare with great reluctance and regret, that the course of proceeding under Major-General Butler in this Commonwealth seems to have been designed and adopted simply to afford means to persons of bad character to make money unscrupulously, and to encourage men whose unfitness had excluded them from any appointment by me to the volunteer militia service, to hope for such appointment over Massachusetts troops from other authority than that of the Executive himself." [26]

When the governor wrote to Butler about two commissions that did not please Andrew, the general replied: "If any grave charge can be substantiated against either of them, I shall be happy to substitute others. I believe however neither of them have ever done anything worse than seducing a mother and making a father wifeless and children motherless, and that you know is no objection to a high military commission in Massachusetts." [27] At length the governor proposed a compromise: he would agree to commission Butler's officers if the War Department would disband the Department of New England and ship Butler off to the seat of the war. [28]

President Lincoln had enough problems without the cares of the Butler-Andrew feud, and he complained, "I am getting mad with the governor and Butler both." [29] But when Andrew personally protested to Lincoln, he was told: "General Butler is cross-eyed; I guess he don't see things the way other people do." [30]

Butler proceeded to recruit his army. Next came the question of its disposition. McClellan wanted the troops as part of his command. [31] Then the Administration in Washington gave consideration to a Southern expedition for Butler's forces. Toward the end of the year, the Attorney General of the United States noted in his diary: "At last, it is given out that Gen. Butler's expedition will go to Ship Island, in the Gulf [of Mexico]. That was not the original destination. But he cannot be sent north of Florida, for Sherman is there, and he being a Maj. Genl., ranks Sherman." [32] The first contingent of

2,500 troops was sent to Ship Island,[33] but the remainder of the soldiers was halted after already aboard ship. The North had become embroiled in a serious dispute with England about the seizure on the high seas of Confederate commissioners Mason and Slidell, and war seemed imminent. With the strong possibility that England might send troops to Canada, it seemed prudent to keep Butler's forces of the Department of New England in their logical locale, to repel invasion or to make one. That was very much to the general's liking. "I can raise fifty thousand additional men in New England alone," he said, "who will follow me into Canada before England can land a single soldier there, and take possession of and hold that province against the combined fleet of Great Britain." [34] Such a war, he felt, could have had a healthy unifying effect upon the entire nation. "If England had attacked us, the vast advantage would have been that it would have made our war a foreign war, in which everybody must have taken part, North and South, who was not a traitor to his country. . . . Canada would not have been in our way at all. Ninety days would have enlisted Irishmen enough to take Canada." [35] But the dispute was settled amicably by December 23rd, and Butler did not get to realize his boyhood ambition of shooting down Redcoats.

By now an objective was found for Butler's army. It was Commander David Dixon Porter who first thought up the idea of a New Orleans assault; and he developed a convenient "sick-leave" to go to Washington with his ideas.[36] The Navy Department liked the theory of a joint expedition, but the question arose as to who should command the troops. Fortunately for Butler, the Assistant Secretary of the Navy, Gustavus Fox, was an old friend. Fox had been raised in Saugus, Massachusetts, not so far from Butler's home, and later he had been agent of the Bay State Mills in Lawrence,[37] which were quite near Butler's mill interests in Lowell. But there was the need of getting high support. "There was but one ear in Washington that was always open to me, the President's," recalled the general. "It so happened [also] that I was a warm friend of Senator Wade, who was Chairman of the Committee on the Conduct of the War." [38] But General McClellan was the most influential military man in the capital at the time, and he did not take to the idea of a Butler expeditionary force. "He did what he could to thwart it." [39] Therefore Butler visited McClellan, and found occasion to mention his friendship with Lincoln and Wade. "I thought as we parted," noted Butler naïvely, "that General McClellan did not seem quite as cordial as when we met." [40] Meanwhile Edwin Stanton had been appointed Secretary of War, on January 13, 1862, and less than a week later Butler had breakfast with him.[41] Then Butler went back to McClellan and laid his cards on the table. To McClellan he said, "General, shall I call on you before or after I call on the President?"

"Better call before," replied "Little Mac," no mean politician himself.[42] And thus Butler got the highly important post of military commander of the New Orleans expedition.

Since the expedition was to be a joint one, the approval of the Navy Department was still necessary. The Secretary of the Navy raised no objection to Butler as army commander, since, Welles said, the general's "energy, activity, and impulsive force might be employed in desultory aquatic and shore duty in concert with the navy." [43] Besides, Welles was a loyal Administration man, and he realized that it might be dangerous to leave Butler in the neighborhood of Washington.[44] As for the naval commander, there was also a personnel problem. The logical choice was Commodore Goldsborough, a crusty old sea dog, but Welles realized that he would not work in harness with a man like Butler.[45] A case might have been made for Commander Porter, the father of the expedition's concept, but he was of too lowly a rank.[46] Furthermore, Porter was too much like Butler in favoring direct action without bothering to consult his immediate superiors, and his superiors had no desire to be by-passed.[47] The choice therefore finally centered upon Farragut, whose abilities seemed even to include the maintenance of satisfactory relations with Butler.[48]

On February 23, 1862, McClellan wrote to Butler: "You are assigned command of the land forces destined to co-operate with the navy in the attack upon New Orleans. . . . Should the navy fail to reduce the works you will land your forces and siege-train, and en-

deavor to breach the works, silence their fire, and carry them by assault." [49] The following day McClellan issued General Orders No. 20,
which created a new "Department of the Gulf," which would "com-
prise all the coast of the Gulf of Mexico west of Pensacola Harbor,
and so much of the Gulf States as may be occupied by the forces
under Major General B. F. Butler, U.S. Volunteers." [50]

But "Little Mac" apparently was not pleased at all by the rising
Butler, for the Massachusetts general's "secret service" reported that
McClellan's chief of staff (and father-in-law) R. B. Marcy said of the
New Orleans project, "I guess we have found a hole to bury this
Yankee elephant in." [51]

The importance of the project was well appreciated by the War Department. When Butler told Stanton, in Lincoln's presence, "I'm going to take New Orleans or you will never see me again," the War
Secretary replied, "Well, you take New Orleans and you shall be
lieutenant-general." [52]

At 9:00 P.M., on February 25th, Butler left Fortress Monroe aboard
the ship aptly named *Mississippi,* a 1,500-ton brig-rigged iron craft,[53]
with 1,600 soldiers aboard and his wife. He had only $75 in gold for
the expedition,[54] but Stanton must have known that Butler himself
had inexhaustible resources. On the morning of the second succeeding day, the ship ran on Frying Pan Shoals, off Cape Fear; and in the
excitement of dropping the anchor the ship's hull was pierced by the
heavy fluke.[55] Only five miles away was the Confederate Fort Macom,
the garrison of which seemed interested in the ship; and lest the
Southerners think that she was a harmless foreign or neutral vessel
Butler at once had a 6-inch gun fired at the fort.[56] But the first ship
to arrive was the U.S.S. *Mt. Vernon* of the Federal blockading fleet,
and Captain O. C. Glisson took most of the soldiers aboard, as well
as Mrs. Butler. The army chaplain asked permission to leave with
the others, but Butler replied: "The devil you do! Look here, chaplain, the government has trusted the bodies of fifteen hundred of its
soldiers to my care, and their souls to your care, and if your prayers
are ever going to be of any use it will be about now, as it looks to
me." [57] Ultimately the ship got afloat and was towed to Port Royal
for repairs.[58] When the *Mississippi* finally got under way again, she

once more struck a shoal. Butler ordered a court of inquiry in the best army style, deposed the captain, and placed him under arrest.[59] "The general, in effect, took command of the ship." [60] It is not recorded whether Butler also took over the duties of the army chaplain, who had resigned his commission in the meantime.[61]

CHAPTER VI

THE FIGHT FOR
NEW ORLEANS

ON March 23, 1862, Butler's ship arrived at its destination, Ship Island, in the Gulf of Mexico, but for two days no landing was possible in the face of a raging gale. Thirty days after the *Mississippi* had cleared Hampton Roads, the seasick soldiers felt the earth again; [1] it had taken Farragut only eighteen days to make the same trip. [2] Ship Island was situated about fifteen miles from the north coast of the Gulf of Mexico, forming Mississippi Sound. It was seven miles long, less than a mile wide, some sixty-five miles from New Orleans. [3] There was not a house on the island, and the soldiers were miserable in the intense heat, amidst disheartening flies and rumors. It was understood that the attack would take place in a week, and meanwhile the soldiers could reflect upon the fact that the Wellingtonian heroes of the British General Pakenham had not been able to capture New Orleans in 1815, even though the city had been defended only by weak militia at that time. [4]

Butler's forces consisted of 15,255 men, chiefly his own New England recruits, together with the well seasoned 21st Indiana, 4th Wisconsin, and 6th Michigan regiments. [5] Numerically, his command consisted of 14,400 infantry troops, 275 cavalry, and 580 artillery. [6] His objective was to participate in the assault upon New Orleans and to hold the city when it had been taken. In the words of this country's greatest naval strategist:

62

It was . . . to be a purely naval attack. . . . The works to be passed— the seaward defenses of New Orleans—, Fort Jackson and St. Philip— were powerful fortifications; but they were ultimately dependent upon the city, ninety miles above them, for a support which could come only by the river. A fleet anchored above the forts lay across their only line of communication, and when thus isolated, their fall became only a ques- tion of time. The work proposed to the United States Navy was, there- fore, to turn the forts by passing their fire, seize their line of communica- tions—the upper river—and their base, New Orleans, and then to give over the latter to the army, which engaged to furnish a force sufficient to hold the conquest.[7]

It was recognized that the role of the military would be secondary; the expedition was made, said General Sherman, "with the cooperat- ing army of General Butler." [8]

At first Butler did cooperate with the navy in a handsome manner. When Flag Officer Farragut mentioned that he was low on medical supplies, Butler offered to share his store.[9] When Farragut found that only soft coal was obtainable, whereas he wanted anthracite for his ships, Butler agreed to turn over a large supply of anthracite to the navy; the Massachusetts businessman knew that he would have to return his troop ships in ballast, and for that purpose he had pur- chased a goodly quantity of hard coal, in anticipation of a price ad- vance. Now, he said, he would use some other form of ballast for the returning unladen troop ships. Farragut was eager to get the coal, but he questioned whether a transfer by the army was not contrary to regulations. "I never read the army regulations," said Butler, "and what is more, I shan't, and then I shall never know I am doing any- thing against them." [10]

The commanders, therefore, laid their plans in an originally har- monious state. New Orleans was the largest and wealthiest city in the Confederacy, and its capture was of first-rate importance, both psy- chologically and materially. But first there were the forts. The larger one was Fort Jackson, with twenty-seven cannon above the 32- pounder size and twenty-five smaller pieces, together with a water battery of six heavy cannon. Nearly opposite was Fort St. Philip, with forty-two guns. They were located at Plaquemine Bend, twenty miles above the Head of the Passes, where the main streams of the Mississippi divide into several passes or channels.[11] In addition, the Confederates had some fifteen gunboats, a huge ironclad (the *Louisiana*), that was nearly complete, and fire rafts for use against the Union wooden ships.[12] The Federal fleet consisted of forty-seven armed vessels, including eight large steam sloops, seventeen steam gunboats, two sailing sloops, and twenty-one mortar schooners that could hurl a 215-pound shell three miles.[13] Under the plan, Porter was to bombard the forts with his mortars until the defenses had been crushed or at least weakened, after which Farragut would run the gantlet with his vessels. If necessary, Butler would assault the unprotected rear of Fort St. Philip, which had no defenses since the swampland there had been deemed impassable. But one of Butler's officers, Lieutenant Weitzel, was certain that the swamps were usable; he had hunted ducks there when he had worked on the building of the fort.[14]

Butler was so busy with his preparations that he almost lost sight of his battle on the home front. Soon it became apparent that the necessary food and supplies were not arriving, despite orders that he had left with his quartermaster and commissary in Boston. The true nature of things was revealed when Butler's brother, Andrew, arrived in a sailing vessel. Governor Andrew had revoked the commissions of Butler's rear-echelon officers, and the supplies therefore had not been purchased.[15]

By April 17th the fleet was in battle array, and the battle itself began the following day. Porter's mortar boats poured a furious stream of shells upon the forts, which showed no sign of weakening; [16] each vessel fired one shell every ten minutes.[17] Butler ordered 6,000 of his troops into small vessels, which on April 26th were towed to Sable Island, twelve miles to the rear of Fort St. Philip.[18] He had been watching the engagement from a transport, and he moved his troops when the way seemed clear, without awaiting word from Farragut.[19] His troops began their advance on the fort from the three land sides, while Porter, on the water side, was demanding the surrender of the garrison. The Confederate officers refused to surrender, but large numbers of the garrison slipped out through the rear, where they surrendered to Butler's advance units.[20] By midnight virtually the entire garrison had mutinied and escaped to surrender to Butler's men in the swamps to the rear of the fort; at the same time the officers were formally surrendering to Porter.[21] Who had captured the fort? Butler felt that he had been the senior officer present. After all, most of Porter's ships were twenty-five miles away at the time,[22] and it was Butler's men who received the surrender of 250 men that had fled from Fort Jackson.[23]

Butler felt that it was very unmilitary for Farragut to steam past forts that had not been reduced, and he was particularly distressed that Porter had accepted the surrender of *military* officers in the forts; after all, that was a matter for the army, which was braving the perils of the swamps. But the general had no ships to use in approaching the forts; [24] the New York ferry boat that he had been using as his flagship unfortunately had gone aground.[25] "Pray be more careful," Mrs. Butler wrote her husband from Ship Island. "Not when there is a real necessity; but do not expose yourself and others merely to show your *contempt* of danger." [26]

Now began the celebrated Butler-Porter feud that was to last almost thirty years, until the latter's death. The general referred to Porter's contribution to the ultimate victory as "that superbly useless bombardment" which served only to waste eight days' time.[27] Furthermore, how could Porter claim that *he* had captured the forts, when none of his ships even had fired at a fort for three days prior to their surrender? He accused Porter of having given too lenient terms of surrender and of having behaved "untruthfully and villainously" in the whole transaction.[28] Butler was a more worldly man than Porter (who was no slouch himself), and the general got the ear of the newspaper correspondents. The sea dog was furious when he read the New York *Herald*'s account, and he dashed off a letter to the Assistant Secretary of the Navy: "*Butler* did it all!!! So I see it stated by that blackguard reporter of the *Herald*." He recommended a Departmental order "that no reporter should be allowed on board of our ships under any circumstances." [29] That would have been playing directly into Butler's hands.

The fact is, Butler "took" New Orleans without striking a blow.

Six days before Butler reached the city, Farragut reported to Welles from his flagship off New Orleans: "In conclusion, I hope I have done all I proposed to do, which was to take the city of New Orleans; and I will now, in conjunction with the Army, General Butler, reduce the forts, and take care of the outlet from the west." [30] To his superior, the Secretary of War, Butler wrote: "I find the city under the dominion of the mob. They have insulted our flag, torn it down with indignity. This outrage will be punished in such manner as in my judgment will caution both the perpetrators and abettors of the act, so that they shall fear the *stripes* if they do not reverence the stars of our banner." [31]

On May 1st Farragut turned over command of New Orleans to Butler,[32] who arrived that day on the *Mississippi* with his wife.[33] For several hours the transports were held just off shore, while patriotic secessionists shouted insults. An eyewitness noted: "There was a perfect *rush* to see this awful representative of human authority. . . . It was a scene which will not soon be forgotten; all seemed to be fearful that it would be the only chance they might have of seeing 'Picayune Butler.' " [34]

Toward nightfall the troops were disembarked by gangplank at the foot of Canal Street, to face an angry mob,[35] while the general observed, "None of my troops up to this time had ever received or given a hostile shot." [36] But he ordered his men to pay no attention to insults and to reply to no taunts.[37] Behind a drum corps of the 31st Massachusetts Regiment, Butler and his staff marched to the customhouse. "The general, not having a musical ear," wrote his apologist, "was observed to be chiefly anxious upon the point of keeping step to the music—a feat that had never become easy to him." [38] The band played "The Star-Spangled Banner," [39] though the crowd urged it to play "Picayune Butler," a popular Confederate tune.[40]

The crowd became emboldened as the march progressed. "You'll never see home again!" one man shouted at Butler. "Yellow fever will have you before long!" [41] One observer recorded: "As soon . . . as they saw Butler, and the triumphant and pompous strut of the Yankees, and heard the music, the indignation of the *canaille* knew no bounds; they knew no language too gross to accost him with;

the newsboy's screams were music to *their* tongues; every epithet, which could be applied to the vilest, was heaped upon him, and this only ended when he was safely ensconced in the Custom-house." [42]

In time the procession reached the customhouse, where Butler was to make his headquarters; he had to force the doors to gain entry. [43] For the first night he selected the St. Charles Hotel, and a howitzer was mounted on each street corner as Mrs. Butler was conveyed there in a carriage. [44]

Butler immediately issued a lengthy proclamation. All persons who were well disposed toward the United States should renew their oaths of allegiance, and their property would be safeguarded; those still holding allegiance to the Confederacy would be treated as enemies. [45] Confederate notes could still circulate "so long as any one will be inconsiderate enough to receive them, until further orders." All assemblages were forbidden. [46] The New Orleans *True Delta* was ordered to print the proclamation, and when the proprietors refused the newspaper was suspended. [47] By a fortunate circumstance Butler *chanced* to have with him Captain John Clark, editor of the Boston *Courier,* who subsequently was given the assignment of publishing the paper. [48]

The following day, May 2nd, Butler sent for Mayor Monroe. Their conversation was interrupted by the roars of a mob outside, and one stentorian voice could be heard screaming: "Where's old Butler? Let him show himself; let him come out here if he dare!" The general, cap in hand, stepped out on a balcony. "Who calls me? I am here!" [49] The mayor seized upon the incident as a proof that Butler should withdraw from the city with his troops, as otherwise order could not be maintained. When Monroe said that order could not be maintained, Butler stared. Then, as he was to recall, things began to happen at precisely the right time:

Just at that moment a wonderful noise directed my attention up St. Charles Street. . . . The Sixth Maine battery . . . under Captain Thompson, had been encamped in Tivoli Circle. St. Charles Street, down which the battery was coming, was at that time paved with foot square granite blocks, which were in a very uneven condition. Thompson was one of the most dare-devil furious riders I ever saw, and he was leading his battery down the street as if there were nobody in it, every horse driven at the fullest speed and the bugles sounding the charge. No one who had not seen such a charge can imagine the terrible noise and clamor it makes, the cannoneers clinging to their seats, and the wheels of the guns bounding up inches as they thunder over the uneven stones.[50]

There was no more talk about how order could be maintained.

The mayor and his delegation then asked Butler for considerate treatment, as New Orleans was not a captured city. The general interrupted them:

New Orleans *is* a conquered city: else how did we get here, and why are we here? Did you open your arms and bid us welcome? Would you not expel us if you could? . . . I therefore proclaim martial law. . . . I warn you that if a shot is fired from any house, it will never again shelter a mortal head, and if I can discover the perpetrator of the deed, the place that knows him now shall know him no more forever.[51]

That evening Butler drove from his hotel to the river, a distance of about a mile, with no escort except a single orderly.[52] No one ever questioned the general's courage.

CHAPTER VII

THE FIGHT IN
NEW ORLEANS, I

BUTLER had occupied New Orleans, a city of 168,000 population, with 2,500 troops.[1] He adjudged that his first job would be to establish proper respect for the flag.

After Farragut's capture of the city, but before Butler had arrived on the scene, William B. Mumford, a professional gambler, had torn the United States flag from the Mint. That was not all; he had dragged the flag through the streets and then had torn it to tatters.[2] Butler had read of this deed in the local newspaper prior to his own arrival, and he promised then and there that he would hang the fellow; later he recalled that "in such matters I always keep my intention."[3] Nor did Mumford give Butler a chance to let the matter pass. He openly boasted of the episode in front of Butler's headquarters and dared the Federals to arrest him. He was obliged. After his arrest he was sentenced to be hanged; but Mumford now boasted that Butler would never dare to have him executed. On June 7th the general signed Mumford's death warrant.[4]

Butler now was deluged with entreaties to spare the gambler's life. Mumford was a handsome man of forty-two, tall and black-bearded,[5] and his bravery (or rashness) had endeared him to the entire community. Mumford's wife even sought the intervention of Mrs. Butler.[6] A prominent clergyman also sought to intervene. With tears in his eyes, the eighty-year-old Dr. Mercer pleaded: "Give me this man's

life, General. It is but a scratch of your pen." "True," replied Butler;
"but a scratch of my pen could burn New Orleans. I could as soon
do the one as the other. I think one would be as wrong as the other." [7]
Despite pleas and threatening letters, Mumford was hanged in front
of the Mint, in accordance with the Spanish custom of meting out
justice at the scene of the crime.[8]

Back North to General Dix, Butler sent a Federal flag that had
been recaptured from Confederate sympathizers, for the Massachusetts general had been much impressed by the patriotic sentiment
that Dix had uttered at the start of the war: "If any one attempts
to tear down a United States flag, shoot him on the spot!" [9]

A New Orleans bookseller placed in the window of his store a
skeleton labeled "Chickahominy," a place where numerous Union
soldiers had been slain; and he was sentenced to two years' confine-
ment at Ship Island because his deed had been "to bring the authority
of the United States and our army into contempt." [10] When a merchant refused to sell shoes to a Federal soldier, the provost marshal
erected a red flag over the store and sold all of the stock at auction.[11]
Shopkeepers who refused to open their stores were fined $100, and the
same fine was imposed upon dealers who kept their doors partially
shut as a token gesture.[12] A contractor who refused to do work for
the army was imprisoned on bread and water till he agreed to perform the job.[13] The equestrian statue of General Jackson had borne
no inscription on its base until Butler ordered Jackson's own words
to be carved on the granite: "The Union Must and Shall Be Pre-
served." [14] A woman who had laughed when the funeral cortege of a
Federal officer passed her residence was sentenced to two years at
Ship Island.[15] A woman who wore a Confederate flag upon her person was sent to the same place of imprisonment for an indeterminate
sentence.[16]

But such examples of firmness did restore the city to firm discipline, even though Butler used methods of military occupation "which
had been obsolete for several centuries." [17] Mrs. Butler wrote home
to her sister, "I think Mr. Butler would rejoice at some demonstration from a mob that he might sweep the streets, and make these
people feel that there is a power here to sustain or crush them ac-

cording as they merit protection from the government or deserve punishment for their traitorous deeds." [18]

The city's finances drew Butler's prompt attention. On May 16th he ordered the suspension of the circulation of all Confederate bills and notes, on peril of confiscation, "one-fourth thereof to go to the informer." [19] The banks then notified their depositors that all deposits of Confederate currency had to be withdrawn prior to the effective date of the order, May 27th, whereupon the general immediately ordered that the banks pay out no more Confederate paper to depositors or creditors; the banks, he felt, should not pass along any loss resulting from the worthlessness of their Confederate currency, for "They have invested the savings of labor and the pittance of the widow in this paper." [20] The Bank of Louisiana objected, saying that such a decree would force them to close, as they had no specie. Would Butler appoint a committee to see if there was really anything amiss in the conduct of their affairs? The general replied: "With the mismanagement, or the contrary of the bank, I have nothing to do, except so far as either affects the interest of the United States. The assigned reason for this examination, that 'the integrity and good faith of the directors has been impugned,' will not move me. . . . [The directors] took this immense wealth from its legal place of deposit, and sent it flying over the country in company with fugitive property burners, among the masses of a disorganized, retreating, and starving army, whence it is more than likely never to return." [21]

A depositor of Confederate currency when it *was* money now demanded that the bank pay back his deposit in something that was money at the time of withdrawal. The bank refused, offering only Confederate currency, and the depositor sued. The provost court found against the bank, and Butler affirmed the finding: "The bank says the court has made an order which takes away the property of the bank, and gives it to another, and that the court has no power so to act. But is that so? Is it not the commanding general's order which does that of which complaint is made? The bank nowhere complains that the general has not the power to make such an order. . . . The other objection, as to the merits of the decision, can, it seems to me, be disposed of in a word. If the order is a proper one, it must be obeyed. Its propriety can not be discussed by me. . . . Let it stand." [22]

Butler's order of June 2nd called for all Confederate property to be turned over to him. The Citizens' Bank wrote that it had a Confederate Government deposit of $219,090.94; it also had a larger amount of Confederate treasury notes, and it proposed to net the two. "This," replied Butler, "can not be permitted. . . . Confederate States treasury notes are not due till six months after the conclusion of a treaty of peace between the Confederate States and the United States. When that time comes it will be in season to set off such claims. . . . The respectability of the source from which the claim of the bank proceeds alone saves it from ridicule." [23]

Then there was the problem of poor relief. The retreating Southern army had carried away much of the available food supplies; [24] likewise, 15,000 bales of cotton had been burned and millions of dollars' worth of other property.[25] Where would the poor obtain the necessities of life? Butler ordered the city officials to hire the needy to clean up the streets and other public places, in return for $0.50 per day and regular army rations.[26] Later he increased the pay to $1.00 per day. The city council passed a resolution stating that "when the city had had control of its affairs it paid one dollar and a half a day to its laborers; but since the United States had taken charge of the city, it proposed to pay only a dollar a day." Butler noted that "in administering the affairs of the city, to be paid for by its tax, I thought I ought to be economical; but as that was to be paid for by taxation of the city, and the city government wanted to pay fifty cents more, I would raise the price to one dollar and fifty cents, although plenty of good labor had been employed at a dollar a day." [27]

Then Butler devised his own startlingly original plan of poor relief:

Those who have brought upon the city this stagnation of business, this desolation of the hearthstone, this starvation of the poor and helpless should, as far as they may be able, relieve these distresses.

There are two classes whom it would seem peculiarly fit should at first contribute. First, those individuals and corporations who have aided the Rebellion with their means; and, second, those who have endeavored to destroy the commercial prosperity of the city, upon which the welfare of its inhabitants depend.

Subscriptions amounting to $1,250,000 had been made to raise money for treasonable purposes of defending the city against the Government of the United States, continued Butler, and the names and amounts subscribed were listed on Schedule A. Schedule B listed cotton brokers who had advised planters not to bring their produce into the city, a measure which was said to have brought ruin at the same time upon the producers and the city.

It is therefore ordered:—

1st, That the sums in schedules annexed marked "A" and "B," set against the names of the several persons, business firms, and corporations herein described, be and hereby are assessed upon each respectively,

2nd, That said sums be paid to Lieut. David O. O. Field, financial clerk, at his Office in the Custom House, on or before Monday the 11th inst., or that the property of the delinquent be forthwith seized, and sold at public auction to pay the amount, with all necessary charges and expenses, or the party imprisoned till paid.

3rd, The money raised by this assessment to be a fund for the purpose of providing employment and food for the deserving poor people of New Orleans.[28]

The Massachusetts general did not let it be forgotten that he was more than a quartermaster, and he declared, "The hand that cuts your bread can cut your throat." [29]

Butler then turned his attention to the question of loyalty. All civil officers and attorneys were directed to take an oath of allegiance in order to continue their functions; [30] likewise, all persons who sought any privilege or protection from the government (such as the obtaining of permits and licenses) had to take an oath, as did those who claimed the right to have payments made to them.[31] Numerous persons took the oath without protest, feeling that they were not automatically disgraced under the circumstances.[32] After all, one *had* to take some form of oath in order to carry on business, which often meant to live.

From the start Butler let it be known that he favored "business as usual"—whatever the circumstances, he always favored that.[33] But without an oath of allegiance, the privilege of doing business was denied. Persons whose property was subject to confiscation because they could not, or would not, take the oath often resorted to subterfuge, such as transferring property to minors or foreigners; but Butler's sharp legal eye could look through form to substance, and many transfers were disallowed as being without reality.[34]

Butler's days were, of necessity, full. His working schedule called for his receiving female petitioners at his residence from eight to nine in the morning, to discuss confidential matters. At nine o'clock he went to his office in the customhouse, "in some state," as his apologist vouchsafed.[35] In his office there was always a stenographer to record all conversations; and lest any visitor speak in such a low voice that the stenographer could not overhear the words the visitor's chair was tied down a respectable distance from the general's desk.[36] On his desk there was conspicuously displayed a pistol, which was unloaded to prevent incidents.[37] On the wall was a reminding sign: "THERE IS NO DIFFERENCE BETWEEN A HE AND A SHE ADDER IN THEIR VENOM."[38] At 11:00 A.M. the general read his mail. At one o'clock he lunched. The afternoon was devoted to reports and letters, and at four-thirty he returned home for dinner. Then there were reviews to be held, outposts to be inspected. A stenographer toiled in his home till ten o'clock, after which Butler worked over confidential matters until a late hour.[39]

Butler exemplified the majesty of the United States Army in a conquered city. "[T]o the Custom-house he was driven daily in a splendid carriage, surrounded by a numerous mounted body guard, and with more pomp and display than I have ever seen accorded to a European monarch," noted a visiting Englishman. "He then sat in imperial dignity in his judgment seat, and pronounced sentences according to his undisputed will on the numerous unfortunate wights who were daily brought before him. To see such autocratic power vested in such a man, and the lives and liberties of so many thousands in his hand, and subject to his whim or caprice, seemed to me to be strangely anomalous in a nation which had so long borne the name of being the great seat and home of human liberties.

"I had seen this personage only once, . . . bedecked with all the

CONFISCATED

*Contemporary New Orleans sketch
of Butler the Conqueror*

75

feathers and tinsel that could be crowded into a major-general's uniform, and surrounded by his guards. There seemed to be such an amount of pomp and vanity displayed about his person, which contrasted so much with the ragged and dirt-begrimed generals in the field, that I thought he looked like a vain old jackanapes, and I could not attribute to him all the diabolical cunning he was said to possess." [40]

A contemporary account thus described Butler in action: "Not tall, but of well-developed form, and fine, massive head; not graceful in movement, but of firm, solid aspect; self-possessed; not silver-tongued, not fluent . . . ; on the contrary, he is slow of speech, often hesitates and labors, can not at once bring down the sledge-hammer squarely on the anvil; but down it comes at last with a ring that is remembered. It is only in the heat and tempest of contention, that he acquires the perfect use of his parts of speech." [41] But the author of those words was Butler's paid apologist, variously referred to as a "ghost-writer," [42] "press agent," [43] and the creator of "as thorough a job of whitewashing as can be found in American literature." [44] A less flattering portrayal was furnished by one who had been hauled before the general:

His appearance did not so much portray the cunning trickster, as betokened a sort of compromise between the proud, semi-sanctified autocrat and the depraved sot.

He had two eyes vastly different in expression. From one seemed to look out benignity, and from the other, malignity. . . .

His head was large and flabby, and nearly destitute of hair—except a little at the sides, which was just the colour of his epaulets.

He maintained the contention with his opponent with a coolness which showed that in that system of warfare at least his generalship excelled. He lay back in his chair and retorted with a provoking smile of ironical politeness, which acted strongly upon the temper of his opponent. [45]

A captain was given the job of screening out applicants for passes through the military lines. On one occasion this officer begged Butler to listen to some of the applicants himself, for he would be far more lenient if he could hear their stories, to which Butler replied: "You are entirely correct. I am sure I should; and that is precisely why I want you to screen them for me." [46] But he could be generous when the spirit moved him. To two elderly ladies who requested a pass, he wrote: "I have an aged mother at home. . . . For her sake you shall have the pass you ask, which is sent herewith." [47] When the wife of the Confederate General Beauregard became gravely ill in New Orleans, Butler offered to send the Southern officer a safe-conduct pass and full protection for a visit.[48]

The financial news from Lowell was good. Butler's business agent there wrote him: "The Middlesex flourishes wonderfully. I think we must pay 10% this 6 months in spite of all I can do to keep down the profit and loss account." [49]

For several months the general was to be deprived of his wife's presence in New Orleans. On June 10, 1862, she returned to Lowell to avoid the unhealthy season,[50] but the correspondence between them was remarkably regular. Almost every conceivable subject was touched upon in their letters: introspection, business matters, military affairs, and sentiment. "Do what is right by 'instinct'—that is best," he advised in one of his epistles. "All my well-considered acts pretty much have been failures. My instinct is better than my reason." [51]

"My dear, dear, good wife, you ask me not to scold you," declared one of his letters. "I am your baby, but may not the petulant child cry when an awry pin pricks him?" [52] A few days later he wrote: "I got your kind note where *you* praised me. How sweet to be praised by one we love!" [53] Another letter detailed many things to be attended to at home; but the general concluded: "Here I am at business again. What shall I say, dearest, that I love you, pshaw! you know that." [54]

But some of her letters were of a complaining, petty tone, and the general replied: "Your note of August 10th, finished on the 12th, reached me on the 26th. It was a dear, kind, loving letter—such a one as gives me new life to receive. I read it over twice. Do write me such letters or none. I cannot live if you write others like those you have written. They are causeless, useless, hurtful." [55] At one point, nettled by her letters, he even requested that she stop writing to him.[56]

Sometimes his letters to her were written in a playful vein. "I must lose my housekeeper. She has done very well, but is not *afflicted* with neatness. I shall have to get another. What say you to a young, dashing, black-eyed brunette, with a strong tongue and a sharp nose, that will make us all stand around?" [57] Other letters that he wrote her were more serious. "I am changing my opinions," declared a letter dated July 28th. "There is nothing of the people worth saving. I am inclined to give it all up to the blacks. Such lying, meanness, wrong, and wickedness, that I am inclined to think that the story of Sodom and Gomorrah a myth, else why not rain and brimstone upon this city? I am afraid the Lord will do so in the shape of the negroes." [58]

Butler kept an eye on the scene at home. "We are in receipt here of very terrible news from the Potomac," he wrote to his wife, "nothing less than the rout of McClellan's entire army. If true, I shall have trouble enough here, but fear not. We shall hold New Orleans. Indeed I think they had better move the Capital here as the safest place." [59] A few days later he asked Mrs. Butler, "Why will not the Administration send for the Army of the Gulf, and let us whip those Rebels in Virginia?" [60]

In reply to his momentous doings, Mrs. Butler could only reply with details of home life, including many recitals of illness. "How far away this looks to you with health, hope, and ambition, all your own, satisfied, as your picture shows you, yet eager to win more," she wrote. "Long may you wear that look, and you will, too; hope with you is triumphant, if it were darkened or killed, you could easier die than bear the difference." [61] But after a four months' absence, Mrs. Butler returned to New Orleans, and to her sister she wrote of the general, "He does not look so alive as he has before, but the cold weather may bring back the old fiery look." [62]

Purely military matters did not occupy too much of Butler's time. His force was supposedly 18,000 men, but actually it never exceeded 15,000, and sometimes it was several thousand smaller in strength. [63] Most of his troops were not in the city. One brigade had been sent to seize and hold Baton Rouge. [64] But the general considered that his troops were sufficient to preserve law and order, and accordingly he directed that all weapons must be turned over to his command. The citizens objected that without weapons they could not protect themselves; so he solved that dilemma by ordering that "robbery by violence or aggravated assault, that ought to be repelled by the use of deadly weapons, burglaries, rapes, and murders, whether committed by blacks or whites, will be, on conviction, punished by death." [65]

But these problems were as nothing compared to Butler's foreign relations. The foreign consuls were very important in New Orleans because the city throve so largely through the use of foreign capital. In addition, there was a tremendous foreign population.[66] The consuls, for their part, assumed the role of protecting their nationals from what they regarded as Butler's unconstitutional laws; and, more importantly, they knew that they had access to the State Department in case of need.[67] The first important source of friction was Butler's required loyalty oath; and when the consuls collectively protested the general replied on June 16th: "Indeed, gentlemen, if any subject of a foreign state does not like our laws, or the administration of them, he has an immediate, effectual, and appropriate remedy in his own hands, alike pleasant to him and to us; and that is, not to annoy his consul with complaints of those laws or the administration of them, or his consul wearying the authorities with verbose protests, but simply to go home—'stay not on the order of his going, but go at once.' Such a person came here without our invitation; he will be parted with without our regrets. But he must not have committed crimes against our laws, and then expect to be allowed to go home to escape the punishment of these crimes." [68]

When the consuls protested against Butler's forced poor-relief contributions from those who had purchased Confederate bonds, the general wrote to the Secretary of War:

There seems to be no such fit subjects for such taxation as the cotton-brokers who had brought the distress upon the city by paralyzing commerce, and the subscribers to the rebel loan. . . . Before their Excellencies, the French and Prussian ministers, complain of my exactions upon foreigners at New Orleans, I desire that they should look at the documents, and consider for a moment the facts and figures set forth in this report. They will find that out of ten thousand four hundred and ninety families who have been fed from the fund, with the raising of which they find fault, *less than one-tenth are Americans;* nine thousand four hundred and eighty are foreigners. . . . I should need no extraordinary taxation to feed the poor of New Orleans, if the bellies of the foreigners were as actively with the rebels as are the heads of those who claim exemption thus far from this taxation, made and used for the purposes set forth above, upon the ground of their neutrality.[69]

When the Prussian consul Kruttschnidt objected to the forced levy in the amount of bond purchases, Butler wrote to Stanton, "Indeed, I suppose another Jew—one Judas—thought his investment in the thirty pieces of silver was a profitable one, until the penalty of treachery reached him." [70]

Several months before the Federal forces assaulted New Orleans, the city was faced with a situation of possible internal disorders. The Confederate troops were gradually being withdrawn for service in the field, whereupon a number of army-trained foreigners organized themselves into groups on a military pattern, in order to help preserve order in the city. Three European brigades were formed, aggregating about 10,000 men in all. When the last Southern forces withdrew from the attacked city, the mayor formally placed the protection of the inhabitants in the hands of the foreign brigades.[71] When Butler entered the city, the British Guard sent all of its equipment to the Confederate General Beauregard. Butler ordered that the men must follow their weapons out of the city, despite the protests of Coppell, the British consul; and the only two men who remained were forthwith arrested.[72] "These people thought it of consequence," wrote Butler, "that Beauregard should have sixty more uniforms and rifles. I think it of the same consequence that he should have sixty more of these faithless men." [73] Coppell reported the matter to the British minister in Washington, Lord Lyons, who hurried to Secretary of State Seward, and the men were liberated.[74] When the funeral procession of a Union officer passed the British consulate, which failed to lower its flag as a sign of respect, Butler demanded a satisfactory explanation and apology.[75]

The French consul had his problems as well. Federal officers arrested Charles Heidsieck, the head of the great French champagne company, under curious circumstances: this native and citizen of

France had come to the United States to look after his Southern accounts. But he made five trips between Mobile and New Orleans in the disguise of a bartender on a riverboat, and Butler claimed that he was carrying treasonable letters.[76] Heidsieck was imprisoned, and forthwith complained to Count Mejan, the French consul, that he was obliged to cook his own food in Fort Jackson Prison. Butler was not sympathetic. "I am unable to see the hardship to one who has, by his own confession, turned bar-keeper for a living, cooking his own food." The general also noted: "His complaint that he could not write to his wife, because the officer, admitted by him to be 'a perfect gentleman,' who was to examine his letter, was too young to be trusted with the delicate revelations of a husband to his wife, who was three thousand miles away, is too absurd for comment." [77] But when the French minister appealed to Seward, the champagne king was released.[78]

Another dispute concerned Confederate uniforms that had been purchased in France ; the money was turned over to the French consul in New Orleans. Butler obtained the consul's promise that the money would not leave his hands until there could be a thorough investigation ; but the State Department released the Frenchman from his promise.[79] The consul reported to the French Minister in Washington, "General Butler can be very polite when he chooses." [80]

The Netherlands consul was similarly aggrieved ; $800,000 in silver had been withdrawn from the Citizens' Bank and deposited in the liquor store of Conturie, who also served as Dutch consul. Butler claimed that this was really Confederate treasure, which had been deposited with the consul to avoid confiscation ; [81] and when the consul refused to part with the silver a military delegation called upon him. Conturie was outraged when one of the officers referred to him as "fellow." "That word is never applied to a gentleman, far less to a foreign consul, acting in his consular capacity, as I am now. I ask you to remember that you used that word." [82] The Secretary of State hastened to apologize to the Dutch minister, van Limburg: "The government disapproves of these proceedings, and also the sanction which was given to them by Major-General Butler, and expresses its regret that the misconduct thus censured has occurred." [83]

The Spanish consul was involved when Federal forces captured the *Fox,* with huge contraband cargoes owned by Avedano Brothers. Butler not only confiscated the cargo, but he required the brothers to make good all bills of exchange that he found for the proceeds of similar blockade running.[84]

The Greek consul was not to be outdone, and he protested the seizure of 3,205 hogsheads of sugar that allegedly had been marked for export to build up the Confederate Government's credit in Europe. M. W. Benachi, the consul, obtained the release of the sugar for lack of proof, and the merchandise was returned with Lincoln's approval,[85] whereupon Butler wrote to the owners and congratulated them on the value enhancement that had occurred during the period of sequestration.[86]

When the Russian consul protested that his incoming mail had been opened, the Massachusetts general replied, "Gen. Butler begs to assure the Consul of his Imperial Majesty of Russia that no letters sent through the *United States Mail* will be examined coming from his consulate to himself." [87]

The Secretary of State was doing an admirable job of avoiding foreign difficulties, except for those arising out of Butler's administration of New Orleans.[88] In desperation Seward sought to resolve these difficulties by sending down a distinguished attorney to investigate the consular imbroglio. Reverdy Johnson of Maryland was dispatched as a special agent of the State Department "to investigate and report upon the complaints made by foreign consuls against the late military proceedings." [89] Johnson was an old enemy of Butler's whom the general had accused of being a secessionist at the time war began.[90] Knowing this, the Postmaster General wrote to Butler of his having objected to the Secretary of State about Johnson's assignment; yet when Blair reminded Seward that Johnson had lied to Butler in Baltimore the Secretary of State replied: "Yes; but he was paid to do that. Now he is paid to lie the other way." [91]

After six weeks of investigation, Johnson decided all the pending cases adversely to Butler.[92] "Unless the almost universal belief of gentlemen of intelligence and integrity in the city, having every means of knowledge, be wholly unfounded," declared the Johnson report, "and the reports of officers of the highest character in the service of the government, who have officially visited the city since it has been in the possession of the military, be also wholly unfounded, a state of fraud and corruption exists there that is without parallel in the history of the country." [93] In vain did the general protest these findings, arguing that the Marylander "has done more to strengthen the hand of secession than any other occurrence of the southwest since my advent in New Orleans." [94] Later Butler wrote to the Secretary of State that "another such commissioner as Mr. Johnson sent to New Orleans would render the city untenable. The town itself got into such a state while Mr. Johnson was here, that he confessed to me that he could hardly sleep from nervousness from fear of a rising, and hurried away, hardly completing his work, as soon as he heard that Baton Rouge was about to be attacked. . . . [T]he only fear I now have is, that if the last accounts are true [about a Confederate invasion of Maryland], Mr. Johnson will have so much more nervous apprehension for his personal safety in Baltimore than he had in New Orleans, that he will want to come back here, now the yellow fever season is over, as to a place of security." [95]

Ben Butler took his reversals in good part. After Seward had apologized to the Dutch minister, the general noted: "I bow to the mandate of 'state necessity' without a murmur. I have made larger sacrifices than this for my country." [96] His being over-ruled in Washington, he thought, was not a matter of right but of *grosse politik*.

The protests of the foreign consuls became so numerous that the *Delta* declared: "If Gen. Butler rides up street, the consuls are sure to come in a body, and protest that he did not ride down. If he smokes a pipe in the morning, a deputation calls upon him in the evening to know why he did not smoke a cigar. If he drinks coffee, they will send some crude messenger with a note asking in the name of some tottering dynasty why he did not drink tea." [97] Since this newspaper could only exist at Butler's pleasure, the author of those lines is not difficult to discern. But the Supreme Court was to give Butler a more judicial approval. A Prussian subject sought damages against the United States because of the detention of the *Essex*, which had a cargo of bullion received in return for a shipment of Belgian clothing.

Butler informed the Prussian consul that the ship could not clear with contraband aboard, intelligence which, the consul declared, was contrary to existing treaties of peace and friendship. On May 8, 1876, Mr. Chief Justice Waite said for the Supreme Court: "Martial law is the law of military necessity in the actual presence of war. It is administered by the general of the army, and is, in fact, his will. Of necessity it is arbitrary; but it must be obeyed. New Orleans was, at this time, the theater of the most active and important military operations. The civil authority was overthrown. General Butler, in command, was the military ruler. His will was law, and necessarily so." [98]

But sex was to raise its head in Butler's international relations. His "Woman Order" not only elicited more foreign disapproval than anything else he ever did, but it ranks as his most discussed domestic act as well.

During the occupation of Baltimore, Butler was perplexed as to the treatment to be afforded to excessively loyal Confederate women. In New Orleans the situation was even worse. Women defiantly wore Southern flags in their hats or on their persons. On the streets, they conspicuously pulled aside their skirts when a Federal soldier was passing, as though to avoid contamination by contact. They sneered at the Union troops, and made sarcastic references to them. [99] If a Northern soldier entered a church or even a streetcar, Southern women would edge away as far as possible, or even get up and leave. They played secessionist airs at public gatherings and taught their children to sing them. One patriotic woman twirled her skirts so violently to express disdain for a Federal trooper that she fell in the gutter; and she indignantly refused the soldier's offer to help her, saying she would rather lie in the gutter than be assisted by a Yankee. [100] When a Southern lady ostentatiously turned her back on Butler, he remarked loudly, "Those women evidently know which end of them looks best." [101] But his slower-witted soldiers could not cope with the insults. One of his generals noted: "Such venom one must see to believe. Such unsexing was hardly ever before in any cause or country so marked and so universal. I look at them and think of fallen angels." [102] The crowning insult came when Admiral Farragut was doused with a vessel of what Butler euphemistically called "not very clean water." [103]

Therefore on May 15, 1862, Butler issued General Order No. 28 from his office, Headquarters of the Department of the Gulf: "As the officers and soldiers of the United States have been subjected to repeated insults from the women (calling themselves ladies) of New Orleans, in return for the most scrupulous non-interference and courtesy on our part, it is ordered, that hereafter, when any female shall, by word, gesture, or movement, insult or show contempt for any officer or soldier of the United States, she shall be regarded and held liable to be treated as a woman of the town plying her avocation." [104]

Mayor Monroe immediately objected to Butler, saying: "As chief magistrate of this city, I cannot allow such an order published without my protest. The passions of our people already aroused, this must exasperate them beyond control; and I will not undertake to be responsible for the peace of the city while such an edict remains in force." Butler replied at once: "John T. Monroe, late mayor of New Orleans, is hereby relieved from all responsibility for the peace of the city, and suspended from any official functions, and committed to Fort Jackson until further orders." [105]

The mayor backed down, and signed an apology that Butler obligingly prepared; but under pressure from his advisers Monroe then declared that it was not really an apology, for the whole affair had been a misunderstanding. Butler hastened to disabuse him of this notion in plain words:

There can be, there has been, no room for misunderstanding of General Order No. 28. No lady will take any notice of a strange gentleman in such a form as to attract attention. Common women do.

Therefore, whatever woman, lady or mistress, gentle or simple, who by gesture, look, or word insults, shows contempt for, thus attracting to herself the notice of my officers or soldiers, will be deemed to act as becomes the vocation of common woman, and will be liable to be treated accordingly.

I shall not, as I have not abated, a single word of that order; it was well considered. If obeyed, it will protect the true and modest woman from all possible insult: the others will take care of themselves.[106]

The mayor went to prison, along with his principal advisers, including the chief of police. Butler then assumed the active handling of the municipal government.[107] By proclamation he informed the populace that he would handle the mayoralty functions in "the absence of the late Mayor of New Orleans, by order of Major-General B. F. Butler, commanding the Department of the Gulf." [108]

Southerners were appalled at the order. A Confederate newspaper published this editorial:

AN APPEAL TO EVERY SOUTHERN SOLDIER.—We turn to you in mute agony! Behold our wrongs! Fathers! husbands! brothers! sons! we know these bitter, burning wrongs will be fully avenged—*never* did southern women appeal in vain for protection from insult! But, for the sake of your sisters throughout the south, with tears we implore you not to surrender your cities, "in consideration of the defenseless women and children!" Do not leave your women to the mercy of this merciless foe! Would it not have been better for New Orleans to have been laid in ruins, and we buried up beneath the mass, than that we should be subjected to these untold sufferings? Is life so precious a boon that, for the preservation of it, *no* sacrifice is too great? Ah, no! ah, no! Rather let us die with you, oh, our fathers! Rather, like Virginius, plunge your own swords into our breasts, saying, "This is all we can give our daughters." THE DAUGHTERS OF NEW ORLEANS.[109]

For several issues, the Darlingston, South Carolina, *Southerner* printed Butler's order on page one, under the word "Notice." [110] In the same state a young girl noted in her diary: "New England's Butler, best known to us as 'Beast' Butler, is famous or infamous now. His amazing order to his soldiers in New Orleans and comments on it are now in everybody's mouth. We hardly expected from Massachusetts behavior to shame a Comanche." [111]

In the British House of Commons, Palmerston, the Prime Minister, declared:

I am quite prepared to say that I think no man could have read the proclamation to which our attention has been drawn, without a feeling of the deepest indignation—a proclamation to which I do not scruple to attach the epithet infamous. Sir, an Englishman must blush to think that such an act has been committed by one belonging to the Anglo-Saxon race. If it had come from some barbarous race that was not within the pale of civilization, one might have regretted it, but that such an order should have been promulgated by a soldier—by one who had raised himself to the rank of general, is a subject undoubtedly of not less astonishment than pain.[112]

The United States Minister to the Court of St. James's, Charles Francis Adams, received an official note, and his first reaction was, "Palmerston wants a quarrel!" His well educated son explained that "The matter of quarrel was General Butler's famous woman-order at New Orleans." [113] The note itself declared:

I cannot refrain from taking the liberty of saying to you that it is difficult if not impossible to express adequately the disgust which must be excited in the mind of every honourable man by the general order of General Butler given in the enclosed extract from yesterday's *Times*. Even when a town is taken by assault it is the practice of the commander of the conquering army to protect to his utmost the inhabitants and especially the female part of them, and I venture to say that no example can be found in the history of civilized nations, till the publication of this order, of a general guilty in cold blood of so infamous an act as deliberately to hand over the female inhabitants of a conquered city to the unbridled license of an unrestrained soldiery.

If the Federal Government chooses to be served by men capable of such revolting outrages, they must submit or abide by the deserved opinion which mankind will form of their conduct.[114]

Adams replied that he could not take cognizance of such a note unless it were official; Palmerston replied that it most assuredly was.[115]

In both the House of Commons and the House of Lords, the British Government was asked to protest. Palmerston then told Adams that he hoped Lincoln would peremptorily remove Butler.[116] Public opinion in England swayed sharply to the Confederate cause, and it was felt that an army which could give high command to a fiend such as Butler was worthy of the worst that its enemies could say about it. How could the North continue to protest that it was fighting for liberty and decency against slave drivers? [117] The London *Times* demanded intervention by England, to stop this "tyranny of victor over vanquished." [118]

Adams, the American minister, dutifully reported all this to the Secretary of State; the vocal pro-secessionist element in England had been greatly encouraged, and Adams pointed out that "In this connection, it is not to be denied that General Butler is furnishing a good deal of material." [119] Seward apologized to the British chargé d'affaires for "a phraseology which could be mistaken or perverted." [120]

But Butler was completely defiant. "Why," he said, "these she-adders of New Orleans themselves were at once tamed into propriety of conduct by the order, and from that day no woman has either insulted or annoyed any live soldier or officer, and of a certainty no soldier has insulted any woman." [121]

In New Orleans the potential characterization of patriots as "women of the town" was particularly resented by the prostitutes. They acquired quantities of Butler pictures, which were affixed to the bottoms of their toilets. Soldiers were instructed to destroy any equipment thus marked.[122]

Butler finally dismissed the whole matter in these words: "Palmerston said my government would revoke the order when it heard it. It did not hear of anything else for many weeks, but the order was never revoked, but, on the contrary, the government gave my administration its highest sanction. The President did not confer on me, however, the 'Order of the Garter.' " [123]

England was not the only nation to express disgust about the matter. Charles Sumner wrote to Butler: "I understand that the French government has forbidden the papers to mention your name. The name of Marlboro was once used in France to frighten children,—more than a century ago. You have taken his place." [124]

CHAPTER VIII

THE FIGHT IN
NEW ORLEANS, II

HAVING thus successfully antagonized foreign governments and women, Butler next proceeded to get embroiled with the clergy. Dr. Leacock, an Episcopalian clergyman, protested to Butler that the general's insistence upon an oath of allegiance to the United States would cause half of his church members to perjure themselves. "Well," replied the commander, "if that is the result of your nine years' preaching; if your people will commit perjury so freely, the sooner you leave your pulpit the better." [1] Dr. Leacock claimed that he himself was a pro-Union man, even though he did not care to take the oath; but Butler unearthed one of Leacock's sermons in November, 1860, in which secession sentiments seemed unquestionable.[2]

The venerable Dr. Mercer claimed that he did not choose to take the oath, for he was a strict neutral. "In my opinion," declared Butler, "there can be no such thing as neutrality by a citizen of the United States. He that is not for us is against us. As an officer, I cannot recognize such neutrality. All good citizens are called upon to lend their influence to the United States: all who do not do so are the enemies of the United States." [3]

An Episcopalian member of Butler's staff, Major Strong, went into the Reverend Dr. Goodrich's church on a sabbath; when the customary prayer for the President of the United States was omitted, the major arose and cried: "Stop, sir! It is my duty to bring these exercises to a close. I came here for the sole purpose of worshipping

God; but, as you omit invoking the blessing our church-service requires upon the President of the nation, I propose to close the services." [4] The next day Butler summoned all the Episcopalian clergymen, who claimed that they were only obeying the orders of their bishop, the Right Reverend Major General Polk. Butler refused to recognize his authority.[5] Dr. Goodrich of St. Paul's endeavored to bypass this difficulty by omitting the service entirely, whereupon Butler ordered the church to be closed.[6]

Word was received at headquarters that a fast day had been ordered, and Butler hastened to cancel it. "It having come to the knowledge of the commanding general that Friday next is proposed to be observed as a day of fasting and prayer in obedience to some supposed proclamation of one Jefferson Davis, in the several churches of this city, it is ordered that no such observance be had.

" 'Churches and religious houses are to be kept open as in time of profound peace,' but no religious exercises can be had upon the supposed authority above mentioned." [7]

Several churches added to their services a period of silent prayer, which, it was well understood, would be for the President of the Confederate States of America. Butler ordered that the silent act of devotion be omitted, on pain of the minister's being sent to Fort Lafayette, the military prison in New York.[8]

At length Dr. Leacock sought out Butler and asked, "Well, general, are you going to shut up the churches?" "No, sir," the officer replied; "I am more likely to shut up the ministers." He did so, filling the places of the deposed clergymen with army chaplains.[9] As a result of this supposedly anticlerical attitude, Butler was suspected when the Reverend Mr. Hodges's church was burned down *"accidentally* one windy night," as a patriotic New Orleans lady believed.[10]

Amidst other fighting, Butler had time for a few more skirmishes with Admiral Porter of the United States Navy. In reading through some reports, Porter discovered that Butler had written of how the Confederate steamer *Arkansas* had been blown up by its own crew, whereas the admiral claimed that his own ship, *Essex,* had caused the destruction of the Southern ironclad. In an angry letter to Butler, the admiral demanded a retraction, as "The 'Essex' was the only vessel present at the action. . . . You, Sir, were one hundred and fifty miles off, and could know nothing of it." [11] The Massachusetts general quickly found material for a reply in a comment that Porter had made about the army's assault on Fort St. Philip, and he warned the admiral (whose commission had not yet been received) : "Please, Captain, do not judge of our profession, yours will furnish you with sufficient scope." [12]

But Butler's disputes did not extend to the New Orleans business-men. He not only authorized merchants and tradesmen to carry on their regular businesses, but he fined those who failed to do so.[13] He even entered the field himself. His troopships were about to return without their passengers, which meant that the vessels would have to be laden with some form of ballast. Rent of each ship was $1,500 per day, and it would require ten days to collect sand and carry it aboard, with another four days' time to unload the sand at the other end. That meant $21,000 in time charges. Therefore Butler purchased sugar from the Louisiana planters and ballasted the ships with it, saving the government (he said) the $21,000 charges.[14] It would appear that sugar did not require any time for loading, unlike sand; it would also appear that there was a handsome profit to be made on the sugar when it reached the North. "The details of this transaction," wrote Butler's man of letters, "were ably arranged by the general's brother, a shrewd and experienced man of business, who was allowed a commission for his trouble. The affair succeeded to admiration." [15]

In June, 1862, a Treasury Department official in New Orleans re-ported to the Secretary of the Treasury that Butler was using his position "to engage in mercantile speculation and had already made considerable shipments North on private account." [16] But the gen-eral had hard work in reopening trade. He found that the Confeder-ates were not anxious to sell such commodities as cotton, for planters had been officially urged to burn their cotton; and now it was embarrassing to find that those who had ignored the government's orders would thereby profit handsomely.[17] But soon the general was able to write: "These difficulties are gradually being smoothed over. I think now that the trade can be opened." [18] Yet much diplomacy was required. When Butler first issued passes that permitted trading through enemy lines, Governor Thomas O. Moore of Louisiana announced that any person found with a Butler pass would be hanged instantly without trial.[19]

The great profits to be realized, however, could not be ignored by enterprising businessmen. Commodities could be purchased very cheaply in the war areas of Louisiana by any one who had cash, a permit from Butler, and the available shipping; and these same commodities could be sold at high prices up North. Butler's apologist quite frankly stated the situation: "The general's brother was one of the lucky men who chanced to be in business in New Orleans at the critical moment. . . . Later in the year, came the confiscations of rebel property, with frequent sales at auction of valuable commodities. Of this business, too, he had an ample share—just the share his means and talents entitled him to." [20] Andrew Jackson Butler, said the admiring writer, "who found himself, by the action of the senate, without employment in New Orleans, and having both capital and credit at command, embarked in the business of bringing cattle from Texas, to the great advantage of the city and his own considerable profit. The quartermaster's chest being empty, General Butler placed all the money of his own, which he could raise, at his disposal. Provisions soon began to arrive." [21]

On August 26, 1862, a special agent of the Treasury Department wrote to Secretary Chase that Andrew Butler "is here for the sole purpose of making money." Two weeks later he reported that "Circumstances look very suspicious"—when Butler explained the situation, "suspicion almost entirely disappears," but "it is the general impression here that money will accomplish anything with the authorities." [22] The Treasury Department agent, George D. Denison, wrote to Chase about Andrew Butler: "He is here for the sole purpose of making money, and is stated by secessionists—and by some Union men—that he has made half a million dollars, or more. I regret his being here at all, for it is not proper that the brother of the commanding General should devote himself to such an object. It leads to the belief that the General himself is interested with him, and such is the belief of our enemies and some of our friends. The effect is bad." [23]

On the day following Denison's report, the Massachusetts general wrote to his wife: "Andrew is shipping Fisher some thousand hogsheads of sugar. It will be of prime quality and will pay, he thinks." [24] On the succeeding day the general wrote, "Andrew is shipping much larger amounts of sugar to Fisher than I supposed." [25] In time the matter reached the attention of Admiral Farragut, who wrote to Butler:

While no one appreciates more highly than myself the energetic, persevering, and skilful merchant, I must confess that no one has a greater abhorrence and detestation of the unscrupulous speculator who takes advantage of every necessity of his fellow-beings, and, regardless of consequences, by bribing and corruption forces his trade into the enemy's country, drawing down dishonor upon the cause as well as the country we serve, and upon us who are exerting every nerve to sustain our honor among nations, and even claim the respect of our enemies, however unwilling they may be to yield it. I have therefore determined to call to your attention the case of the Schooner 'L. L. Davis,' whose cargo is owned by one Mr. Wyer of New Orleans. [26]

On the very day of Farragut's letter, December 10, 1862, Denison wrote to the Secretary of the Treasury that "Col. Butler has three or four men in his employ who manage his business for him. The principal one is Mr. Wyer." [27] Not unnaturally these activities reached congressional ears, but Zachariah Chandler successfully defended Butler against a charge made by Senator Davis that the Massachusetts general had connived with his brother to seize abandoned property in Louisiana for private gains. [28] Butler later was able to reciprocate by publishing a certificate attesting to Chandler's sobriety. [29]

A popular New Orleans song of the day concerned the brothers Butler:

> Two brothers came to New Orleans,
>   Both were the name of "Butler."
> The one was a major-general,
>   The other merely sutler.

The first made proclamations
That were fearful to behold,
While the sutler dealt out rations
And took his pay in gold.[30]

There were eight or nine river steamboats available for army purposes, and Andrew Butler was able to make use of these. On trips through the enemy lines for trading purposes, a company or so of infantry would accompany each ship; bushwhacking could not be permitted.[31] Such contraband items as salt [32] and medicines [33] were sold to the Confederates under General Butler's permits. In return for these contraband items, Andrew Butler would accept cotton and sugar, which were worth four or five times as much in New York as they were in New Orleans.[34] Yet the general indignantly denied that his brother had made a real financial killing because of his connections; despite rumors, said the general, his brother's profits in the four-month period were less than $200,000.[35]

Admiral Porter was distressed to find that the shipping he had helped to capture was now being used to sell contraband to the enemy. But he felt that the people of New Orleans were "great fools" for objecting to Butler's rule, since no other administrator would have permitted any contraband articles to enter the city.[36] The Secretary of the Treasury was advised by his New Orleans representative that the Unionists in that city wished Butler "was President for though he would make millions for himself during the first three months he would finish the war in three months more!"[37] Even in Richmond a diarist heard that salt was being traded for cotton. "The Governor [Pettus, of Mississippi] says he don't *know* that he has received the consent of 'Butler, the Beast' (but he knows the trade is impossible without it)."[38] Three days later, on November 10th, he wrote, "Is it not *certain* that 'Butler, the Beast,' is a party to the speculation?"[39] A few days later the diarist commented that "Butler is preparing to do a great business—and no objection to the illicit traffic is filed by the Secretaries of State or Treasury."[40]

There is no direct proof that General Butler personally profited from trading with the enemy or from the issuance of passes only to his brother and other favorites. The Treasury Department representative in New Orleans reported that the general "is such a smart man that it would in any case be difficult to discover what he wished to conceal." [41] A contemporary review observed: "We are bound to say that we never lighted on the slightest trace of proof against him personally and directly. . . . But, on the other hand, numerous competent witnesses testify that his brother was in New Orleans during the greater part of his administration; that his brother was a man whose antecedents and character were bad; and that he did use, night and day, the facilities which the relationship and constant intercourse with the commanding general gave him to perpetuate various frauds and jobs and violations of the regulations for his own benefit; and that in the doing of these things he accumulated a large fortune which, at his death [in 1868], he bequeathed to the general. What the public refuses to believe about this is, that so shrewd an observer as the general did not know what his brother was about; and what disgusts it is that he should not have sent him out of the department, at least when his performances began to create scandal. A man of the nicest sense of honor would, of course, not have waited for the scandal." [42] An esteemed historian reported that when General Butler went to New Orleans in 1862, he was worth $150,000; by 1868 his wealth was estimated to be $3,000,000. [43]

One of General Butler's more serious problems was yellow fever. He never forgot that his father had been killed by the disease; now he was to have his chance to fight back at it. In an ordinary year, it was not unusual for as many as 10 per cent of the city's population to be killed off; [44] in 1853 the yellow fever death toll was 25 per cent. [45] In some years New Orleans had escaped entirely, but never when there were large epidemics in ports with which commerce was carried on, or when there were large numbers of people in the city who were unaccustomed to the climate—such as Butler's sizable army of Northerners. [46] When Butler first questioned the local physicians about control of the disease, he found some doctors who refused to advise him; they hoped the potential pestilence would drive the hated Federals from the city. [47]

In the face of local professional resistance, Butler consulted his army physicians; but none of them had had any experience with yellow fever. So the general undertook to become a specialist himself. He studied the history of past epidemics and consulted such books as could be found. He found that the worst death rate had been in that part of New Orleans known as "Frenchtown," which was the dirtiest of all sections; hence there seemed to be a connection between filth and the disease. In addition, there had been a particularly heavy death toll around the markets, which suggested that food was a source of passing the disease.[48] He believed that yellow fever had to be imported, as there were no traces of it in any part of the United States that experienced frost.[49] Armed with this knowledge and surmise, he set up his yellow-fever-control program: first, a ship quarantine station was set up seventy miles below the city, with waiting periods of as long as forty days if there were illness aboard. Second, the streets and canals were thoroughly cleaned. Third, no refuse could be deposited in yards or streets; army wagons would call for all refuse at stated times, and chloride of lime was used to clean individual receptacles of householders.[50] There were stiff fines for any one who threw refuse into the streets; one bold fellow who decided to make a test case of this was rewarded with three years in prison.[51] There was considerable opposition to the severity of Butler's methods, and many persons thought it was patriotic to resist, so that yellow fever could rout the Federal army even if the Confederates couldn't.[52] Tarsara, the Spanish minister, protested in Washington that Butler had no right to quarantine the *Cardenas,* which actually had yellow fever aboard; [53] and Callejon, the local consul, threatened as retaliation that no more Spanish ships would come to the United States. Butler replied that this country could receive no greater favor. The dispute grew more heated, and Butler expelled the consul after an argument in which neither man could understand the other because of lack of a suitable interpreter.[54]

Not unnaturally, the Spanish consul wanted to know why *his* ships could not pass quarantine and unload cargo, if a ship with another flag could do so. A United States Navy steamer, the *Tennessee,* was permitted to discharge her cargo upon the captain's representation that the ship was about to sink. When the vessel remained afloat, Butler wrote an angry letter to Commodore Henry W. Wilson, complaining that "The 'Tennessee' still lays in the stream, has lain there for thirty-six hours, and yet does not sink. It shows well for the quality of the water at New Orleans. I am now so far relieved that I can officially assure the Spanish authorities that the 'Tennessee' was only allowed to come up to save her from sinking." [55]

But only two cases of yellow fever were reported in New Orleans that year, the result of a false statement by a ship's master that his vessel had not stopped at Nassau, where an epidemic was raging. Butler quarantined the square where these persons resided, posted sentries to see that the sick men had no contact except with the "acclimated men" he had assigned, set fires burning at all four corners of the square to keep an upward current of air; [56] and, when the men died, he had the bodies cremated and all their effects burned.[57]

But with all his severity Butler had kept yellow fever from the city. His own staff was treated as sternly as the local population. When he was deluged with requests from his men for furloughs as the yellow-fever season approached, he published all the applications in the New Orleans *Delta,* with his own endorsements that definitely discouraged other requests: "A surgeon who would make his private and domestic affairs an excuse for leaving his regiment, and exposing his fellow-citizens to the want of medical attendance at this season of the year . . . deserves to be cashiered for cowardice or neglect of duty.—B. F. B." [58] After Butler saw that he had won the battle with disease, he wrote: "This science is not taught at West Point. The want of its proper application to the troops in the field kills more men than are killed by bullets, for it takes nearly a man's weight in lead to be shot at him before he is killed." [59]

Butler's relations with foreign powers continued to be strained. H.M.S. *Rinaldo* caused some embarrassment when the British sailors sang secessionist songs; and it became known that a Confederate flag would be displayed the following day. Butler informed the captain that he would have his artillery fire on any vessel displaying an enemy banner; and the flag never was raised.[60] But he was regarded very suspiciously in England, and Bernal Osborne stated in Parliament: "If this were the proper time, I could point to outrages committed by the militia of New York in one of the Southern States occupied by them, where the General commanding, on the pretext that one of his men had been poisoned by strychnine, issued an order of the day, threatening to put a slave into every man's house to incite the slaves to murder their masters. Such was the general order issued by General Butler." [61] And England was ready to believe anything that was said about Butler.

More friction was engendered when Butler claimed the right to search not only departing merchantmen but also warships, as they might contain contraband. The Spanish people were outraged when Butler sent a search party to scrutinize the contents of the *Blasco de Garay.*[62]

There were more complicated aspects to the French situation. New Orleans had a huge French population; and when it became known that Napoleon III's fleet might pay a call the City Council voted to extend the hospitality of the city to the sailors. Butler canceled the invitation, for, he said, "the tender of its hospitalities by a government to which police duties and sanitary regulations only are intrusted, is simply an invitation to the calaboose or the hospital." [63] But when the fleet did arrive, Butler had a problem. The Secretary of State had told him in rather veiled language that the French ships were there to help the Confederacy, in return for aid to Napoleon III's Mexican venture; and Butler thought that Seward was trying to tell him that the fleet should be kept away from New Orleans, even though no orders to that effect could be given.[64] Butler did not know how he could fire on the French navy without orders; he even examined French law for a possible precedent. Finally he recalled that the sanitary regulations of a garrisoned place had the effect of military regulations, and hence the commanding general could enforce them, especially when martial law had been declared. As the French fleet had come from the yellow-fever port of Martinique, he would hold it in quarantine; and the admiral would be given his standard notification that any ship breaking quarantine would be fired upon.[65] But he received Admiral Reynaud himself; and with the thought of showing the Frenchman how difficult it would be to carry the city by assault he personally conducted the admiral through all the harbor fortifications, explaining in detail how the city would be defended.[66] With all the secrets thus disclosed, the French admiral (whose name could be translated as "Fox") doubtless could have taken the city even as Farragut had done, without the benefit of a blueprint.

Butler always was well informed about what was happening. His press agent admitted that "no man ever had a better spy system than he, or paid more liberally for intelligence." [67] When Butler first had entered New Orleans, the free Negro regiment in the city had offered him its services; he had no work for the men militarily, but he utilized their services none the less. As a result, he contrived to have spies in innumerable homes.[68] When the general called for a surrender of arms by the citizenry, he published a price list of informers' fees: $10 for each serviceable gun, musket, or rifle; $7 for a revolver; $5 for a pistol; $5 for a saber or officer's sword; $3 apiece for dirks, sword canes, daggers, or Bowie knives.[69] He even developed a reliable method for sifting out the rumors about Confederate successes. He found that there was a brisk market in Confederate notes, which rose in value upon the news of Southern successes and fell just as certainly when there were military setbacks. The brokers, Butler found, "were principally Jews, and as Benjamin, the Confederate Secretary of State, was a Jew, and his brother-in-law was a broker, I supposed there were some of the Jew brokers who could get true intelligence from Richmond." [70] Butler therefore had spies to study brokerage transactions.

By September, Butler felt that the oath of allegiance to the United States should have been taken by even more persons, so he published a new Confiscation Order: all who ever had been United States citizens and had not renewed their allegiance, or who owed allegiance or sympathy to the Confederacy, were obliged to report to the provost marshal with inventories of property. So said General Order No. 76.[71] From Confederate General Jeff Thompson, commanding forces that opposed Butler's troops in Louisiana, came a prompt reply: "We thank you for General Order No. 76. It will answer us for a precedent at New Orleans, St. Louis, Louisville, Baltimore, Washington, each of which we will have in a few days. We were undetermined how to act. Please 'pile it on.' " [72]

Meanwhile there was some fighting to be done by Butler's army. On August 5th his brigade at Baton Rouge was attacked by the Confederates, under General Breckinridge, whose candidacy for the Presidency of the United States Butler had supported fewer than two years ago. General Williams successfully fought off the attack at the cost of his own life; [73] but Butler withdrew the brigade before a second attack could be mounted. [74]

Butler was now worried about the possibility of other attacks. Because he could get no reinforcements from the War Department by the regular channels, he wrote to his friend Senator Wilson for aid, saying: "I beg you, as chairman of the Military Committee, to use your influence to have more troops sent here—Mass. troops especially." [75] This type of appeal struck a sympathetic note in the ears of the Massachusetts Senator, "whose tears in their flow never for a moment distorted his count of the votes to be gained for his party." [76] But when even that stratagem did not work to his complete satisfaction, Butler decided to form his own colored regiments, something that no other commander had dared to do in the face of Lincoln's known objection. [77] To the Secretary of War Butler wrote of his accomplished fact: "I shall also have within ten days a regiment, one thousand strong, of native guards (colored), the darkest of whom will be about the complexion of the late Mr. Webster." [78] In all, he formed three regiments of infantry and two companies of artillery. One of these groups got into a squabble with some Frenchmen; and when the French consul protested about the disgraceful conduct of the Negroes Butler tartly replied that they had the same blood as Alexandre Dumas, who was treated by the Paris aristocracy with the greatest respect. [79]

The creation of Negro regiments was only an additional grievance against Butler that the Southerners harbored. General Beauregard of Louisiana first coined the lasting phrase "Butler the Beast." [80] Others embroidered on this theme; thus one female diarist referred to him as a "hideous, cross-eyed beast." [81] And the name has stuck to this day. "[H]e is still referred to there [New Orleans] as Butler the Beast, and if one-twentieth of the stories told about him are true he was veritably a scoundrel of the deepest dye." [82] "No other Federal commander," wrote a Southern historian, "was ever to be regarded with as loathing a contempt as General Benjamin F. Butler for his activities in New Orleans, and no other commander was to be awarded the special title of 'Beast.' " [83] It was even rumored that many squint-eyed yellow babies were born in that city by reason of their mothers' fright at Butler's presence.[84] "When the needy barbarians of the upper plains of Asia descended upon the classic fields of Italy," wrote the Confederate President, "their atrocities were such as shocked the common-sense of humanity; but, if any one should inquire minutely into the conduct of Butler and his followers at New Orleans, he will find there a history yet more revolting." [85]

If Butler's concept of martial law was severe, he had good precedent. In a letter he wrote:

Now, my theory of the law martial is this—that it is a . . . well-defined part of the common law of this country, . . . recognized in its proper place by the Constitution, and that proper place . . . is in the camp and garrison. Now, the best definition of martial law that I have ever heard was that by Sir Arthur Wellesly, afterwards Duke of Wellington . . . : "The will of the Comdg. General exercised according to . . . natural equity." . . . Thus civil government may well exist in subordination to martial law . . . when . . . efficient to the end desired. When [not] . . . , that government is . . . to be cast aside.[86]

Objectively, it must seem that any man in his position in New Orleans would have been unpopular.[87] His personality magnified his shortcomings, real or imaginary. When he moved from the St. Charles Hotel to a private residence, he not inappropriately selected the mansion of the Confederate General Twiggs; and finding one of Twiggs's swords there, he sent it to the Patent Office in Washington with the recommendation that it be prominently displayed as a memento of the injudiciousness of such an invention as secession.[88] Another sword of General Twiggs (the gift of the State of Georgia) was sent by Butler to President Lincoln, with the recommendation that it be deposited in the library at West Point, "with an appropriate inscription, as a perpetual memento to the youths there, how worse than useless are all education and military training, even when allied to gallantry and courage, if heartfelt patriotism and undying fidelity to the Constitution and the Flag are wanting." [89] The story then started that Butler had even stolen the silver spoons from the Twiggs mansion,[90] and soon it was being charged that he stole silverware whenever he dined out.[91] The sobriquet of "Spoons" Butler was to be permanent.

Finally President Davis issued a most remarkable proclamation on the subject of Butler, naming as his specific crimes the execution of Mumford, the imprisonment of peaceful and aged citizens, the encouraging of soldiers to insult women, the imprisonment of paroled soldiers, the obtaining of allegiance by duress, the inciting of slaves, and the plundering of a community. The peroration was tremendous:

Now therefore, I, Jefferson Davis, President of the Confederate States of America, and in their name, do pronounce and declare that said Benjamin F. Butler to be a felon, deserving of capital punishment. I do order that he shall no longer be considered or treated simply as a public enemy of the Confederate States of America, but as an outlaw and common enemy of mankind, and that, in the event of his capture, the officer in charge of the capturing force do cause him to be immediately executed by hanging.

And I do further order that no commissioned officer of the United States, taken captive, shall be released on parole, before exchanged, until the said Butler shall have met with due punishment for his crimes. . . . I . . . do order . . . That all commissioned officers in the command of said Benjamin F. Butler be declared not entitled to be considered as soldiers engaged in honorable warfare, but as robbers and criminals, deserving death; and that they and each of them, whenever captured, reserved for execution.[92]

One wonders whether Davis, in writing these angry words, remembered how Butler had voted for him fifty times as the Democratic candidate for President of the United States not two years previously.

Immediately after the proclamation, the Charleston *Courier* printed a letter from a woman in South Carolina: "I propose to spin the thread to make the cord to execute the order of our noble President Davis when old Butler is caught and my daughter asks that she may be allowed to adjust it around his neck." [93]

But Butler's deeds were beginning to creep up on him, deservedly or not. As early as August 2, 1862, the general wrote to his wife about another Bay State politician: "They have an absurd story here that Banks is to be sent down here to take my place. I wish to heaven he would come!" [94] Within a few months people in the fashionable New Orleans clubs were betting, ten to one, that he would be recalled before the end of the year.[95] When Butler was informed of this, he wrote to the general in chief in Washington: "I learn . . . that I am to be relieved of this command. If that be so, might I ask that my successor be sent as early as possible, as my own health is not the strongest, and it would seem but fair that he should take some part in the yellow-fever season." [96] The Secretary of War himself replied and "expressed his confidence in you, and his approval of your vigor and ability." [97] Yet Stanton already had appointed Banks to succeed Butler, who was later to ask, "Can lying, injustice, deceit, and tergiversation farther go?" [98]

On November 29th Butler wrote lengthily to Lincoln, stating that "I see by the papers that Gen'l Banks is about being sent into this Department with troops upon an independent expedition and command. This seems to imply a want of confidence in the Commander of this Department, perhaps deserved, but still painful to me." Butler then offered to depart rather than to embarrass the administration.[99] Secretary of the Treasury Chase wrote reassuringly to Butler on December 14th: "Don't think that the appointment of General Banks will really harm you. It will not. Your retirement would, for it would be ascribed to wounded self-love. . . . Our friends in Congress are unanimous in your praise. Nobody finds fault except some honest people who really believe what has been said about your connection with trade." [100]

The order relieving Butler (as the one relieving General McClellan) was dated the day after the 1862 elections, "so that," said the Massachusetts general, "it might appear as if the Republican administration had determined to put out of command all generals who had heretofore been Democrats, and to supply true Republican generals in their places." [101]

But there were other possible reasons for the removal. A Seward biographer wrote that half of the Secretary of State's time was spent on complaints of foreign ministers about Butler's administration.[102] It has been said that the United States Government yielded to the pressure of foreign governments, the good will of which had to be kept at all costs.[103] Many persons believed that the removal had been contrived by the French because of their plans for seizing Mexico or even annexing Texas.[104] Certainly the French plans for aiding the Confederacy by opening the New Orleans blockade had been broken by the Farragut-Butler team.[105] A military writer felt that Butler had been removed "for obvious reasons." [106] Yet a year after Butler's death it was stated, "Why he was removed is as great a problem today as it was at the date of his removal." [107]

On December 12, 1862, Butler received his first official information of the order of removal when Banks presented it in person.[108] Four days later General Banks asked that certain of Butler's officers retain their duties for a time; and Butler at once replied: "In compliance with your request I have directed all my staff who are heads of departments to remain such time as will enable them to turn over the property in their hands and fully instruct the corresponding officers of your staff so that there may be the least possible embarrassment from the change." [109] On December 18th Butler wrote to Lincoln of the removal in favor of Banks, and in conclusion he stated: "Having received no further orders, either to report to him or otherwise, I have taken the liberty to suppose that I was permitted to return home, my services being no longer needed here. . . . I have the honor to inform you that, until further orders, my address will be Lowell, Massachusetts." [110]

Butler then made a farewell address to the people of New Orleans —and England:

I have not been too harsh. I might have smoked you to death in caverns as were the Covenanters of Scotland by a royal British general, or roasted you like the people of Algiers were roasted by the French; your wives and daughters might have been given over to the ravisher as were the women of Spain in the Peninsular War, and your property turned over to indiscriminate plunder like that of the Chinese when the English captured their capital; you might have been blown from the mouths of cannon as were the sepoys of Delhi,—and yet kept within the rules of civilized war as practiced by the most polished and hypocritical capitals of Europe. But I have not done so.[111]

In Washington this speech greatly moved an exiled Polish count and revolutionary, who now worked in the State Department, so he said, to "keep Seward from making a fool of himself." [112] "Gen. Butler's farewell proclamation to New Orleans," he wrote, "rings the purest and most patriotic harmony. Compare Butler's with Lincoln's writings. All the hearts in the country resounded with Butler; and because he acted as he did, Lincoln-Seward-Blair-Halleck's policy shelved Butler." [113] Said another admirer of Butler's final New Orleans speech: "His language resembled, in its terse, laconic character, the eloquence of Napoleon, whom he may almost be said to have rivalled in the vigor of his administration." [114]

On the morning of December 24th, General Butler left New Orleans in an unarmed transport.[115] "Good-bye, honey," cried an old Negress, "you never stole nothing from me!" [116]

CHAPTER IX

INTERREGNUM

BUTLER'S ship reached the harbor of New York on New Year's Day, 1863. A revenue cutter met the vessel, and a holograph letter from Lincoln was handed to the general: "I believe you have a family, and I dislike to deprive you of an early visit to them. But I really wish to see you at the earliest moment. I am contemplating a peculiar and important service for you, which I think, and hope you will think, is as honorable as it is important. I wish to confer with you about it. Please come immediately after your arrival at New York." [1]

Butler hurried to Washington, but he was more interested in his past assignment than in a future one. "Mr. President," he demanded, "will you please tell me for what acts of mine I am recalled from New Orleans?"

"I am not at liberty to tell you," Lincoln answered, "but you may ask Mr. Stanton." So the irate general rushed to the Secretary of War and repeated his question to him. "The reason," explained Stanton, "was one which does not imply, on the part of the government, any want of confidence in your honor as a man, or in your ability as a commander."

"Well, you have told me what I was *not* recalled for. I now ask you to tell me what I *was* recalled for."

"You and I are both lawyers," Stanton continued, "and it is of no use your filing a bill of discovery upon *me*, for I shan't tell you." [2]

So Butler hurried to interrogate the Secretary of State; and Seward declared: "I do not know what you were recalled for, I assure you, but Halleck knows all about it. He is the general-in-chief, and had everything to do with it." But Halleck was not more communicative than the others. "I do not know, General," he stated; "no reasons were ever given to me. It was done solely under the direction of the Secretary of State." [3]

Butler realized the impossibility of learning anything from this "ring-around-a-rosie" set-up, so he went back to Lincoln. He told the President that he would give back his commission, for he was returning to his home in Lowell. "Oh, you shall go where you please, General, but keep your commission." [4] Perhaps the President was thinking of Butler's words when he had accepted that very commission: "I shall do no political act and loyally support your administration as long as I hold your commission." [5] Butler could not be allowed to go away angry, at least angry enough to return his commission. But the President would not explain what was back of the recall.

Butler stayed around Washington for a time, demanding that some one have the courage to say that he had been removed at the request of Napoleon III.[6] But he was officially ignored. The only members of the diplomatic corps in Washington to call on him were the ministers of Russia and of the Free City of Bremen; [7] virtually all the other ministers had had angry strife with Butler over the treatment of their nationals (and their consuls) in New Orleans.

Salmon P. Chase, the Secretary of the Treasury, sided with Butler in his troubles; [8] perhaps he found this another opportunity to embarrass Lincoln. Or perhaps the secretary was impressed by a letter he had received from his New Orleans representative, which said of Butler: "In two weeks he could restore everything, but I do not suppose he will be sent here, for he is too earnest a man to suit Mr. Seward, and if placed in a high position, he might become dangerous as candidate for the Presidency." [9] To Butler, Chase's representative also wrote directly: "Come back to New Orleans. . . . [T]he happiest day of my life will be the day when a steamer arrives with you on board." [10]

The Secretary of the Navy likewise regretted the turn of events. He had noted in his diary: "Information reaches us that General Butler has been superseded at New Orleans by General Banks. The

wisdom of this change I question. . . . I have not a very exalted
opinion of the military qualities of either. . . . [Banks] has not the
energy, power, ability of Butler, nor, though of loose and fluctuating
principles, will he be so reckless and unscrupulous." [11] Ability Butler
unquestionably had—but that was not all. As one eminent historian
observed, "In fairness to Butler it must be said that his administration was in some respects intelligent and able. . . . But there was an
amount of confiscation unparalleled elsewhere during the war; and
a swarm of adventurers, with Butler's connivance, made their fortunes in speculating with the property thus seized." [12]

Welles went to the trouble of protesting Butler's removal to Lincoln, feeling that his civil administration had been successful.[13] On
January 23rd the President wrote to his Secretary of War: "I think
General Butler should go to New Orleans again. He is unwilling to
go unless he is restored to the command of the department. . . . I
think we cannot longer dispense with General Butler's services." [14]
But that was not to be.

To his brother Andrew, Butler wrote: "There are possibilities that
I shall return to N. Orleans. . . . Believe nothing about me you
see in the newspapers." [15] And the Massachusetts general had reason
for his optimism. The Butler papers in the Library of Congress contain several drafts, on War Department stationery, of tentative orders "That Maj Gen Butler return to the Department of the Gulf
via the Mississippi River to assume command thereof when he arrives within the Same." [16] There is also a draft letter from Lincoln
ordering all officers on the Mississippi to extend courtesies to Butler,
who would be there "at my request, for observation." [17]

If Butler's reception in some administration circles was cold, it
was anything but frigid elsewhere. One admirer wrote the general:
"Only after I had the honor and the pleasure to shake hands with
you, I read your parting word to the people of New-Orleans. I master
not my feelings, my rapture. I bring to you my homage. You speak
deeds not words; deeds of eternal honor to a noble and true patriot
and citizen, to a lofty-minded and genuine statesman." [18]

Butler was in great demand as a speaker not only on the New
Orleans situation but on broader vistas. Invitations poured in from

General Butler

Butler and his staff

such varied sources as the Mercantile Library Association of Boston, the citizens of Manchester, and Tiger Engine Company Number 5 of Lowell.[19] To a gathering of important citizens at the Fifth Avenue Hotel in New York he said: "Let us bring the South into subjection to the Union. . . . But, at all events, they must come under the power of the Union."[20] That was the first indication that Butler had become a "hard peace" man: he had been regarded generally as a great friend of the South, who could understand the people and the philosophy. But after New Orleans he knew that he was bitterly hated by the South; and hatred begets hatred. In another speech Butler had his say on the question of British intervention in the war. "Let us proclaim non-intercourse," he declared, "so that no ounce of food from the United States shall ever by any accident get into an Englishman's mouth until this rebellion ceases."[21]

The British did not trust the utterer of such sentiments. Sir Henry Holland, Queen Victoria's physician-in-ordinary and the friend of many highly placed Englishmen, wrote to Thurlow Weed on the deterioration of Anglo-American relations. Certain specific actions were responsible, he believed. "I would name as such . . . the conduct of General Butler, and some other local authorities, on the scene of the war."[22]

But at home Butler's actions were generally applauded. The House of Representatives adopted resolutions expressing its appreciation of "your able, energetic and humane administration of the Department of the Gulf."[23] Both houses of the Massachusetts legislature thanked him "for the energy, ability and success, characterizing his late administration and command of the Department of the Gulf."[24] By joint resolution the Ohio legislature declared that Butler "is entitled to the grateful acknowledgement and thanks of the loyal people of the Country."[25] The Women's National League sent to Lincoln a copy of its resolution, which stated, "When Butler, in the chief city of the southern despotism, hung a traitor we felt a glow of pride; for that one act proved that we had a government and one man brave enough to administer its laws."[26]

Harper's Weekly approvingly depicted in cartoon form the Massachusetts general freshly returned from New Orleans with soap and scrubbing brush. Has Mr. Lincoln any further clean-up jobs?[27] Thurlow Weed wrote to the American consul general in Paris: *"We are in a bad way.* I wish that Ben Butler had been elected president, —or that even now he was in Halleck's place."[28]

The Committee on the Conduct of the War summoned Butler to Washington to express his opinions on the operation of the Department of the Gulf,[29] and the resultant session has been described as a meeting of a mutual admiration society.[30]

Then, since there was nothing further for him to do, Butler returned to his home in Lowell, from where he wrote to his brother in New Orleans: "I am at home. My reception has been all I could have desired. I can go back to N.O. I may do so but awaiting [*sic*] the culminating of events here. All well. Mother sends love. No news. Banks put his foot in it by his proclamation. If the battle now being fought is not successful we shall have a change of Government. Come to New York as soon as you can do so without sacrifice."[31]

In return the general's brother reported: "I have drawn for 274683 Dollars to pay for 892 Hlds Tobacco shipped to New York. . . . I am closing up as fast as possible but have innumerable obstacles thrown in my way."[32] Two weeks later he wrote from New Orleans: "I will not be able to leave here for 20 or 30 days. It will take that long to wind up—they seize everything that comes from below, and it takes from 1 to 8 days to get it passed that bullet-headed commission, but it will pay me something after all the drawbacks and charges."[33]

The general attempted to devote his attention to his own affairs, but there were many interruptions from the outside world. He was not regarded as being outside the active army. Thus the Secretary of the Treasury wrote to introduce his brother-in-law as a "capital cavalry officer for any service."[34] General Hooker's new chief of staff asked how to set up an espionage system, for "I feel that I am not mistaken, when I judge that your experience in this line will prove valuable."[35]

There was a veritable rain of letters upon the general. Men wanted to sign up for Butler's next expedition, or to sign up for their sons. There were letters of appreciation, and not a few threats. A Lowell

alderman offered to accompany Butler to the next battle as barber.
A woman was willing to see service as Mrs. Butler's seamstress. A
nephew wrote to the general of his desire to be transferred from field
activity with the Army of the Potomac to recruiting service, for.
"Even as a mustering officer I can at least get on a white shirt now
and then, which is looked upon here as effeminacy." [36]

The Massachusetts general was obliged to devote a considerable
amount of his time to explaining details of what he had done in
New Orleans. To Stanton, the Secretary of War, there were such letters as claims of British subjects; [37] to the Secretary of State went
justifications of the treatment of foreign nationals.[38] Butler received
so much correspondence that he could not give all of it his personal
attention, but when a packer wrote on his business stationery a reply seemed due. His secretary wrote: "Yours of the 4th is rec'd, in
which you advise Maj. Gen. Butler if *you* were *he,* you would, or
would not, do so and so. I am instructed by the General to say that
as you attempt to advise him what to do, if *you* were *he, he* would if
he were you, stick to 'packing pork.' " [39]

The general also sought to answer the numerous charges that were
being made about him. He wrote to his biographer that "no sense of
delicacy of position in relation to myself shall interfere with the
closest investigation of every act alleged to have been done or permitted by me." [40]

In February, 1863, Radical Republican leaders such as Wade and
Chandler sought to get Butler a military command in the West,
in order to build up Western support for the general's rising political
ambitions.[41] After Chase resigned his post as Secretary of the Treasury, the Radicals looked most hopefully at Butler, Frémont, and
Wade.[42]

Butler continued his active correspondence with Chase, and to
the Ohioan he poured forth his most intensive analysis of the war:

I do not understand our plan of carrying on war, although I have
never written a treatise on either the law of nations or the art of war in
any of its branches, for what education I have has been by reading a few
good books, not by writing poor ones, still I may venture to assert that
I cannot see the use of five or six little armies who never co-operate with

each other—considerably too large for garrisons and quite too small for armies—too little to move—too large to lie still; enough to swallow up men, less than needed for effective action; too large to afford to lose them as garrisons of posts, which by the rules of war are supposed to be captured after their resistance has cost the enemy enough for the outlay, and yet so small as to keep us in constant trepidation lest they be overpowered. . . .

Perhaps the disappointment of the country at the Bull Run defeat has determined the course of our battles, but so is the fact. We have risked nothing, and we have gained nothing but delays. Nothing was ever greatly gained without something *greatly risked.* . . .

Permit me to congratulate you upon the eminent success which has attended the finances of the Government under your administration. It is admirable; but was it greatly won without the courage greatly to risk a failure? [43]

In July, 1863, New York was wracked by bloody draft riots, which were not brought under control till troops were rushed back from the battlefields of Gettysburg.[44] Within a week's time a number of Congressmen asked Lincoln to declare martial law in New York, with General Butler to enforce it; [45] no commander was better fitted for the assignment. Welles noted in his diary on July 15th: "In many respects General Butler would at this time have best fitted that position. As a municipal and police officer he has audacity and certain other qualities in which most military men are deficient, while as a general in the field he is likely to accomplish but little." [46] Butler was not called at that time, but he was to be remembered when New York again seemed ripe for rioting.

Another ugly situation brought forth a demand for Butler. In Missouri the radical element (known as the "Charcoals" [47]) was disturbed by the Frémont-Blair political machine and by the generalship of Schofield, and Lincoln was urged to place Butler in command of the Department of Missouri.[48]

But Butler seemed far removed from war and its train, and finally the chairman of the Committee on the Conduct of the War, John Covode of Pennsylvania, journeyed to Lowell to ascertain whether the general would still participate in the war. "I told him," said Butler, "that . . . if the matters which I should propose could be carried out that I would again take part in the war. I said that it seemed to me that the management of the war had got entirely mixed up with politics." [49]

Butler had his terms, but at first they could not be met. He wanted to take command of the Army of Tennessee, which would cut the Confederacy in two by marching to Savannah; and it is interesting to note that Sherman, who eventually made that march, was the only Federal soldier whom the Southerners linked with Butler—and with Satan.[50] Butler told the Committee on the Conduct of the War that he could make the march with 75,000 men spared from the Army of the Potomac, and from Washington, "doing nothing there but keeping rebels off." [51] But keeping the rebels off apparently was considered a full-time job, for the 75,000 troops were not reassigned.

That summer Butler was invited by Lincoln to ride with him one evening to the Soldiers' Home, some two miles from the White House on a lonely road. The President had no guard or escort; and when Butler criticized his lack of precaution Lincoln argued that assassination was not an American crime. He did agree, however, that he would accept a guard if the Secretary of War should assign one; and that was done. Butler took credit for seeing that the President was properly safeguarded.[52]

After nearly a year of military inactivity, Butler was appointed to the command of the Department of Virginia and North Carolina.[53] In November, 1863, he was ordered to relieve General Foster in that capacity.[54] On his way from Lowell to take over his new assignment, Butler called upon Lincoln, who counseled: "Don't let Davis catch you, General; he has put a price on your head; he will hang you for sure."

"That's a game two can play at, Mr. President," replied Butler. "If I ever catch him I will remember your scruples about capital punishment, and relieve you from any trouble with them in his case. He has outlawed me and if I get hold of him I shall give him the law of the outlaw after a reasonable time to say his prayers." [55]

Butler took up his new assignment with enthusiasm, which was not shared by the people in his bailiwick. "They regret Genl. Butler is in command there," the Attorney General of the United States noted in his diary. "He is, they think, the last man to soften and conciliate. His name is a fear, not a hope—The people have a vague dread that makes them shrink from contact with him." [56]

CHAPTER X

ON TO RICHMOND

BUTLER'S new Department had its headquarters at Fortress Monroe; and here he received a visit from his new commander, Ulysses S. Grant. "This was the first time I had ever met him," the latter recalled.[1] Appraising the commander and his subaltern, the Assistant Secretary of War declared: "It is much to be regretted that he could not have had, in some places, the assistance of men better able to comprehend and perform the duty allotted them."[2] The commander's military secretary related that "Butler, whom Grant found in command of the Department of Virginia and North Carolina, was not a professional soldier, and his military career had not been brilliant, but his energy was great, his ability undoubted, and his political influence such that the government was unwilling to disturb him. Grant, therefore, did not insist on his removal."[3] John Rawlins, Grant's chief of staff, shared with his superior a disappointment in Butler's military merits as well as an appreciation of his political status.[4] As Admiral Porter wrote, "All men seemed afraid of Butler's political power: it was even potential. with the President."[5] But it was necessary that he should have military command; that would keep him out of politics, if anything could.[6] A colonel complained, none the less, that the "military element did not enter in any degree into Butler's composition, and the Army of the Potomac, including myself, paid the penalty."[7]

Grant endeavored to bolster Butler's military weaknesses; he "gave him two of the ablest professional soldiers in the army to command his corps, in the hope that Butler would avail himself of their talent and experience; he sent him a promising general officer for his cavalry; and offered him the opportunity of capturing the rebel capital; leaving thus what seemed to most men the prize of the campaign within the reach of a subordinate, while he assumed for himself the more difficult task of conquering the greatest army of the Confederacy." [8] But Butler did not take kindly to these well regarded generals, and he said that "my two corps commanders agreed upon but one thing and that was, how they could thwart and interfere with me." [9] He described how Generals Gillmore and Smith responded to his orders: "Gillmore got his dinner, picked his teeth, waited." [10] "Smith's curse was that he had graduated as a topographical engineer,—that is, a picture drawer or map maker,—and he was continually making maps before he made his assaults." [11]

But the grand assault had to be mounted, and Grant drew up his plans with care. He warned Butler pointedly: "Start on the date given in my letter. There will be no delay with this Army." [12] Early on the morning of May 4, 1864, the advance got under way. [13] Grant led the main army overland from the north in the direction of Richmond, while Siegel went up the Shenandoah Valley toward Lynchburg and Averell operated in the southwest. The fourth prong in the attack was to be Butler's thrust from Fortress Monroe on the line of the James River. [14] The plan called for Butler to advance up the James, to approach Richmond from the rear, and then to prevent reinforcements from reaching Lee's main army, which would be grappling with Grant's. [15] On May 5th Butler occupied City Point and Bermuda Hundred with 12,000 troops, designated as the Army of the James. [16] He was now only twelve miles from Richmond, where one of his spies, Elizabeth Van Lew, already was operating. [17] Reported the Assistant Secretary of War:

No fairer opportunity was ever lost than Butler had after landing at Bermuda Hundred. Had that General been adequate to the part assigned him, he would have marched instantly against the communications of Richmond, and the rebel troops from the Carolinas hastening to its defense. . . . [18] It was a great misfortune to the national cause, that Butler did not pursue a vigorous and determined policy, immediately after his landing on the south side of the James; but he seems to have had no perception of the strategic importance of his operations, or of the relative value of the points before him. . . . He neither marched rapidly nor fought vigorously in any direction, and hence did no serious damage to the enemy.[19]

"It was in the chances," related Rhodes, "that a skilful and daring general might have captured Petersburg or Richmond. Butler was neither, and dallied while Beauregard energetically gathered together the loose forces in North and South Carolina, and brought them to the defence of the two places." [20] One of his officers thus described General Butler on that campaign: "Eager for military distinction, inordinately self-confident until face-to-face with an opponent in actual battle, when, on the night of May 5, the Army of the James was landed from the transports at Bermuda Hundreds, Butler was there in full command." [21]

Pickett bluffed Butler into thinking that the Petersburg fortifications were adequately manned,[22] for which trickery Pickett incurred the Massachusetts general's permanent enmity.[23] By the time Butler got around to attacking the Confederate lines at Drewry's Bluff on May 13th, the defenses were too strong to be turned; [24] and after two days of fighting, on May 16th Beauregard hurled Butler's forces back to Bermuda Hundred Neck.[25] The James River flows southeastward; the Appomattox flows northeastward into the James, making the land in between in effect a peninsula. As Butler retreated Beauregard stationed his troops at the open end,[26] so that the Federal forces could only resume a ground advance through a narrow, easily defended strip of earth. This opening was only four miles wide,[27] and, noted Grant, "it was therefore as if Butler was in a bottle." [28] In his official report, Grant used that same phrase: "The enemy intrenched strongly in his [Butler's] front which cut him off from his railroads, the city, and all that was valuable to him. His army, therefore, though in a position of great security, was as completely shut off from further operations directly against Richmond as if it had been in a bottle, strongly corked." [29]

"Butler, like Grouchy,[30] was left by the commander in chief to act, under general instructions, as the conditions of time and place, and the movements of the enemy in his front, might make more expedient," noted a disgruntled officer, "the plan of campaign and general strategic situation being always clearly in mind. Both failed, and failed utterly." [31] Even when the Confederate forces were not at the neck of the peninsula, the Massachusetts general did not again undertake a determined advance. Said a distinguished British military strategist: "Meanwhile Butler, finding himself uncorked, like the jinn in the Arabian Nights, was persuaded, even with less trouble than the time before, to creep back into his bottle." [32]

That ended Butler's dream of winning the war by capturing Richmond, and his wife shared his sorrow. In one of the most poignant letters in the history of warfare, she confided to her general: "I actually have bought a carriage hat of straw, white velvet, and a long white feather. I thought it would but barely answer to grace the taking of Richmond. I will instantly send it home and order it put in the darkest closet in the attic." [33]

Butler's army being thus effectively corked up on Bermuda Hundred, it was militarily ineffective as a major offensive force; and the troops were gradually siphoned off in large measure as reinforcements for Grant.[34] But Butler was in a fighting mood; and as he could not get at the Confederate army he turned his vast energies to his own subalterns. The obstreperous General "Baldy" Smith in particular had to be put in his place.

During the campaign Smith's corps had been forced back at one point. "His front," said the Assistant Secretary of War, "was too much extended already for a defensive battle and an offensive one with such a leader as Butler, was out of the question." [35] Butler accused him of having bungled a troop movement; and when Smith retorted Butler reminded him that *he* was the superior officer. Smith wrote back that he had moved troops longer than Butler and was *his* superior in that. "I did not think that I should be insulted by a second grade West Pointer," Butler declared; [36] and his reply seemed so insulting in turn that Smith went to Grant and asked to be relieved from serving under such a general.[37] The friction became so heated that the Assistant Secretary of War wrote to the Secretary on July 1st, "Butler is pretty deep in controversial correspondence with 'Baldy' Smith, in which Grant says Butler is clearly in the wrong." [38]

Smith complained to Grant of "the terrible waste of life that has resulted from what I had considered a want of generalship in its present commander." But Grant replied hopelessly that he "could not relieve General Butler." [39]

Grant's fear of antagonizing Butler is one of the great mysteries of the war. There is no reason to believe that Grant was politically ambitious at this stage of things, and hence Butler's power in that sphere should not have deterred him from what he knew was his proper course. Then what did Butler have on Grant? One of Grant's biographers has suggested that the lieutenant general was afraid lest Butler publicize the well known stories of drunkenness; [40] and "Baldy" Smith himself thought that that was the answer. [41] Yet everyone knew about Grant's weakness in that direction, and blackmail hence would seem illogical.

Early in July, Grant had occasion to visit Smith's headquarters; and as the commander left, "Baldy" said to a staff officer: "General Grant has gone away drunk. General Butler has seen it, and will never fail to use the weapon which has been put into his hands." [42] It is known that the lieutenant general had succumbed to his old habits during this period. His chief of staff, who had undertaken the responsibility of keeping his superior from the bottle, recorded on July 28th: "I find the General in my absence digressed from his true path. The God of Heaven only knows how long I am to serve my country as the guardian of the habits of him whom it has honored." [43] Rhodes related: "It was commonly believed in the army that his misfortunes had driven him again to drink, and on this account and others, Butler, with crafty method, acquired a hold on him which prevented him from acting for the best interests of the service. It is not a grateful task to relate the story of Butler using Grant as a tool to accomplish his own ends. The picture of such a relation between the two is repulsive, but it may be fraught with instruction, as men of the type of Butler are never absent from our political life." [44] At this time Butler wrote to his wife that "Grant was *sick* all day yesterday, so he could not be seen." [45] One may speculate on what the Massachusetts general intended to convey by the underscoring.

Smith knew his way around a bit, too, and he went to Washington to seek the aid of Senator Foote of Vermont. Immediately thereafter Order No. 225 was issued from the War Department, to the effect that Smith would take charge of the XVIII Corps, with Butler to command the remainder of the troops of the Department of North Carolina and Virginia, with headquarters at Fortress Monroe instead of in the field.[46] When Butler heard that he was to be replaced in large measure by Smith, he at once set out for Grant's headquarters at City Point. To his staff he said, "Gentlemen, the order will be revoked tomorrow";[47] to Colonel Shaffer, his chief of staff, he declared: "Do not trouble yourself about the order. It is all right now and better than if it had not been disturbed."[48]

When the Massachusetts general arrived at City Point, Grant was engaged in a discussion with Dana, the Assistant Secretary of War; but Butler burst right into their presence without announcement and demanded, "General Grant, did you issue this order?"

Grant was visibly disturbed as he answered, "No, not in that form." Dana immediately departed, noting Grant's embarrassment. Butler remained closeted with his military superior for an hour.[49] "I did not mean that you should have seen that order," explained Grant. "It is a mistake. I suppressed all the copies that were transmitted through me. How did you get this?"

"Some friend in the War Department, fearing perhaps I should not see it, forwarded me one direct," replied Butler.

"Well, I don't want this at all. I want Smith to report to you— you to have the full command," Grant declared.[50]

Butler wrote to his wife that this was the work of Halleck and his crew, "those people—whom God and his humble instrument will take care of before we get through."[51]

The very next day Grant wrote to Halleck in Washington not to effect the change.[52] On the same day Butler wrote triumphantly to his wife: "Thanks for your kind letter of condolence, but 'I ain't dead yet.' The Washington people better look out for themselves or Early[53] will get them." The letter was signed, "Benj. F. Butler, Maj. General, 'commanding all the troops he ever commanded, and more too.'"[54]

That was the end of Smith. He was relieved of his command within a few days.[55] Concerning his own removal, Smith wrote, "I was convinced that General Grant, under the pressure of the great burden he was carrying, had temporarily become the victim of a habit which had at one time disqualified him from command, to force him to act against his judgment and inclination."[56] Butler scoffed at Smith's charge that Grant's intoxication was as a weapon placed in his (Butler's) hands: "General Smith, who put it there?"[57] It was in *Smith's* headquarters that Grant had had the drink(s) which inaugurated this affair.

Butler's other corps commander, Quincy A. Gillmore, had a similar though less explosive end, even though Mrs. Butler meanwhile was advising her husband: "Avoid hostility as much as possible; keep it for the rebels."[58] Butler drew up a scathing indictment of Gillmore's maneuvers on the field,[59] and with angry accusations the Massachusetts general had him arrested for disobedience to orders and military incapacity. Grant released him from arrest, but that was all he could do.[60] When Gillmore answered his accuser in kind, Butler replied not to him but to the useful Senator Henry Wilson: "I must take the responsibility of asking you to bring before the Senate at once the name of Genl. Gillmore, and have his name rejected by your body."[61]

Next, lest there be any remote chance that the Senate might not refuse to approve Gillmore's pending promotion to major general, Butler sent a communication to one of his agents, who reported back from Washington: "I arrived here at 11 A.M. to-day. It is now 2.30 P.M. I have seen Senators Wade, Chandler, Pomeroy, Harlan, Lane (Ind.), Fessenden, Wilkinson, Sumner, and as soon as Morrill comes in I will see him. I have read the letter to the gentlemen, and said that in addition to the justice of the desired rejection, you would esteem it a personal favor if their prompt action should relieve you of a nuisance (or a worse thing) as Gen. G. has proven himself to be, so far."[62] That letter is one of the very few traces that remain of how Butler worked.

When Gillmore sent Butler a copy of his counter-complaint, the latter was in position to reply that Gillmore had been relieved of his command, and "a steamer will be ready at once to take out to Fortress Monroe." [63] Thus Butler disposed of the two well regarded generals that were supposed to guide him. The only time that the paths of Butler and Gillmore were to cross again was nine years later, when the latter served as president of a military board which recommended further adoption of the Gatling gun, the use of which Butler had pioneered in the field.[64]

But not all Congressmen were so docile to Butler's desires, and Senator Garret Davis was audacious enough to propose that the Massachusetts general be the subject of an inquiry. To him Butler wrote, "You can do me no greater favor than to have every act of my political life, which began on the first Tuesday of November, 1839, and ended on the 15th day of April, 1861, most thoroughly scrutinized." [65] The invitation thus extended did not include Butler's military life.

Butler was able to salvage his own command, and he probably did not even know at that time that on July 1st, less than a week before General Order No. 228 had been issued, Grant had written to Halleck:

Whilst I have no difficulty with General Butler, finding him always clear in his conception of orders and prompt to obey, yet there is want of knowledge how to execute, and particularly a prejudice against him as commander, that operates against his usefulness. . . . I would dislike removing him from his present command unless it was to increase it, but, as I say, may have to do it yet if General Butler remains. As an administrative officer General Butler has no superior. In taking charge of a department where there are no great battles to be fought, but a dissatisfied element to control, no one could manage it better than he. . . . I regret the necessity of asking for a change in commanders here, but General Butler, not being a soldier by education or experience, is in the hands of his subordinates in the execution of all operations military. . . . At the same time, as I have here stated, General Butler has always been prompt in his obedience to orders from me, and clear in his understanding of them. I would not, therefore, be willing to recommend his retirement.[66]

That Butler's assignment was a problem, Halleck admitted two days later in his reply to Grant's strangely vacillating report:

It was foreseen from the first that you would eventually find it necessary to relieve General B. on account of his total unfitness to command in the field, and his generally quarrelsome character. What shall be done with him has, therefore, already been, as I am informed, a matter of consultation. To send him to Kentucky would probably cause an insurrection in that State and an immediate call for large reinforcements. Moreover, he would probably greatly embarrass Sherman, if he did not attempt to supersede him, by using against him all his talent at political intrigue, and his facilities for newspaper abuse. If you send him to Missouri, nearly the same thing will occur there. Although it might not be objectionable to have a free fight between him and Rosecrans, the Government would be seriously embarrassed by the local difficulties and calls for reinforcements likely to follow. Inveterate as is Rosecrans' habit of continually calling for more troops, Butler differs only in demanding instead of calling. As things now stand in the West, I think we can keep the peace, but if Butler be thrown in as a disturbing element, I anticipate very serious results. Why not leave General Butler in command of his department, including North Carolina, Norfolk, Fort Monroe, Yorktown, etc. and make a new army corps of the part of the Eighteenth under Smith? This would leave B. under your immediate control, and at the same time would relieve you of his presence in the field. Moreover, it would save the necessity of organizing a new department. If he must be relieved entirely, I think it would be best to make a new department for him in New England. I make these remarks merely as suggestions. Whatever you may finally determine on I will try to have done. As General B. claims to rank me, I shall give him no orders wherever he may go, without the special directions of yourself or the Secretary of War.[67]

But that part of Halleck's troubled recommendation which *was* adopted, as to Smith, had to be reversed. The problems of an army chief of staff who could not give orders to a general claiming to outrank him were unenviable. As to dismissing Butler, no one even dared to entertain such a thought.

Butler's thoughts about the scholarly Halleck were equally interesting. "Now there is General Halleck, what has *he* to do?" asked the Massachusetts general. "At a moment when every true man is laboring to his utmost, when the days ought to be forty hours long, General Halleck is translating French books at nine cents a page; and, sir, if you should put those nine cents in a box and shake them up, you would form a clear idea of General Halleck's soul!" [68]

The Grant-Butler situation was scarcely a secret, and a contemporary pamphleteer wrote: "The famous prehistoric story of Ulysses and Polyphemus has received its counterpart in the case of two well-known personages of our own age and country. Ulysses of old contrived, with a burning stake, to put out the glaring eye of Polyphemus, the man-eating Cyclops, and thereby to abridge his power for cannibal indulgence; while our modern Ulysses, perhaps, mindful of his classical prototype, is content to leave the new Polyphemus safely 'bottled-up' under the hermetical seal of the saucy Rebel Beauregard." [69] Butler with his one good eye made an acceptable modern Cyclops.

Meanwhile, Butler was having trouble with another Smith. Shortly after the capture of New Orleans, Butler's auditors discovered that the books of Samuel Smith and Company showed $50,000 in gold; but the vault was empty. The gold had been hidden during the uncertain last days of Confederate domination; whereupon Butler claimed that the bank's books were fraudulent, and Samuel Smith was imprisoned until the gold could be returned from its place of hiding. Butler did not report the subsequent receipt of the gold to the government for two months, at which time he wrote to the Secretary of the Treasury that he needed the cash for troop salaries. Almost a year later Smith applied to the Treasury Department for the return of his gold, but he was told that as the Treasury Department had never received it this was a War Department problem.[70] Smith dutifully applied to the War Department, but records were lacking as to this transaction. Therefore Smith's lawyer, Judge Pierrepont of New York, wrote to Butler at Fortress Monroe; and after three letters, Butler replied as follows: "As you are aware, I am in the field, and have, therefore, no books or papers with me relating to former transactions, and was obliged to wait until I had examined some memoranda before I could make as full an answer as I could wish." But he kept the funds. Pierrepont then asked that the money be turned over to the War Department so that a legal remedy could be sought. Butler answered that he had informed the Secretary of War that "as a lawyer, I supposed that I might be held personally for the sum, and that if he would give me an order to pay over the money to the War Office in such form to release me from the responsibility if hereafter called upon by Smith and Co., I should be glad to pay the money over. He doubted whether this could be done." [71]

But without a War Department order, Butler refused to part with the funds; whereas Stanton felt that since the funds never had reached his Department he could issue no order. Eight months after Pierrepont first wrote to Butler, he had the general served with a summons. Butler declared that he was not amenable to the jurisdiction of New York courts; Pierrepont replied that "You have been a general since you were a lawyer; and when you speak of jurisdiction I think you have not read our recent statute." [72] Butler asked the Solicitor of the War Department whether the government would defend the suit, but the government refused to be a party at all. "The Government declined to aid the General in longer keeping Smith's gold," Pierrepont wrote to Schuyler Colfax, Speaker of the House: "and yet the General still holds on to it. Parting with $50,000 of gold, long kept, seems to be attended with reluctance;—perhaps it is natural. Take $50,000 of another man's gold—keep it two years and nine months without giving security to any one—use it as your own; let it rise to 285, and a natural affection springs up for the increasing treasure not to be severed without a pang; natural affections are to be respected, but Mr. Smith has also a lingering attachment to that gold—the honest earnings of many long and weary years." [73]

When Butler took over the Department of North Carolina and Virginia, he found that jurisdiction over part of his bailiwick was claimed by the pro-Union government of the western part of Virginia; [74] the forty so-called "loyal counties" had "seceded" from Virginia and formed a government at Alexandria, under Francis H. Pierpont (not to be confused with Butler's legal adversary Edwards Pierrepont). The governor was distressed when he heard that the military government embracing his territory was to be headed by Butler: "I sighed when I heard it—I remembered New Orleans." [75] It was not long before questions arose on the constitutional interpretation of the status of the West Virginia government, as well as the rights and prerogatives of the civil and military authorities. Butler

drastically suppressed the civil government at every point of juris-
dictional conflict.[76] He demanded that all business permits be reissued
by him; he imposed a 1 per cent import tax on goods entering his
military district, the funds going to a provost marshal instead of to
a civil treasurer.[77] He released prisoners that Pierpont was holding
for civil trial,[78] and he established his own monopoly over the liquor
trade.[79]

Butler referred to Pierpont as "a person who calls himself Governor," [80] and he said that his state government was a "useless, ex-
pensive and inefficient thing, unrecognized by Congress, unknown to
the Constitution of the United States, and of such character that
there is no command in the Decalogue against worshipping it, it being in the likeness of nothing in the heavens above or the earth beneath, or the waters under the earth." [81] Lincoln wrote to Butler to
go easy on the whole arrangement, to do nothing except on the
ground of military necessity.[82] Therefore the Massachusetts general
decided that he would hold a plebiscite, letting the people vote on
whether they would prefer to be governed by civil or martial law.
The adherents of a civil administration denied Butler's authority
to hold such an election, which they boycotted; as a result, the
military-law advocates won handily.

The Secretary of the Navy noted in his diary: "This exhibition
of popular sovereignty destroying itself pleases Butler. . . . While
Butler has talents and capacity, he is not to be trusted, . . . The more
I see of him, the greater is my distrust of his integrity." [83] The
Cabinet took a dim view of the proceedings. Stanton wrote to Butler of hearing "that you have ordered all the Municipal officers of
Norfolk and Portsmouth to report to you in detail the amounts of
all money received by them, etc., and also that you have constituted
a Commission to investigate the conditions of the Savings Funds and
Banking institutions there and [Pierpont], as Governor, feels aggrieved by these measures. The President directs me to request you
to suspend these measures, until you can state to him, in writing
or otherwise, your views of the necessity or propriety of them." [84]

But Butler could explain anything. The Attorney General of the
United States was concerned about a report from General Wilde that

Butler had illegally confiscated certain property. After the Massachusetts general had an opportunity to offer an explanation, the Attorney General noted in his diary: "And Gen. Butler says that Gen. Wilde, *being no lawyer,* made a mistake of a word— He did not mean *confiscate,* but *sequestrate !*" [85] Lincoln did nothing whatsoever about disciplining or over-ruling Butler, and the Attorney General wrote further in his diary: "Alas! that I should live to see such abject fear —such stolid indifference to duty. . . . My heart is sick, when I see the President shrinking from the correction of gross and heinous wrong because he is afraid 'Genl. Butler will raise a hub-bub about it!' . . . The Prest knows what is right, as well as any man, and will be glad to *see it done,* but, unhappily, lacks the nerve to do it." [86]

CHAPTER XI

BUSINESS AS USUAL

IN 1863 Butler created a system of Negro administration in his Department. A General Superintendent of Negro Affairs was appointed, with superintendents under him. A census was taken of colored persons, and shelter and medical care were provided on an organized basis. Land was made available to Negroes, and various educational projects were inaugurated.[1] Nor did Butler overlook the fact that he was a soldier. "We have raised a full company of cavalry in three days," he wrote to the Secretary of War. "The 1st company of colored cavalry." [2]

The general took a great interest in Negro affairs. "I never saw a loyal Virginian who was worth a curse whose skin was lighter than the ace of spades!" he declared.[3] When a citizen objected to the presence of colored soldiers, the general replied, "If you do not die until the negroes hurt you, if you behave yourself, you will live forever." [4] But he could see difficult times ahead for the freedmen, since Congress had taken no action. "The Administration has put the negro, his liberty, his future, into the hands of the Supreme Court," he wrote to Wendell Phillips, the great Abolitionist. "God help him if he has no other refuge!" [5]

Yet Butler's benevolent despotism did not extend very far. When he felt the need of serving as an avenging deity, his retribution was swift and sure. Thus when Early's Confederate raiders burned the Blair home at Silver Spring, Maryland, Butler at once dispatched troops to burn the country mansion of James Seddon, sometime Secretary of War for the Southern cause.[6] When Pickett was outwitting Butler at Petersburg, another Confederate general well understood what the Massachusetts general's reaction would be, for he reported to Richmond: "I have sent a small force to protect . . . General Pickett's property." [7] But the Northern detachment arrived first, and Pickett was obliged to write to his wife: "If it had been burned in line of battle, it would have been all right; but it was not. It was burned by General Butler at a great expense to the Government and in revenge for having been outgeneraled by a little handful of men at Petersburg." [8] Fortunately this form of retribution did not start a chain reaction. "Even the fact that Ben Butler's troops had looted and burned his ancestral homestead did not alter the fine regard of the gallant General Pickett for the amenities of civilized warfare." [9] Pickett was to get his revenge in another form; and the next time his troops met those of Butler, Lee reported: "We tried very hard to keep Pickett's men from capturing the breastworks of the enemy but couldn't do it." [10]

Butler was never too busy for details. The most precise use of words was necessary to his lawyer's mind. When the Assistant Adjutant General wrote to him about the transfer of very young soldiers who should not have been on the firing line, the general replied that "how boys 13, 14, and 15 years of age are to be 'Veteran Reserves' is a question I shall leave to the Department to settle." [11] When one of his subordinates referred to the fact that "Many of the troops have been in the field since the outbreak of the Revolution," Butler replied with asperity: "What revolution do you mean? The revolution of our ancestors, against England? There has been no other revolution in the United States since, but there has been and is a *rebellion*. It is not usual for officers in the United States service to style the *rebellion* as a *revolution*." [12]

He was not so meticulous about correcting newspaper stories about himself, for he generally ignored all newspapers and newsmen. He did write to the editor of the Baltimore *American* about one offending article,[13] but three days later Butler indicated that he could take care of himself without writing letters to *editors*. To a colonel he wrote, "Find out who the correspondent of the Baltimore *American* is at Point Lookout. Caution him against giving any more movements of troops, or else shut him up in the rebel prison." [14]

Another reporter, Butler believed, was actually a spy that the Secretary of War had sent to keep an eye on the Massachusetts general. This man was deliberately ordered "to remain in the trenches, where they say it is impossible he should escape being shot." [15]

Butler continued to fight some of the same opponents (generically) he had opposed at New Orleans. He arrested a clergyman in Norfolk for alleged disloyalty and set him at hard labor on public works; but Lincoln changed the sentence to banishment from the Department.[16] When Chaplain Hudson of the 1st New York Volunteer Engineers ("who was a sort of actor-chaplain") left without permission, Butler made a mental note; and the next time he was in New York on private business, "I hunted him up with a detective." [17] When the chaplain was brought back to camp for trial, he claimed that he had left to be at the bedside of his dying child, but Butler showed that the desertion had been after the child's death.[18]

The general also had some friction with the Jewish faith. An Associated Press dispatch from Butler at Fortress Monroe stated that his troops had captured 150 rebels, 90 mules, 60 combatants, and four Jews. A young graduate of the Ohio Law College went to complain to Lincoln, who was amused only at first; he gave the attorney a pass to see Butler. The general explained that the error really had been that of a subordinate and that the matter would not recur.[19] But when another Butler report stated that five Jews had been captured while trying to run the blockade, Meyer S. Isaacs asked why the religion had to be specified. The general replied that he had used the language of the original dispatch to him, and actually he had meant nativity.[20] Isaacs then asked why the nationalities of others should not be mentioned in dispatches, to which Butler replied: "I admit that my experience with men of the Jewish faith or nation, has been an unfortunate one." [21]

Two French war vessels and two merchantmen were ordered by Butler to leave his harbor at once, as they had stayed too long, whereupon the squadron commander, Captain Marivault, went at once to Richmond,[22] where, in his aggrieved condition, he doubtless had much to say about what he had seen behind the Federal lines. Butler then wrote the Secretary of State that he believed the French consul at Richmond was carrying dispatches through the lines, and the general wanted to search him. Seward hastily wrote to the Secretary of War that "In the present state of relations between the United States and France, it is not deemed advisable to comply with this request." [23]

The Secretary of State also had to engage in correspondence with Lord Lyons, the British minister, about Butler's arrest of an English subject for an alleged breach of the blockade.[24]

By this time Butler was one of the few political generals remaining in uniform.[25] But his contempt for generals of the regular army had not lessened. "Sometimes it was discussed before me," he wrote, "how superior all West Pointers were to volunteer officers.

"I thought I would put a stop to that, so I invited some of the officers to a dinner party at my headquarters with some of my personal staff who were volunteers. I believed that at that dinner party such discussions might be renewed, so I called Captain Haggerty of my staff, a very bright young lawyer, and told him to go to the library and read the descriptions of one or two of Napoleon's famous battles, naming Marengo, and to ascertain the pivotal point or movement upon which the battles turned, so as to be able clearly to tell me what it was when I asked him." Needless to say, when Butler maneuvered the conversation to Marengo, only Haggerty could explain it. Butler exclaimed triumphantly: "I am very much obliged to you, Captain. You see, gentlemen, it will be convenient during this war to have some volunteer officers along with us, so that if we get into a like predicament with Napoleon we shall have somebody who, knows what was done under like circumstances." Butler later recalled that "The conversation was not renewed. In due time we separated, and the question of the military superiority of West Pointers was never discussed in my hearing by that set of officers afterwards." [26] A favorite expression of his was, "I don't trust them West Point fellows, they're trying to keep me from being successful." [27]

By virtue of his early commissioning as a major general, Butler was the senior major general in the army, outranked only by Grant's three stars of a lieutenant general. Knowing that persons from Lincoln down had tried to find a way of by-passing this seniority, Butler commented: "The president has power to do many things; but it has been said that even 'an act of parliament could not make one's uncle his aunt.' How then can the president make a junior officer a senior officer in the same grade?" [28] Yet there was a technical difficulty in Butler's rank: he was a major general of volunteers and not in the regular army. Although each designation involved the same rank and the same two stars upon one's shoulder straps, the Massachusetts general was aware of the distinction. He was not the only officer to notice it.

General Halleck wrote to Grant and suggested that Meade and Sherman be promoted to major generals, for "I do not wish to see these vacancies so long unfilled, lest some outside political influences cause the President to fill them by the promotion of persons totally unworthy. I know that influences have been exerted in favor of a man utterly unfit to hold any commission in the army." [29] Indeed, on the very next day Butler asked Lincoln, "Do you think I have done enough to entitle me to one of the vacant commissions in the army to date from May 18, 1861; otherwise I should prefer my present one, if you think me fit to hold either, and I can hold on to it." [30] Butler was very cognizant of the fact that the earliest dating of a commission gave the holder thereof seniority over all other men of the same rank. Lincoln replied that he would not dispose of another major generalship in the regular army until operations then in progress were terminated; [31] and as Butler did not distinguish himself in this campaign he was scarcely in position to remind the wily Lincoln of their discussion.

Naturally a commission was no slight thing to Butler. When officers wanted to resign in a combat area, he would accept their resignations—and then put them to work at building fortifications. He could justify this: "If I found civilians within my lines with nothing to do and no right there, I could put them anywhere. After they were dismissed they were civilians, and had no business there." [32] Grant intervened when the ex-officers complained; but resignations stopped.[33]

The Massachusetts general was not well regarded by his companions in arms. General Robert Schenck thus wrote about Stanton to General Lew Wallace (of *Ben Hur* fame) : "Ben Butler is the only man he fears. Butler can do the most atrocious things—steal or murder—and be let alone. . . . I always think of old Ben as a cross-eyed cuttle-fish swimming about in waters of his own muddying." [34] In vain had "Baldy" Smith demanded of Grant: "I want simply . . . to ask you how you can place a man in command of two army corps who is as helpless as a child on the field of battle and as visionary as an opium-eater in council?" [35] Ordinary soldiers shouted at Butler from the anonymity of the ranks, "Who stole the silver spoons?" [36] When he visited the Federal prison camp at Point Lookout, Confederate prisoners screamed such pleasantries as, "You damn lobster-eyed son of a bitch!" "Pay me the money you robbed me of in New Orleans!" "Why don't you fight men and not women?" and "How much are you worth, you burglar?" [37] It is not recorded that the Federal jailers disciplined these vocal prisoners.

But Butler sought to gain support from his men by incentive plans. On September 28, 1864, he published this inducement: "[T]he commanding general will recommend for promotion to the next highest grade . . . all officers and soldiers of the leading division, brigade, or regiment first entering the city, to each officer and man six (6) months' extra pay." [38] He looked after the men who pleased him. Thus he promoted Weitzel from first lieutenant of engineers to brigadier general. [39] But that officer was a first-class engineer; in fact, on one occasion Lincoln asked him various technical questions, to which ready replies were given, at which the President declared, "Hold on, Weitzel, I can't beat you, but I think I can beat Butler." [40]

Butler found that Norfolk, Virginia, had annual yellow-fever epidemics, which, though not so severe as those in New Orleans, were of no small proportions. In 1857, for example, more than 10 per cent of the population was thus killed off. Therefore he introduced the methods that he had used so successfully in New Orleans. For heavy cleaning and sanitation duty, he took 250 prisoners from Fort Norfolk, who worked in the streets without close guard; [41] to lessen the chance of escape he borrowed clothing for them from the Massachusetts House of Correction, the regular prison garb of half black, half gray uniforms, with scarlet caps.[42]

While Butler was campaigning in the field with the Army of the James, his wife remained at Fortress Monroe. Hence he could keep in close communication with her. "I send you flowers from City Point where they are blooming in wild and sweet profusion in deserted gardens," he wrote in one letter. "They will be withered before you get them, but the gift is in the heart of the giver." [43]

His wife was no less sentimental in her letters. "I do not often praise you," she wrote in a letter from Fortress Monroe, "but it is my firm belief that there is but *one man* known to the people who can save this country in its present critical state from utter loss and confusion irremediable; and that is yourself. Not only in time of peace and plenty you would be the best or only man; but I have seen, nor heard, of no man but you with broad and comprehensive views, and also a determined will and grasp of power (when within your reach) to carry them into effect. I think the country is doomed if Lincoln is again elected. We shall never conquer." [44] And that was the woman to whom Butler had written that "no man is a hero to his wife. She sees too much of him in his unheroic moods." [45]

But sentiment was not always the hallmark of their letters. When Grant mentioned that he was going to Fortress Monroe to meet Lincoln, Butler telegraphed him: "A pleasant voyage. I could wish I was going with you, but use my house. Mrs. Butler will be happy to entertain you." [46] Then he quickly dashed off a note to his wife: "You are continually saying cultivate good feeling with the officers. So I do all I can. Now I will give you a chance to aid me, and you must do it. Gen'l. Grant this morning asked me if there was a house at the fortress in which Mrs. Grant and her two boys could live while he was up here. I of course told him that you were there in my house all alone, and that you would be glad to have his wife and her children come and stop with you, . . . Mrs. G. is coming down in a few days, and you must do [*sic*] the *most agreeable*." [47]

But by August, 1864, Mrs. Butler had to return to Lowell, as her sister had been taken with a fatal illness. "Your going away seems

to break away our ties and leave me oh! so lonely," the general wrote
to her.[48] A week later he suggested that she seek the consolation of
religion. "If I *could* believe," he said, "I would become a member of
the church, but alas! I haven't faith. You may have." [49]
"You must not write me any more about coming home," declared
one of his letters. "You have made me so homesick now I am almost
unfit for duty. . . . It would not be fit that I should come now." [50]
Yet a week later he was in Lowell for a visit.[51]

One of Butler's major assignments was the direction of the exchange of military prisoners with the Confederates. He was given the
assignment not only to keep him occupied at nonmilitary matters but
because Grant was not interested in making exchanges; he knew
that the Southerners were at the bottom of the man-power barrel,
whereas the North's personnel resources were almost unlimited. Grant
believed that exchanges would not be made, as Butler was *persona
non grata* in the South; [52] and at first this seemed to be the case,
for Robert Ould, the Confederate States Agent of Exchange, would
not deal with Butler by reason of his having been declared an outlaw
by President Davis.[53] Ould wrote to E. A. Hitchcock, United States
Commissioner of Exchange: "Although we do not pretend to prescribe
what agents your Government shall employ in connection with the
cartel, yet when one who has been proclaimed to be so obnoxious
as General Butler is selected, self-respect requires that the Confederate authorities should refuse to treat with him or establish
such relations with him as properly pertain to an agent of exchange." [54] From Fortress Monroe the Massachusetts general engaged
in long-distance legal battles with Judge Ould about the status of
the exchanges (and himself), [55] and eventually the officials found
a basis for negotiations. Military prisoners were being exchanged
without difficulty at such places as New Orleans, Port Royal, and
Atlanta; but Butler greatly antagonized Ould by insisting that whites
and Negroes be exchanged equally.[56] When the Confederates talked
about executing Federal prisoners whose acts had been overly severe,
Butler reminded them that he had more prisoners than they had,
and he would surely retaliate.[57] And if Northern prisoners were not

given proper living and working conditions, he threatened to duplicate all of these conditions in *his* prison camps, with this novel addition: he would give his Southern prisoners full writing equipment
so that they could tell the folks at home what it meant to be a
prisoner of war.[58] He was concerned only with soldiers; he made no
effort whatsoever to exchange naval prisoners until the Secretary of
the Navy personally intervened.[59]

If Butler showed severity toward prisoners of war, he was no less
so toward his own men who violated regulations. His discipline was
so strict that Lincoln was moved to object: "How can I have a
butcher's day every Friday in the Army of the Potomac?" "Better
have that," Butler replied, "than have the Army of the Potomac so
depleted by desertions that good men will be butchered on other
days than Friday." [60] On one occasion Lincoln wrote to Butler:
"Please suspend executions in any and all sentences of death in your
department until further order." [61] The President hesitated about pardoning one sentenced soldier; finally he signed the pardon, exclaiming, "By jingo, Butler or no Butler, here goes!" [62]

Butler's relations with the navy were never good. He quarreled
with the sister service because it would not take monitors of fifteen-
foot draft up rivers ten feet deep.[63] When confronted with arithmetic,
Butler set out to correct it. He wanted naval support for his troops
at Trent's Beach; but the ironclads available drew sixteen feet of
water, and the James was only seven feet deep at that point. "The
river at this point is so crooked," observed a contemporary account,
"that Butler must have laid it out with his wrong eye." [64] The river
pursued a winding course, bending in horseshoe manner at Dutch
Gap; and here Butler had his idea. The shallow arms of the horseshoe could be avoided; from one parallel side to the other he would
build a canal sixteen feet deep, sixty feet wide; and then the Federal
gunboats could accompany any advance his army might make.[65]
But when the construction work was well advanced, the senior naval
officer present, Commander Parker, announced that he could no
longer promise to protect the army workers from Southern gunboats
if the canal also enabled Confederate vessels to sail up the James.
"Here was a situation," complained Butler; "I had been trying to

make an opening by which the dog could get at the fox and destroy him, and the dog begged of me that I would not, lest the fox should eat him up. And so I never did a stroke more work on the canal, and the country rang with 'another of Butler's failures' at Dutch Gap Canal." [66]

But the hatred of Butler in the Union forces was as nothing compared to the repulsion he engendered in the South. One Confederate soldier wrote home, "But here let me say that the inhuman barbarities and insulting ruffianism was not so often the action (perhaps was never so) of the veteran Northern soldier as of the low hirelings who skulked in forts and cities distant from the battle field and who continually fashioned their conduct on such leaders as Ben Butler." [67] The then Colonel John B. Gordon of the Sixth Alabama rallied his men on the battlefield with a reference to "the infamous Butler." [68] Louisiana regiments charged with the slogans "Butler and New Orleans!" and "Boys, remember Butler!" [69] Even civilians fell into line. A popular acrostic spelled out with the first letter of each line the fiend that all Southerners should despise:

> Brutal and vulgar, a coward and knave;
> Famed for no action, noble or brave;
> Beastly by instinct, a drunkard and sot;
> Ugly, venomous, on mankind a blot;
> Thief, liar and scoundrel in highest degree,
> Let Yankeedom boast of such heros as thee;
> Every woman and child shall for ages to come,
> Remember thee, monster, thou vilest of scum. [70]

When the game of charades was played, "Beauty and the Beast" would be acted out by showing a portrait of Butler as the last word. [71]

The very name of Butler struck terror, or horror, into Confederate generals. When Pickett heard of a movement of the Army of the James, the Southern Gettysburg hero wrote to Adjutant General Cooper: "Butler's plan, evidently, is to let loose his swarm of blacks upon our ladies and defenseless families, plunder and devastate the country. Against such a warfare there is but one resource—to hang at once every one captured belonging to the expedition, and afterwards every one caught who belongs to Butler's department. Let us come to a definite understanding with these heathen at once. Butler cannot be allowed to rule here as he did in New Orleans. His course must be stopped." [72] When Robert E. Lee learned that his captured son was being sent to New York instead of being taken to a prison camp in Virginia, he was well satisfied, "as any place would be better than Fort Monroe, with Butler in command." [73]

When the 1864 presidential election drew near, Butler was in many minds. He was such a champion of the Negro that the Abolitionist Wendell Phillips would have liked to see Butler as President rather than Lincoln. [74] As the war progressed, dissatisfied radicals, both Republican and Democrat, began to turn to him. [75] He was widely regarded as a man who could save the Union Party. [76] Horace Greeley was an enthusiastic champion. "Mr. Lincoln is already beaten," he explained. "He cannot be elected. And we must have another ticket to save us from utter overthrow. If we had such a ticket as could be made by naming Grant, Butler, or Sherman for President, and Farragut for Vice, we could make a fight yet. And such a ticket we ought to have anyhow, with or without a convention." [77] It was his biographer, Parton, that Butler had delegated to arrange his initial meeting with Greeley, and Parton reported back that he had not told the editor of his object. "The chastest virgin may have desires—may be tormented with desires, but she will not confess them to herself. However, you know mankind and will know how to shape your course." [78]

Butler did not stay aloof from this campaigning, for he found it possible to leave his troops for several days at a time to come to New York for political discussions. [79] Senator William E. Chandler wrote to Butler from the Union Republican State Committee in Concord, New Hampshire, to be sure that certain of his constituents were furloughed for voting purposes. [80]

Chase, the ambitious Secretary of the Treasury, offered Butler the Vice Presidency on *his* ticket; but the Massachusetts general declined, saying, "I should not, at my time of life, wish to be Vice-

President, even if I had no other position." [81] Besides, he added craftily, he might still capture Richmond and thereby gain the first position on *any* ticket. It was believed that any considerable success before Richmond would place Butler in such a position.[82] As a Richmond newspaper noted, "If either Grant or Butler had taken Richmond before the Baltimore Convention, then Grant or Butler would have been nominated." [83] But Grant was too busily occupied at his military duties to participate in such conjectures.[84]

For his running mate in 1864, Lincoln wanted a Democrat. His Vice President, Hannibal Hamlin, could have been called that; but he was not a "war Democrat." Lincoln's first choice within this limitation was Butler.[85] Perhaps this choice was dictated by smart political considerations; Butler as a leading Democrat and a soldier with a popular war record was a great menace even to Lincoln.[86] The menace was very real, and John Hay, Lincoln's secretary, referred to Butler as the "smartest damned rascal that ever lived." [87]

Simon Cameron, the deposed Secretary of War who was still the political boss of Pennsylvania, made overtures to Butler, who wrote back: "Is it not possible for you to come here? I think it would be worth your while." [88] According to Cameron, "It was the desire of Lincoln, and also of Stanton . . . that Butler should run as the candidate for Vice-President. I was called into consultation and heartily endorsed the scheme. Accordingly, Lincoln sent me on a mission to Fort Monroe to see General Butler, and to say to him that it was his [Lincoln's] request that he [Butler] should allow himself to run as second on the ticket. I, accompanied by William H. Armstrong, afterward a member of Congress, did visit General Butler and made the tender according to instructions. To our astonishment, Butler refused to agree to the proposition. He said there was nothing in the Vice-Presidency." [89] Tell Lincoln, said Butler, that "with the prospects of the campaign, I would not quit the field to be Vice-President, even with himself as President, unless he will give me bond with sureties, in the full amount of his four years' salary, that he will die or resign within three months after his inauguration." [90] Just six weeks after his inauguration, Lincoln was dead.

Therefore, at the 1864 convention, Andrew Johnson of Tennessee was selected as Lincoln's "war Democrat" instead, gaining the designation with 200 votes.[91] Although avowedly not a candidate, Butler received Vice Presidential votes from Missouri and from some of the New England states,[92] and he was fourth place in the balloting with 26 votes.[93] "Hurrah for Lincoln and Johnson!" Butler wrote to his wife on June 11th. "That's the ticket! This country has more vitality than any other on earth if it can stand this sort of administration for another four years."[94]

As Election Day drew near, anxiety was felt about New York City. The draft riots had taken place scarcely a year ago, and "It was feared that without the restraining presence of a resolute soldier, backed by an imposing military force, a lawless mob would take possession of the ballot boxes and the city."[95] The Commander of the Department of the East, General Dix, was believed to be too weak for the job, as he would eschew any use of force, being a candidate for governor of the state.[96] Some Radical Republicans wanted Butler to be sent to New York to supervise the election, as a riot might very well be the result of his presence, and a few hundred "Copperhead corpses" would have had a salubrious effect in inciting people to vote for the war (that is, Republican) party.[97] In any event, the Secretary of War summoned Butler and asked whether he could handle New York on Election Day, with due regard to General Dix's position. Replied Butler, "I will coddle the general and be his obedient servant until it becomes necessary to be something else, and of that you must leave me to judge."[98]

Butler's designation for the responsibility of a peaceful New York was well received. The New York *Times* approved his choice as the hero who "scattered the howling rabble of New Orleans like chaff."[99] "His name alone," commented Grant's military secretary, "would be a terror to those who plotted against the republic."[100] But August Belmont, the prominent banker, addressed a crowd at Cooper Institute on November 2, 1864, and savagely denounced the friends of the Southern leaders who were still in the North. "Here we have, first and foremost, Benjamin F. Butler, of Massachusetts, who, at Charleston, gave, during fifty-two ballots, his vote for Jeff. Davis,

(*Margaret Noyes Knowles*)

The Butler home in Lowell
(Built about 1845)

Butler, the civilian

the only vote cast for him in the convention, and then left that body to sit in council with the Southern traitors." [101]

Butler arrived at the Hoffman House in New York on November 4th, to the great embarrassment of Judge Henry Clay Dean, who had announced only the night before that if Butler marched up Broadway he would be hanged. The Massachusetts general took time to send for the judge, who promised he would "correct" his statement.[102] Next came General Sandford, in command of the New York State Militia, who said he would not put his troops under Butler's orders on Election Day, whereupon Butler announced that any armed men not under his orders would be treated as enemies. Sandford replied that he would appeal to Governor Seymour for orders, but Butler answered that he regarded the governor as a very high militia officer —no more.[103]

On the night before the election Butler went to the opera house, where he had a stage box, "having got a new uniform so that I could go in full feather." [104] That was meant literally, and the general did not even pay for this finery; for when he had gotten his orders to report to New York post haste he told Stanton, "I want a new uniform, and if you order me off in this condition of rig I shall put it in the bill." [105] At the opera August Belmont offered to bet $1,000 that McClellan, Lincoln's Democratic opponent, would be elected. Butler covered the bet.[106]

On Election Day, November 8th, Butler had 3,500 troops under his direct orders. Troops were stationed on ferry boats, which had Western Union telegraph connections with his headquarters; other telegraph wires extended from each polling place to Butler's headquarters.[107] A regiment with artillery would have been landed at the ferry slip nearest any point of disorder.[108] But the only disorder noted was at the polling place where August Belmont tried to vote; *someone* had reported that he had made a wager on the election, contrary to law.[109]

On the following Monday, November 14th, distinguished citizens of New York gave Butler a huge banquet at the Fifth Avenue Hotel.[110] The Reverend Henry Ward Beecher proposed Butler for President of the United States in 1868.[111]

After the election excitement Butler returned to his Department. As usual, he managed to keep himself occupied. Gustavus Fox, the Assistant Secretary of the Navy, wrote that Lincoln was undecided about the new Chief Justice of the United States. Would Butler recommend Montgomery Blair? "I beg of you, by the long and confidential intercourse which has existed between us, wherein on one great occasion, when the scales balanced between McClellan's hostility and my influence in your favor, I won, that you write a letter in the Judge's behalf. He, as you are aware, stood by you before the President in our early troubles, and you can now not only repay him but put the Blairs under obligations to you that will do you no injury in the future." [112]

Rumors hinted that Butler might be in line for a new post. Some people believed that Stanton would become Chief Justice, with Butler succeeding him as Secretary of War. "I should esteem it a great misfortune to see either Banks or Butler there," wrote General Meade to his wife.[113] Mrs. Butler also heard the rumor, and told her husband that the idea was a pleasing one. He replied mischievously: "So the dear little puss wants to be Mrs. Secretary of War, does she? Sly little puss! Why does she not cry for a piece of the moon? She shall have it, so she shall! Don't she wish she may get it, but how? That's the question. . . . Goodbye, Mrs. Maj. General, how poor that title sounds now, doesn't it?" [114]

But Butler had more pressing duties. A rival noted that "wherever he was in command came rumors of jobs, frauds, trading with rebels through the lines, and the putting of unfit persons in responsible positions." [115] A vigorous trade with the enemy had sprung up in medicines, coffee, sugar, bacon, salt, boots, hats, and dry goods, payment being made in Southern cotton.[116] Butler had gotten Lincoln's general approval to send plows, harrows, and farming utensils to loyal North Carolina farmers for cotton,[117] and a ship was sent out under this authorization. At Baltimore the provost marshal became suspicious and took possession of the vessel's customhouse papers; he also posted a guard, but as the ship did not have steam in its boilers he felt that a *shore* guard was sufficient. Suddenly a tug appeared and hauled the ship away from the guards. Meanwhile the provost marshal felt that as he had the customhouse papers, the steamer would have difficulties ahead; but G. W. Lane, the ship's agent, later informed the provost marshal that the papers really weren't needed at all, as "General Butler intended to give him a pass at Fortress Monroe." [118] The pass was issued all right, though Captain Melancthon Smith, senior officer in the sounds of North Carolina, reported to the commander of the North Atlantic Blockading Squadron, "There are many articles in the manifest that would afford comfort to the enemy." [119]

In fact, E. H. Willett, a Treasury agent, reported that after Lane had got his various approvals and permits, "on last Thursday night a lot of his goods were landed at the wharf at Edenton (North Carolina) to a Confederate Government agent. I have good authority for saying Friday night some goods, or part of them, were on their way to the Confederate army, all of which was done without my permission. It is out of my power to carry out the trade regulations according to my instructions, and ask to be relieved from its duties on this occasion." [120] Upon receipt of this report, Captain J. P. Bankhead of the U.S.S. *Otsego* arrested Lane and sent him to the provost marshal at Roanoke Island. Bankhead reported that "Gen. Palmer had the Rebel agent brought before him who was said to have purchased the supplies, and who acknowledged the same." [121] A witness identified as Lane's partner in the venture one Fisher Hildreth, who was Butler's brother-in-law.[122] Andrew Butler had died of consumption in February, 1864,[123] his last words having been, "God bless all my friends." [124] But the family was still able to carry on, thanks to Fisher Hildreth. Meanwhile the Massachusetts general acted as executor of his brother's estate, which had been estimated to be worth several hundred thousand dollars in the New Orleans days of little more than a year ago but which was now valued by the general at merely $76,391.04 in the probate accounting.[125]

A military commission under Brigadier General Devons tried six persons for trading with the enemy, and fines and prison sentences were imposed; [126] but Butler revoked the punishment on the grounds that the trading was in accordance with Treasury regulations.[127] The Secretary of the Treasury denied that there were such regulations.[128]

General George H. Gordon, in charge of a military commission set up by Congress to investigate the methods by which Lee's army was receiving supplies from the North, reported that the guilty parties had been arrested, tried, convicted, and sentenced to imprisonment, but that Butler would do nothing about it. If Butler knew about this trading with the enemy, Gordon explained, he was guilty of violating the Articles of War; if he did not know what was going on literally and figuratively under his nose, he was incompetent to command a Department. "He may hang on either horn of the dilemma that pleases him." [129]

But Butler was not sufficiently interested in Gordon's charges to refute them. Who was Gordon, anyway? "In the beginning of the war," stated Butler, "when every man who had seen West Point was supposed to be a Wellington, Gov. Andrew appointed him Colonel of the 2nd Massachusetts Regiment, and regretted it but once, and that was all the time." [130] And he was even now under charges of contempt and disrespect to his superior officer, Benjamin F. Butler.[131]

Grant was disturbed by trading with the enemy. "I have always believed," he wrote, "that entire non-intercourse with 'people in rebellion' would prove the most speedy way to bring about a permanent peace." [132] He also reported, "I have positively refused to adopt this mode of feeding the Southern army unless it is the direct order of the President." Therefore Stanton authorized him to "disregard and annul" all permits "by whomsoever signed." [133]

But Butler did not share his chief's scruples. Welles wrote in his diary: "A week or two since, Admiral Lee sent me certain papers in the case of the steamer *Princeton,* then at Norfolk, among them a permit from General Butler authorizing the vessel to go on a trading voyage in the sounds and rivers of North Carolina, provided Admiral Lee would consent. The latter would not consent without orders from the Navy Department, and I approved his course in refusing." [134] Lee commanded the North Atlantic Blockading Squadron, which had work not dissimilar to that of the fleet that had controlled the Mississippi. There was a large trade in contraband articles to be broken up, and much difficulty was engendered by the fact that many traders had permits from Butler which were embarrassing to the navy. Conditions were far less satisfactory here to the navy than they had been on the Mississippi, for aggrieved traders on the James and Roanoke rivers had much easier access to high army personnel.[135]

In time Butler's business activities in his district reached the attention of David Creamer, the tax assessor, who demanded a schedule of the general's income for Internal Revenue tax purposes. Butler replied that he was out of the assessor's jurisdiction and that "while I remain in this District where martial law is predominant, and I am the executor thereof, it would be exceedingly difficult for you to collect the tax." [136]

It is inconceivable to think that the Cabinet did not know what was going on. Thus on March 19, 1864, the Secretary of the Navy noted in his diary : "At the Cabinet-meeting Chase manifested a little disturbance of mind at my letter respecting the *Ann Hamilton* and the *Princeton,* sent in reply to his somewhat arrogant letter to me. Seward asked him if he had any gold to sell. He said no, if S. wanted to make money he had better get a permit from General Butler to carry in military supplies, and then persuade me to let the vessel pass the blockade." [137]

The trade had far surpassed Butler's original proposal to Lincoln to permit barter with friendly farmers. "It was," wrote Welles, "a little, dirty, speculating intrigue, initiated as early as last March, in a letter from General Butler addressed to the President, proposing to send in ploughs, harrows, and farming utensils to loyal farmers in North Carolina, in exchange for cotton and products of the country,— plausible and taking rascality. The President endorsed that he approved the object. On this General Butler granted a permit." [138]

The large-scale trading that Butler actually developed had to have outlets, and a system of stores was set up. At certain points on the picket line separating the hostile armies, stores had been erected by permission of the military authorities. Military permits were obtained from Butler's headquarters for goods to go to a particular store. The establishment at Coan Jack, North Carolina, was operated by Captain Johnston, assistant adjutant general of the Department under Butler.[139] The store at Ballyhack was operated by Renshaw and Company, Renshaw having been a clerk of a brother-in-law of

Butler's named Reed. At Bernard's Mills, half of the profits went to another Butler brother-in-law, Hildreth, who had not put up a cent of the capital.[140] Other stores were at South Mills, Hamburg, Washington Ditch, Elizabeth City, Gatesville, and Edenton, all operated with goods supplied from above the Northern lines. It was reported to a Congressional investigating committee that some of the goods were supplied by De Witt C. Farrington of Massachusetts, who was identified as "Gen. Butler's special agent." [141] The distinguished scholar Rhodes recorded that "so far as I know there is no evidence of corruption in the trade with the Confederacy which may be properly considered by a historian against any major-general holding a high and responsible position except Benjamin F. Butler of Massachusetts." [142] By some sort of coincidence, wherever Butler was stationed there was "disreputable trade." [143]

Southerners, if realistic, did not mind. One trooper wrote home to his family: "With our onions we have bacon cured in Ohio and shipped to Nassau to be sent us by blockade runners. It is said Beast Butler is engaged in this traffic. It is a good thing for us that he is. It is also said that when he commanded at New Orleans he promised to exchange bacon for cotton, but our departments, with great folly, refused to trade with him because of his violent orders. What difference did that make? They were, to some extent, blinds to enable him to carry out just such profitable schemes." [144]

CHAPTER XII

THE BIG EXPLOSION

IT was one of General Butler's characteristics that he used every circumstance to his own advantage. Thus, when he read in the summer of 1864 of a gunpowder explosion at Alnwick, England,[1] his first thought must have been how he could benefit from it. Soon he concocted a new theory of offensive warfare.

Butler was a vigorous innovator, and unorthodoxy never disturbed him. As early as August 11, 1861, he had aerial reconnaissance made from a balloon,[2] and he purchased the first Gatling guns on his own initiative after the Bureau of Ordnance had turned them down.[3] On November 29, 1864, Colonel Theodore Lyman, General Meade's personal aide, wrote in a letter: "Butler never is happy unless he has half a dozen contrivances on hand. An idea that Benjamin considered highly practical was a fire engine, wherewith he proposed to squirt water on earthworks and wash them all down. Then, with Greek fire, he proposed to hold a redoubt with only five men and a small garden engine. 'Certainly,' said General Meade, 'Only your engine fires thirty feet, and a rifle 3,000 yards, and I am afraid your five men might be killed before they had a chance to burn up their adversaries!' Butler also was going to get a gun that would shoot seven miles and, taking direction by compass, burn the city of Richmond with shells of Greek fire. If that didn't do, he had an auger to bore a tunnel five feet in diameter, and he was going to bore to Richmond and suddenly pop up in somebody's basement while the family were at breakfast! So, you see, he is ingenious!" [4] But *this* time he had some solid basis for his plan: the Alnwick explosion definitely had gone off.

Butler had just the place for his attack by concussion. Fort Fisher commanded the approaches of the Cape Fear River; it was set on a sandy promontory running out into the sea, with very deep water quite close to it; [5] this was the key to Wilmington, the last remaining gateway for war materials from the outer world.[6] It was a favorite jumping-off place for Confederate blockade runners. But to take the fort, a joint army and navy expedition seemed indicated; and the North Carolina fort was in Butler's Department. The Massachusetts general thus felt that it was his province to make a recommendation: cram a steamer with 300 tons of powder, with the proper firing mechanism, and then take the vessel as close to the fort as possible for detonation. The Assistant Secretary of the Navy agreed to the plan, possibly to get army troops for the assault.[7] The Secretary was not so hopeful, and he recorded in his diary, "I have no faith in General Butler's scheme of knocking down Fort Fisher by blowing up a vessel filled with powder." [8] Grant was similarly minded, and he wrote to General Sherman that "I do not believe a particle" in this explosive theory.[9] But Welles threw himself wholeheartedly back of the project, for, as he admitted, "I am not certain we should have been able to engage the army in this expedition but for Butler, and we could not have enlisted Butler had we not assented to the powder-boat." [10]

Grant agreed to provide 6,500 soldiers for the joint expedition, from Butler's command.[11] The lieutenant general selected General Weitzel to go with the troops; but Butler, in whose geographical limits the fort was located, took personal command himself.[12] This was a distinct surprise to Grant, who related: "I had no idea of General Butler's accompanying the expedition until the evening before it got off from Bermuda Hundred, and then did not dream but that General Weitzel had received all the instructions, and would be in command. I rather formed the idea that General Butler was actuated by a desire to witness the effect of the explosion of the powder-boat." [13] He did not know his man.

Admiral Porter was given command of the naval aspects of the expedition. He "merely suggested one thing—namely, that General Butler should not go in command." [14] The Massachusetts general in turn said of Porter: "I had criticized his foolish performances in bombarding Forts St. Philip and Jackson, leaving the latter, upon which he expended most of his work, as defensible as before. . . . Porter . . . hated [me] as the devil hates holy water." [15] This was scarcely a well chosen pair to lead a joint expedition! In point of view of seniority, Butler outranked Porter.[16]

The practical Sherman wrote to Grant, "I would favor an attack on Wilmington, in the belief that Porter and Butler will fail in their present undertaking." [17] But the joint commanders persisted in their plan. Porter, in an effort to improve his personal relations with his new associate, brought his wife with him to call socially on the Butlers at Fortress Monroe, and the Butlers were also entertained on the *Malvern*, Porter's flagship.[18] Grant himself came to Hampton Roads to see what could be done to start the expedition. He visited Porter on the *Malvern*, "but," said the admiral, "he would scarcely put his foot on board ere General Butler would make his appearance. Butler's presence was always enough to make General Grant quiet and meditative, and he soon took his departure." [19] Porter's biographer felt that Grant exercised no actual control whatsoever over Butler.[20]

The plan itself was simple. There were 1,077 Confederate defenders in Fort Fisher, and an armada of fifty vessels was to make the assault, thirty-three ships being designated for attack and seventeen being in reserve.[21] The powder ship was to be placed as near the fort's walls as possible; when it was detonated soldiers would land from transports and overpower the bewildered garrison. As the naval contingent had some slow-moving monitors, the plan called for Porter to sail a day ahead of Butler's swifter transports; but the general dashed off with his vessels at a time that suited him, and the first word that Porter got that the expedition was under way was the report of his own lookouts. Then the admiral had to steam frantically in an effort to overtake the troops he was convoying. Meanwhile Butler had reached Fort Fisher and had performed a full-dress reconnaissance with his transports, thus throwing away the element of surprise.[22] The general led the expedition from his flagship, the *Ben Deford*.[23]

When Porter caught up with Butler, he advised him to move his transports twenty miles away from the contemplated explosion and to let the steam in his boilers run down. In order to take the proper precautions, the general moved his transports to Beaufort, sixty miles from the scene of action.[24]

The powder ship was the *Louisiana,* an old steamer that had been disguised as a blockade runner.[25] This ship was in effect one huge powder magazine, the powder being stored above the water line in order to give the explosion its greatest lateral force. The heads were removed from the powder barrels, and fuses connected the numerous barrels and sacks of powder. Clockwork mechanisms were set to co-ordinate the action of the explosives.[26] Early in the morning of December 24, 1864, Captain Rhind set off the firing mechanism; but it was not until 1:40 A.M., twenty-two minutes later, that the detonation occurred, in four sharp reports.[27] Two hundred and fifteen tons of powder went off within three hundred yards of the northeastern salient of the fort; [28] but the garrison merely felt that there had been an explosion aboard a blockade runner [29] or a burst boiler aboard some Federal vessel.[30] Butler's transports were too far away to land troops at 8:00 A.M. as planned, so troops were landed at eight o'clock the following morning; and 2,500 soldiers went ashore.[31] The army contingent was commanded by General Adelbert Ames, Butler's son-in-law,[32] and they approached within seventy-five yards of the fort. One soldier shot a Confederate courier and escaped on the latter's mule, while other troops captured two hundred prisoners and a flag before withdrawing. Butler did not go ashore; he watched operations from the tug *Chamberlain* [33] and, when he heard that the fort was getting reinforcements, ordered withdrawal so hurriedly that seven hundred of his men were abandoned, to be rescued from the beach by Porter's men.[34] The general informed the admiral that he did not think the fort could be taken, "as it was left substantially un-injured as a defensive work by the Navy fire," but Porter tartly answered: "I wish some more of your gallant fellows had followed the officer who took the flag from the parapet, and the brave fellow who took the horse out from the fort. I think they would have found it an easier conquest than is supposed." [35] Butler claimed that the navy had exploded the powder ship prematurely so that the fleet could hog all the glory.[36]

Butler's hasty withdrawal was sharply criticized. "In doing this," said his superior officer, "Butler made a fearful mistake." [37] Porter commented, "It was, however, nothing more than I expected when General Butler mixed himself up in this expedition." [38] The Secretary of the Navy recorded, "It is to be regretted that Butler went with the expedition, for though possessed of ability as a civilian he has shown no very great military capacity for work like this." [39]

When Butler ordered his withdrawal, he found that his transports were rather low on fuel; so he seized the navy's coal reserve. Fortunately for the fleet, Porter's men were able to locate at Beaufort some army coal, which, under the simple technology existing at that time, also fitted navy furnaces; and this was seized, Porter stating that "necessity knows no law." [40] On his return the admiral remembered to leave at Fortress Monroe "the troops that General Butler, in his hurry to get away, had left on the beach." [41]

Grant sent Lincoln a telegram about the failure, concluding: "Who is to blame, will, I hope, be known." Two days later he wrote to Porter: "Please hold on wherever you are for a few days, and I will endeavor to be back again, with an increased force, and without the former commander." [42] Porter, by now, took the setback calmly, even hopefully. His report stated: "General Weitzel went on shore, determined what the report of the defenses would be, for General Butler had made an opinion for him. . . . If this temporary failure succeeds in sending General Butler into private life it is not to be regretted, for it cost only a certain amount of shells, which I would expend in a month's target practice anyhow." [43]

But the general reaction was bitter. The New York *World* said that Butler should have landed on the beach wearing "those ostrich feathers which he wore in the streets of New York, brandishing his puissant horse-pistols, and fixing on Fort Fisher the terrors of his revolving orb." [44] The Secretary of the Navy declared: "General Butler has won laurels under the smoke and fire and fight of the Navy,—as at Hatteras or at New Orleans,—and he flattered himself that he should in like manner be favored at Wilmington. General Grant ought never to have given him this command. It is unfortunate that Butler is associated with Grant, for he has great mental power which gives him undue ascendancy over his official superior. Certainly Grant must have known that Butler was not the proper officer for such an expedition. Why did he give B. this command?" [45] A Massachusetts Congressman wrote that "the worst example of timidity and inefficiency in American military history, not excepting Hull's surrender, was the attempt and repulse at Ft. Fisher." [46] The crew of Porter's flagship created for Butler a leather medal: on one side was a pair of legs in the act of running, surmounted by a major general's insignia, while on the reverse was the legend, "in commemoration of his heroic conduct before Fort Fisher, Dec. 1864." [47]

After Fort Fisher, Butler resumed his customary functions with his Department and with Grant. As to his commander, the Massachusetts general noted naïvely, "I noticed nothing, except, perhaps, a want of cordiality in his manner." [48] But Grant already had written the Secretary of War to ask for Butler's removal. "I do this," he said, "with reluctance, but the good of the service requires it. In my absence, General Butler necessarily commands, and there is a lack of confidence felt in his military ability, making him an unsafe commander for a large army. His administration of the affairs of his Department is also objectionable." [49] On the following day Grant sent a telegram to Lincoln declaring: "I wrote a letter to the Secretary of War, which was mailed yesterday, asking to have General Butler removed from command. Learning that the Secretary left Washington yesterday, I telegraph you, asking that prompt action may be taken in the matter." [50]

The action was not a surprise. The Secretary of the Navy confided to his diary: "President says Stanton readily gives up Butler." [51] And Butler himself suspected that Grant was being subjected to pressure. "I know very well," stated the Massachusetts general, "where the pressure came from; and also whence it got its vitality in the mind of Grant. The pressure came from his West Point staff of officers, who were trying in every way to have me vilified and abused." [52]

Lincoln's Executive Order No. 1 for 1865 relieved Butler of his command.[53] On January 8th the Adjutant General's office issued the following order: "By direction of the President of the United States,

Maj.-Gen. Benjamin F. Butler is relieved from the command of the Department of North Carolina and Virginia. . . . Major-General Butler on being relieved will repair to Lowell, Mass., and report by letter to the adjutant-general of the army." [54] Butler made a touching farewell address to his army three days later, in which he said: "I have refused to order the useless sacrifice to the lives of such soldiers, and I am relieved from your command. The wasted blood of my men does not stain my garments." [55]

Butler left Fortress Monroe for Lowell on January 15th, and an eyewitness left this picture of his departure:

He was escorted to the boat by a small body of troops, and by Generals Shepley and Marston, both of whom hung about him as a victim of regular army persecution. Once in the cabin of his boat,—where his family had secluded themselves in their staterooms,—none were so poor as to do him reverence. Butler seemed excited and unhappy. Cut down in the spring-tide of his popularity, it was with pleasure that he grasped the hand of a coal-heaver who happened to be passing, and who was much astonished at the unexpected honor.[56]

Major General E. O. C. Ord was designated by Grant to relieve Butler in command of the Department of Virginia and North Carolina.[57] Ord's first question was to ask Grant whether Butler should be permitted to distribute seven hundred copies of his farewell address about the "wasted blood of my men." Grant did not see fit to interfere with the distribution.[58]

The dismissal was widely hailed. General Sherman wrote to Porter: "I am rejoiced that the current of events has carried Butler to Lowell, where he should have stayed and confined his bellicose operations to the factory girls. . . . He has no blood on his skirts and judging from the past, it will be long before his blood stains anything. His solicitude for the blood of his men is as moonshine." [59] General Meade wrote to his wife: "Butler's removal has caused great excitement everywhere. He will have some very powerful influences exerted in his favor, and he will use them efficiently. I see Wilson has moved in the Senate that the Committee on the Conduct of the War enquire and report on the Wilmington fiasco. This is the beginning of a war on Grant." [60]

Harper's Weekly observed: "Of the patriotism, ability and energy of General Butler there can be no doubt. But of the fact that, from Great Bethel to Wilmington, the purely military movements which he has directed have not been successful, there is also no doubt." [61] The New York *World* called Butler's dismissal the "best emancipation proclamation Mr. Lincoln has yet made." [62] The Secretary of the Navy wrote:

Much speculation has been had concerning the dismissal of General Butler. It was anticipated that, being a favorite with the extremists, his dismissal would create a great excitement, but it has passed off without irritation, almost without sensation. The quidnuncs and, indeed, most of the public impute his dismissal from the Army of the James to the Wilmington failure; but it will soon be known that General Grant desired to get rid of him. Butler's greater intellect overshadowed Grant, and annoyed and embarrassed the General-in-Chief.

General Butler's farewell to his army is in many respects skillful and adroit, but in some respects will prove a failure. He does not conceal his chagrin but has hardly discovered whom to strike. . . . I am not his admirer, and should lament to see him in any responsible position without a superior. He has inordinate and irresponsible ambition, and would scruple at nothing to gratify it and his avarice. . . . Seward fears him. There is no love between them, and yet S. would prefer to avoid a conflict. Butler has the reckless audacity attributed to the worst revolutionists in France, in the worst of times, but is deficient in personal courage. He is a suitable idol for Greeley, a profound philanthropist, being the opposite of G. in almost everything except love of notoriety.[63]

Perhaps Welles was a bit surprised when Butler called on him ten days after this remarkable appraisal. Wrote the Secretary:

He has come to testify before the Committee on the Conduct of the War,—called probably on his own suggestion,—greatly preferring Washington, for the present at least, to Lowell. I am sorry he has come here. It is for no good or patriotic purpose, I apprehend. As for the "Committee on the Conduct of the War," who have brought him here, they are most of them narrow and prejudiced partisans, mischievous busybodies, and a discredit to Congress. Mean and contemptible partisanship colors all their acts. Secretly opposed to the President, they hope to make something of Butler, who has ability and is a good deal indignant.[64]

Meanwhile Grant had designated General Terry to succeed to the military command in the joint expedition against Fort Fisher; since Terry and Admiral Porter were on speaking terms they did not have to carry on their discussions through intermediaries.[65] Porter approved of the choice and said of Terry: "He had, however, been a long time under the command of General Butler, who, for a wonder, had treated him very well. . . . Terry had no staff, wore no spurs, and we do not think he owned a sword. He had a well-formed head, full of sense, which served him in lieu of feathers, sword, boots, spurs, and staff—of which a General can have too many." [66] To Grant, Porter declared: "I hold it to be a good rule never to send a boy on a man's errand. . . . There is no use fretting over the past; we must endeavor to avoid mistakes in the future, and if any expedition fails now to take the works, which were comparatively weak ten days ago, the sagacity of the leaders of the late expedition will be applauded." [67]

The Porter-Terry expedition was successful, and Fort Fisher was captured. "This will be severe for Butler," Welles wrote, "who insisted that the place could not be taken but by a siege, since his powder-boat failed." [68] Indeed, the fort fell at a most inopportune time for Butler. He just had finished demonstrating to the Committee on the Conduct of the War that Fort Fisher could not be taken by assault, when newsboys were heard calling out an extra, "Fort Fisher done took!" "Of course, they all laughed," recalled General Sherman, "and none more heartily than General Butler himself." [69]

But Butler brooded about this assault. "By the gallantry of General Terry and his brave troops another expedition which was afterwards sent down was successful in assaulting the fort, I admit most willingly, but this throws no light on the question, and by and by I may consider the motives for sending it down. Sherman with his army had at that time nearly or quite enveloped North Carolina or was proceeding in his victorious march to do so. In less than thirty days he would be behind Wilmington which must of course fall as did Savannah." [70] And as for Porter, *"The fact is, that on the first attack after the failure of the powder-boat, Porter did not intend that the attack of the army should succeed."* [71] Butler's biographer was disturbed at the vehemence of his hero, and to the Massachusetts general he wrote that any report should be moderate. "I hope your report will not contain the word 'Porter,' nor even small beer, nor any illusion to malt." [72]

Porter likewise was convinced that the full story of Fort Fisher had not been told. "Congress did not get the truth,'" he said, "nor did it desire to do so. Wherever it struck down a spade it struck a politician." [73]

But Congress apparently desired to get the truth; at least, the Committee on the Conduct of the War invited Butler to testify. His testimony was not evasive.

> QUESTION: "To what do you attribute the failure of the expedition?"
> ANSWER: "To the delay of the navy in Beaufort, and the refusal of Admiral Porter to run by the fort, and the failure of the bombardment to silence the fire of the fort on the land front."

When he was asked to what he attributed Porter's not passing close to the fort, Butler replied, "Since the loss of the Tennessee at Mobile, some of the officers of the navy have 'torpedo on the brain.' " [74] The testimony continued:

> QUESTION: "Was there harmony between yourself and Admiral Porter . . . ?"
> ANSWER: "Entire; not a word or a thought of a word on my part in any way or form, of controversy." [75]

After Fort Fisher had been exhausted, the committee gave Butler a free hand.

> QUESTION: "Are there any other of your acts which have been criticized which you wish to comment upon?"
> ANSWER: "I do not know. Many things I have done have been criticized."

As examples, the general cited arbitrary arrests, his military record, his appointments, various financial deals, and the exchange of prisoners.[76] The final report of the committee dealt very kindly with the general.[77]

Meanwhile Butler's successor as army commander, General Ord, was endeavoring to straighten things up. He wrote to Grant: "I propose, after thinking the matter over about the huge illicit trade, to order a military commission, with power to call for papers and persons; have them, after investigating thoroughly, try and sentence parties they may deem guilty. . . . Butler is not the only one aimed at." [78] But a few weeks after Butler's removal, Grant reported, "I have put a stop to supplies going out through Norfolk to Lee's army." [79]

Butler was to see Lincoln just once again. The President asked the general's views about the disposition of Negroes. Should they be sent out of the country? "Mr. President," replied Butler, "I have gone very carefully over my calculations as to the power of the country to export the negroes of the South, and I assure you that using all your naval vessels and all the merchant marine fit to cross the seas with safety, it will be impossible for you to transport them to the nearest place that can be found fit for them,—and that is the Island of San Domingo,—half as fast as negro children will be born here."

But Butler had a plan for the employment of 150,000 Negro troops, which he explained:

Now I have had some experience in digging canals. The reason why my canal, which was well dug, did not succeed, you know. My experience during the war has shown me that the army organization is one of the very best for digging. . . . The United States wants a ship canal across the Isthmus of Darien, at some proper and convenient point. Now, I know of a concession made by the United States of Colombia of a strip thirty miles wide across the Isthmus for that purpose. I have the confidence of the negroes. If you will put me in command of them, I will take them down there and dig the canal. It will cost the United States nothing but their pay, the clothing that they wear will otherwise be eaten by the moths, the arms are of no worth, as we have so many of them in excess, the wagons and equipments will otherwise rust out. [80]

"There is meat in that, General Butler," commented Lincoln; "there is meat in that. But how will it affect foreign relations? I want you to go and talk it over with Mr. Seward and get his objections, if he has any, and see how you can answer them." [81]

But Seward was injured that same day; and when he had recovered, Lincoln was dead.

CHAPTER XIII

PRESIDENTIAL
IMPEACHMENT

BUTLER was in New York when he heard the news of Lincoln's assassination on April 15, 1865. To an audience in Wall Street he declared, "Perhaps I may say reverently that this dispensation of God's good providence is sent to teach us that the spirit of the Rebellion has not been broken by the surrender of its armies." [1] This was the spirit that actuated his future course of action, or so one would deduce from the facts. The war was not over. Anyone who believed that the conflict was completed was a visionary and should be superseded by more realistic men.

He went at once to Washington, "in order to be present to give any assistance in this crisis of the country." [2] There was great excitement in Washington, noted a witness, and "General Butler was called out among others, and he made a speech full of surprising liberality and generosity toward the enemy." [3] At the Willard he met with the leaders of the Radical Republican element, who informed him that within eight hours of the President's death a caucus was conferring on plans to rid the government of the "Lincoln influences." It had been decided to push Butler for Secretary of State, in place of the apparently disabled Seward.[4] Lincoln's "bribe of unconditional forgiveness" had been denounced, and Butler was the chief speaker.[5] The assassination of the "soft peace" President was regarded as a gift from Heaven,[6] of which full advantage should be taken. The Massachusetts general fell in completely with the plans and stated, "The President must not administer the estate of Lincoln." [7]

In "informed circles" chaos prevailed. One of Jay Cooke's associates wrote from his bank in Philadelphia: " 'The Beloved remains' are knocking the machinery of social life here into a cocked hat. I could not get a bed at any hotel last night—had to sleep on my shawl on some chairs—fought for my breakfast and am inexorably parted from my baggage." [8]

At first Butler was all kindness and aid to the new President Johnson; perhaps Lincoln's successor could be cajoled or guided into going along with the Radical plan for the South. From his room in Willard's Hotel, Butler called on Johnson frequently with advice, and he helpfully wrote a twenty-page letter on the legal status under the Appomattox Convention of prisoners of war.[9] He advised the President that Lee's officers and men should be tried under municipal law.[10] On hotel stationery he sent the President a twelve-page epistle on the validity of pardons to the Confederate offenders; Butler concluded that "there would seem to be no doubt that these men are amenable to all laws and to the consequences of breaking them like other offenders." The general wrote "citizens" as the last word, but he crossed it out to substitute "offenders." [11] Sometimes his advice may not have been well received, and Welles recorded how when the President was ill, "Ben Butler had pushed his way to the very door of the sick-room to insist on the execution of Davis and Lee, and to urge severity." [12]

The Committee on the Conduct of the War met with the new President, and the feeling was that "he would act upon the advice of General Butler by inaugurating a policy of his own instead of administering on the political estate of his predecessor." [13]

It does not appear that at this period Butler had plans for himself in the government. He was kept very busy with his legal affairs, and the reputation that he had gained during the war of knowing how to get things done in Washington was useful. An Illinois Congressman noted in his diary of attending a trial in the Supreme Court where one attorney "was followed by Genl. B. F. Butler in the opening speech in support of the Military Commissions. He spoke an hour and a half today. His manner pompous and his matter paltry. He is a weak man—a humbug." [14] But General Wallace wrote to his wife about the same case: "The room was crowded, and as this is the first time I have seen him, I was much impressed by the appearance of the famous 'Ben.' " [15]

Immediately after the close of the Civil War there were some large cases arising from the conflict, and Butler's services were in demand. There was the matter of the *Grey Jacket,* a condemned blockade runner with a $500,000 cargo of cotton. Butler got the case for a contingent fee believed to be $125,000, and he tried to effect a settlement with the Secretary of the Navy. Because Welles was not sympathetic, the general threatened to go to Congress to appeal for sympathy for a man who had lost his all as a result of the seizure and condemnation of his cotton. Welles replied that his appeal for the sailors who had done their duty would be as strong. Butler countered with an offer to split the haul, 50 per cent to his client and 50 per cent to the naval pension fund. When Welles refused to compromise, Butler got Thad Stevens in the House of Representatives to get through legislation that would suspend proceedings in matters of this sort until the Supreme Court could render judgment. "Great derangement in order to get a great fee has been effected," noted Welles.[16] Subsequently Butler got McCulloch, the Secretary of the Treasury, to intervene in the proceedings; and the Secretary of the Navy recorded: "I regret it. McCulloch has been imposed upon. Butler is reckless, avaricious, unscrupulous. He knows there is neither law nor justice in his course on this question, but he has the promise of larger fees. For three months he has been annoying me on this subject. He then went to the Attorney-General and for a time made some headway. Failing there, he has now imposed upon McCulloch, who has been deceived by Butler's cunning and browbeaten by his audacity." [17]

The matter reached the Supreme Court after a lower tribunal had condemned vessel and cargo, but Butler was unsuccessful in getting a reversal for his client.[18]

Butler also appeared before the Supreme Court as attorney for the Government in the celebrated *Milligan* case. Milligan had been arrested on the order of the general commanding the military district of Indiana, and he was tried in October, 1864, by a military commission on the charges of conspiracy against the Government, giving aid and comfort to the enemy, inciting insurrection, and violating the laws of war. He was found guilty and was sentenced to be hanged. He petitioned the Circuit Court for a writ of habeas corpus; but when the trial judges could not agree the case was sent up to the Supreme Court.[19] Milligan was represented by some of the greatest lawyers in the land, including Jeremiah S. Black and David Dudley Field. The Attorney General of the United States engaged Butler as special counsel. The Supreme Court ruled in favor of Milligan, holding that the right of habeas corpus could not be suspended and that the constitutional rights of citizens could not be abridged by a military commission despite the exigencies of war. "No graver question was ever considered by this Court," declared Mr. Justice Davis in his opinion, "nor one which more nearly concerns the right of every American citizen when charged with crime, to be tried and punished according to law." [20]

Butler meanwhile was considering his formal reentry into politics. To Ben Wade, one of the Radical Republican leaders, he wrote cautiously; and Wade replied in a letter about a Massachusetts petition that he had to present to the President: "Saw Johnson with it. I made it the occasion of a renewed earnest application to him to reconstruct his Cabinet, and place yourself at the head of it as Secretary of State." [21]

But when Butler decided to enter the national political scene (as a politician this time), his apparent friendship with Johnson was brushed aside. The general firmly declared that "if any man stands in the way of the great march of the country . . . he must be taken out of the way." [22] And Butler quickly became one of the leaders of the Radical element that sought to curb Johnson. The President, after some initial vacillation, decided to follow Lincoln's policy of readmitting the Southern states as rapidly as possible; but the Radicals realized that the restoration of the South to the Union—and to Congress—would threaten the continuance of the Republican party in power. Clearly the new Southern Congressmen would hate the Republicans who had pursued the war to successful conclusion, and legislation would be subject to the same regional pressures as before.²³ In September 1866, the anti-Johnson Soldiers' and Sailors' Convention was held in Pittsburgh, and Butler launched himself as a savior of the Union at this time. He was extremely abusive of Johnson.²⁴ He advocated the hanging of Jefferson Davis and of Lee.²⁵ "Of the four conventions held," remarked one of Butler's political rivals, "this, of the soldiers who had fought the battles of the Union, was far the most influential upon public opinion." ²⁶ Butler was the leading spirit at this convention. He participated in the selection of representatives, arranged the caucuses, wrote and read the resolutions, and guided the proceedings in every respect; the general tone stressed was the inadequacy of the administration in Washington.²⁷ To similar conventions in Cleveland and Cincinnati, Butler said of the President, "Impeach him and remove him now." Johnson should be notified plainly that unless he did what he was told, "the boys in blue will make him." And if the President actually called out the army to enforce his decrees, why, the present audience and its sympathizers would take care of *that*.²⁸ Who *could* represent the country properly in Washington? Butler offered to serve the people.

All this was a prologue to his running for Congress. "The Radicals have elected General Butler to Congress in a district of which he was not a resident," noted the Secretary of the Navy; ²⁹ but that was not technically so. Butler was more meticulous than that. Because he did not wish to antagonize the sitting member of Congress from the Lowell district (Middlesex), he ran as a candidate from the Essex district, where he had a sort of residence. It happened to be a tent on the south side of Cape Ann, next to Ipswich Bay; but it unquestionably *was* a residence—at least, during some of the summer months. Butler ran for the House of Representatives, "feeling a little curiosity to know whether I could be elected in a district where I was only a carpet-bagger." Nevertheless, "I was elected to Congress while I lived in a tent on that beach." ³⁰

From the standpoint of the President's enemies, he was the man of the hour.³¹ As such, he received "perhaps more attention from the House than is usually accorded to a new member." ³² Reported another outstanding political figure:

Though his military career had been the subject of adverse and bitter criticism, it had been marked by certain features which pleased the people, and he came out of the war with an extraordinary popularity in the loyal states. He engaged at once in political strife. During the canvass against the President's policy in 1866 he went through the country, it may with truth be said, at the head of a triumphal procession. He was received everywhere with a remarkable display of enthusiasm, and was fortunate in commending himself to the good will of the most Radical section of the Republican party.[33]

And Butler at once became one of the commanding figures in a Congress of powerful men, such as Hayes, Garfield, John Sherman, General Logan, Blaine, Schuyler Colfax, and Roscoe Conkling.[34] A political observer declared:

One new face was there—a face, once seen, not to be forgotten. The broad forehead shelving up to the top of the bald crown, the fringe of thin hair encircling the lower head, the eyes asquint and half-hidden by pointed lids, the sharp nose with its nervous sniff, the spasmodic puffing out of the cheeks, the turned-down collar exposing the wide throat, and the right hand uplifted in the attitude of affirming without book;—these striking peculiarities betokened the presence of Benjamin F. Butler. His appearance on the floor meant business.[35]

Butler quickly took a place at the head of those who were gunning for President Johnson. He introduced a resolution calling for the investigation of Johnson's connection with Lincoln's murder.[36] He headed a special "Assassination Committee" of the House to examine into the crime, a committee which had as its real objective the involvement of Johnson in the killing.[37] He believed (or let others think that he believed) that Johnson had been a party to the assassination.[38] He was interested in discovering "who it was that could profit by assassination who could not profit by capture and abduction; who it was expected would succeed to Lincoln, if the knife made a vacancy." [39] When John Wilkes Booth's diary was found to contain an entry, "I have almost a mind to return to Washington and . . . clear my name, which I feel I can do," Butler demanded: "How clear himself? By disclosing his accomplices? Who were they? . . . If we had only the advantage of all that testimony, we might have been able . . . to find who, indeed, were all the accomplices of Booth." [40]

Butler was a bitter opponent of Johnson's policy of conciliation toward the South, of readmitting the former Confederate states in quick order. Three days after Lincoln's death, Butler had said that "the time has not yet come for holding any relations with her but that of the conqueror to the conquered." [41] To Ben Wade he wrote: "The most vivid hope I have is that the rebels will behave so outrageously as to awaken the Government and the North once more out of the dream of brotherly Union where brotherly love is not. My ground for that hope is that heretofore, under Providence, whenever all looked gloomy for our cause, something of outrage or extravagant pretensions have been put forth on the part of the South which has brought our people to their senses. May it so happen again. I think it is happening." [42]

When he had attained nominal (and eventually titular) leadership of the Committee on Reconstruction, he was able to keep out all the Southern states that would not accept the sternest of conditions. [43] He assured his followers that there would be requirements for readmission more drastic than a mere application. [44] An editorial declared that "Ben. Butler, in his New Year speech, declared a war of race impossible; but Ben. Butler has proven himself more skilful in confiscating spoons and other private property of Southern people than wise in legislation." [45]

By now it was obvious to the Radicals that they had been wrong in having thought that Johnson would act upon Butler's advice. Therefore Butler really went to work in attacking the President on a personal plane. He declared that Johnson's leniency was only for personal gain; thus the pardoning of deserters from the army was to have them available as loyal voters. [46] He tried to manufacture a murder case against the President and consorted with jailbirds as a possible source of evidence. [47] Finally the desperate Johnson resorted to the same sort of tactics: he had the adjutant general of the army search the files for any helpful information on Butler's war record. [48]

A New York attorney noted in his diary that "A. Johnson disgraces his high place and deserves to be impeached, but these ultraists, as, for example, B. F. Butler, are no less violent in talk and revolutionary in aspiration than A. Johnson himself." [49] That part of the nation which was not disgusted found the contest hilarious. With reference to the trips through the hustings that Johnson and Butler each made, Representative Thad Stevens of Pennsylvania declared: "I have amused myself with a little light frivolous reading. For instance, there was a serial account of a very remarkable circus that travelled through the country from Washington to Chicago and St. Louis and from Louisville back to Washington. . . . I expected great wit from the celebrated character of the clowns." [50]

But the game was in deadly earnest. The conspirators eagerly awaited an opportunity to bring charges against the President. The actual pretext found was Johnson's removal of Stanton, the Secretary of War, without the consent of the Senate; this was contrary to the Tenure of Office Act and was a ground for impeachment proceedings.[51] General Lorenzo Thomas was appointed temporary Secretary of War,[52] but Stanton refused to yield his office; he placed armed patrols to guard the building.[53] The Radicals were exultant; they "rejoiced that the madness of Johnson had at last compelled Congress to face the great duty." [54]

On March 2nd and 3rd, 1868, the House of Representatives adopted eleven wordy articles of impeachment. Article 10, better known as the "Butler article," accused the President of having made "inflammatory and scandalous harangues" by which he had tried to bring Congress into disgrace. Johnson was charged with having degraded his office "to the great scandal of all good citizens"; and cumulatively, he was declared "guilty of a high misdemeanor in office." [55] The Secretary of the Navy condemned the impeachment resolutions. "Infamous charges, infamous testimony, and infamous proceedings could be produced as easily, honestly, and legally as Butler could get spoons in New Orleans." [56]

Butler threw all his vast energy into the impeachment trial. For months he had been studying assiduously the various English trials involving impeachment; [57] and for his opening speech he worked like a Trojan. He slept but nine hours in the three days preceding the trial.[58] Much curiosity surrounded his opening speech, and hun-

dreds of dollars were offered for an advance copy. Butler had the
speech printed, but to circumvent leaks portions of it were farmed
out to various publishers.[59]

The fifty-four Senators from the twenty-seven states were to hear
the impeachment proceedings as presented by the House Managers,
who sat in a semicircle of desks before the Senate.[60] Some oversized
armchairs were borrowed from the now empty office of the Vice
President and were placed in the front for the Managers of the Impeachment.[61] The Managers, Butler noted, were "the ablest men of
the house," and he modestly added, "barring myself." [62] The trial
itself opened on March 13th before the Senate sitting as a court of
impeachment. Johnson was represented by Henry Stanbery, who had
resigned his post of Attorney General so that he could try the case
without embarrassment; William M. Evarts, the celebrated New
York Attorney; and Benjamin R. Curtis, a former Justice of the
United States Supreme Court.[63] It was an imposing defense counsel,
and Butler particularly admired the great legal talent of Justice Curtis, who had dissented in the Dred Scott case. "Much as I admire that
opinion," said the Massachusetts general, "still, I think it was the
second ablest effort of Curtis, the first, in my judgment, being Mr.
Curtis's opening argument in defense of Andrew Johnson upon the
trial of his impeachment." [64]

The presiding officer at the trial was Salmon Portland Chase, Chief
Justice of the United States. He could scarcely have viewed the matter with complete detachment; barely four years ago he had sought
Butler for the Vice President's position on the Chase presidential
ticket.[65] On the other hand, he did not relish the idea of his old rival,
Ben Wade, the President of the Senate, being next in line of succession if Johnson *were* removed.[66] Chase's perplexity was furthered
when, during the course of the trial, he let his friends put forth his
name for the 1868 presidential nomination.[67]

Much back-of-the-scene maneuvering went on up to the very start
of the trial. The Secretary of the Navy noted:

Butler, Stevens, and men like them, taking advantage of prejudices and
as yet unforgiving hate growing out of the war, do not attempt to cover
up intended villainy. One of the schemes now on foot is to admit the

bogus Senators, elected under the bogus constitutions which the carpet-baggers, aided by negroes under military dictation, have imposed on the Southern States. Strengthened in numbers by these interlopers, they hope to carry conviction. How long can a government stand which is the hands of such profligate and unprincipled wretches? [68]

That failing, Butler tried to insist that Johnson actually be brought in and placed at the bar of the Senate, to stand until the Senate offered him a chair. "But," the disappointed Representative declared, "our band of managers was too weak in the knees or back to insist upon this." [69] When Johnson's counsel asked for a forty-day postponement to perfect their case, Butler objected, saying that it had taken God only forty days to destroy the world by flood.[70] Unlike most of his fellow Managers, Butler was not a bit nervous. He said, "I came to the conclusion to try the case upon the same rules of evidence, and in the same manner, as I should try a horse case, and I knew how to do that." [71]

But this was not an ordinary horse case. Butler began the proceedings of the Managers of the Impeachment on March 30th with a four-hour speech.[72]

[T]he interest of the audience immediately centered upon one of the leaders—a man whose large pudgy body seemed literally bursting out of his extraordinary swallow tail coat, exposing a broad expanse of not too immaculate linen, and whose massive bald head with its little fringe of oily curls was probably familiar to every occupant of the galleries, for Benjamin F. Butler had not hidden his light under a bushel. There was power in the man's coarse, big-featured face, force and aggressiveness in every line, but his curiously ill-mated eyes with their half-closed lids, his hard mouth and small, drooping mustache, all combined to create an uncomfortable impression of cunning and insincerity, and his whole personality was unattractive.[73]

Although his speech was in the afternoon, Butler was dressed in evening attire, with a white necktie; [74] and one recorder thought that he could detect a histrionic, if not comic, air about the presentation.[75] The Massachusetts general read his speech from small printed slips of paper,[76] and at times his nose seemed to touch the notes.[77] Johnson, he said, had succeeded to the Presidency "by murder most foul." He was the "elect of an assassin." The Senators were informed that the "hopes of free institutions" awaited their verdict. "We have brought the criminal to your bar, and demanded judgment at your hands for his so great crimes." In short (*sic*), Johnson should be removed, not for his crimes, but for his unfitness for office.[78] And it was the Senators' duty "to inquire into and determine whether Andrew Johnson, because of malversation in office, is longer fit to retain the office of President of the United States, or hereafter to hold any office of honor or profit. . . . You are a law unto yourselves." [79]

Butler defined impeachment: "We define, therefore, an impeachable crime or misdemeanor to be one in its nature or consequences subversive of some fundamental or essential principle of government, or highly prejudicial to the public interest, and this may consist of a violation of the Constitution, of law, of an official oath, or of duty, by an act committed or omitted, or, without violating a positive law, by the abuse of discretionary powers from improper motives, or for any improper purpose." [80] This conveniently elastic definition could scarcely miss. He ended his opening oration with these words: "I speak, therefore, not the language of exaggeration, but the words of truth and soberness, that the future political welfare and liberties of all men hang trembling on the decision of the hour." [81]

"The speech itself," declared a contemporary review, "as it appears in print, without the aid of the general's tones, is both carefully prepared and able. It is all argument, or, at least, as close an approach to mere argument as is necessary, till he gets to the last charge, that of bad language—what canon lawyers call 'brawling'—in the speeches delivered at the West, and here he belabors the President without mercy, and, on the whole, in language not unjustifiably strong; but too strong to be very effective before any calmer or more critical audiences than a jury." [82] Yet the speech was included in a ten-volume set of the greatest orations of all time.[83]

The deposed Secretary of War, whose removal had uncorked the impeachment charges, was understandably touched by Butler's speech, and he wrote to the Massachusetts general:

Please accept my thanks for a copy of your great argument in the impeachment case. I have carefully read and pondered every word. In arrangement, style, tone, and manner of treating the subject it is admirable; and as an instructive argument the world, to all time, is enriched by it. I can add no more to express my judgment, than that it is worthy of you, and of "all the people" in whose name you spoke. Be the result of the case what it may, the "welfare and liberties of all men" are more secure for your vindication of them yesterday. As an American citizen, and as your friend I rejoice at the mighty blow you struck against the great enemy of the nation.[84]

Butler later said that the first three days of the trial were the hardest of his life. No other Manager offered him help. He assembled corps of stenographers, dictated by the hour, revised his words repeatedly, and saw that his speeches were set in type for distribution to the nation's press. The New York *Herald* of March 31st noted the curious fact that the text of his speeches (prepared before the actual delivery) was well interlarded with "applause" and "prolonged cheers." [85]

The Secretary of the Navy reported, "On the part of Butler and some others there is an inclination to play the part of buffoons, and display levity in a matter of the gravest importance to the nation." [86] But they meant business. Butler objected literally to every statement of the President's counsel or witnesses, and he insisted upon discussions on every point of order.[87] He objected to every question until it was reduced to writing and argued.[88] When the law seemed to be going against him, he argued that the Senate was not a court. in a *judicial* sense but a *political* body empowered to try and to determine the *political* fitness of Johnson.[89] On other occasions he forgot that the "jurors" were United States Senators and he resorted to all the tricks of the courtroom.[90] A great criminal lawyer of a later day believed that Butler even used the minatory manners of a cheap police court.[91]

But the President's counsel fought fire with fire. When Evarts defended Johnson against the charge of undignified attacks upon members of Congress, he did so by showing from published proceedings

how Managers Butler and Bingham had abused each other with frank-
ness and vocabulary that made the President's attempts at scurrility
seem amateurish.[92]

Yet nothing could faze Butler. Young Georges Clemenceau, who
was attending the trial as correspondent for *Le Temps,* thus reported
on the fiery politician who was partially to mold "The Tiger": "Always ready with a retort, impossible to embarrass, bold to any length
in attack, wily to an extreme in defense, he speaks simply and clearly,
without too much rhetoric, enlivening his remarks now and then with
a vein of irony. . . . One might have feared that he would try to
emulate Burke or Sheridan in the trial of Warren Hastings and, by
trying to fly too high, singe his wings in the sun. But Mr. Butler had
the good taste to be himself." [93] Another reporter declared that Butler, "although not profound in his knowledge of law, had few equals,
and probably no superior, at the bar in readiness, ingenuity, and the
ability to overshadow an antagonist with ridicule and abuse." [94]

Day after day the impassioned trial went on. When Stanbery, Johnson's counsel in chief, was ill, Butler refused to postpone the hearings. "Gentlemen of the Senate," he declared in his adaptation of
courtroom tactics, "this is the closing of a war wherein 300,000 men
laid down their lives to save the country. In one day we sacrificed
them by tens and twenties of thousands on the field of battle, and
shall the country wait now in its march to safety because of the
sickness of one man?" [95] Nor did Butler endear himself to the President's other defenders. Thomas A. R. Nelson, one of Johnson's counsel, objected to Butler's reference to him as "the veriest tyro in the
law in the most benighted portion of the Southern country," and he
tartly suggested that the Impeachment Manager make his remark
elsewhere. Butler chose to regard this as a challenge, and the next
day Nelson was obliged to make a public apology, which he did by
saying that he was not a "duelist by profession" and that no offense
had been intended.[96]

As the trial progressed, Butler became quite confident of the result. "The removal of the great obstruction is certain," he declared in
May. "Wade and prosperity are sure to come with the apple-
blossoms." [97] But he tried to leave nothing to chance. "There is a per-

fect inquisition by Butler and the chief conspirators," Welles noted, "where individual rights are stricken down, and the outrage is sanctioned and enforced by this Radical Congress!"[98] Every pressure was exerted to bring wavering Senators into line. The Massachusetts general said to one Senator during the trial, "Tell the damn scoundrel that if he wants money there is a bushel of it to be had."[99]

The Secretary of the Navy was horrified to find Butler engaged in private conversation with Senator Conkling, and he wrote: "It was an ominous and discreditable conjunction,—the principal Manager, an unscrupulous, corrupt, and villainous character, holding concourse with one of the Senatorial triers, a conceited coxcomb of some talents and individual party aspirations."[100] Butler was even said to have had spies go through the wastebaskets of the opposing counsel.[101]

Eventually the trial came to an end; and on May 26th the Senate voted. Of the 54 votes cast, two-thirds, or 36, would be necessary to find the President guilty as charged. The action failed by a single vote, as 35 Senators found the President "Guilty" and 19, "Not Guilty."[102] Stanton immediately resigned.[103] Directly after the verdict, an extra was sold in Washington with the sensational headlines, "Suicide of Ben Butler";[104] but the general had other things to do. He at once had a congressional committee formed to investigate possible bribery of Senators; every telegraph office in Washington had its messages impounded by his order, and financial institutions had to furnish analyses of senatorial bank accounts.[105]

Butler's new committee pursued the trail of suspected tampering of Senators with vigor; and on July 3rd the committee report was filed. Four Senators who had voted for acquittal were indirectly charged with corruption, and the taint of suspicion was left on three others. The general's co-Managers declined to sign the report with him.[106] Rhodes declared that "Butler's conception of humanity was so low that he could not conceive of men doing what was certain to lose them social consideration and political preferment unless they were paid for it in money."[107] But no evidence of this could be found.

Butler's impassioned fury against Johnson had been so marked during the abortive impeachment proceedings that Washington's population was shocked to see the Massachusetts general call upon the President at the New Year's Reception at the White House on January 1, 1869; Butler actually smiled as he spoke to Johnson for a full five minutes. But to the former Impeachment Manager there was nothing illogical in all this. "My unpleasantness was political," he explained. "I don't believe in carrying political disputes into social life." [108]

CHAPTER XIV

RECONSTRUCTION

BUTLER'S greatest energies in the three-year period follow-ing the close of the Civil War were devoted to the impeachment bat-tle. In order not to disturb the continuity of that struggle, the previ-ous chapter did not examine his other activities in any detail. A certain amount of temporal backtracking is indicated at this point.

Aside from the mad fight for position that every national politician experienced in the chaotic days following Lincoln's assassination, Butler must have wondered about his *personal* position. That he had been superseded as commander of the Army of the James was not in itself decisive; after all, he had been superseded as commander in Baltimore, at Fortress Monroe, at New Orleans. But now—was he even *General* Butler any more? It was only natural to enjoy being a general, but Butler did not want to have someone else take the rank away from him. Therefore he cautiously asked the Secretary of War when the wartime commissions would be canceled. On October 26, 1865, Stanton informed him that Lieutenant General Grant was about to cancel these commissions. Two days later Butler wrote to the President of the United States: "Having entered the service of the country for the war in the position I now hold, the only official posi-tion ever held by me under the Government, and the war being now closed so far as military operations are concerned, learning that the Government has no further need of service from me as a Major Gen-eral of Volunteers, I respectfully beg leave to resign my commis-sion from this date." [1] No one was going to fire *him!* Butler claimed he held on to his commission from May to November so that he could be employed on Jefferson Davis's trial if the Confederate President were tried by a *military* commission.[2]

Of course, he was known as General Butler for the rest of his life. And just to make it official, the Massachusetts legislature named him as major general of the state militia.[3]

Various business enterprises demanded some of his time. His Lowell textile mills were progressing well, but there were always new fields. Because the ending of the Civil War meant that patriotic societies would become active, and such organizations would need banners, Butler organized the U.S. Bunting Company to supply the necessary flags.[4] With two other men he incorporated the Pentucket Navigation Company, for freighting merchandise on the Merrimack River.[5]

But his work as a lawyer and as a member of Congress were most demanding of his time. One of his colleagues has left this remarkable picture of Congressman Butler in action:

General Butler had long been regarded as a powerful antagonist at the bar and he fully maintained his reputation in the parliamentary conflicts in which he became at once involved. He exhibited an extraordinary capacity for agitation, possessing in a high degree what John Randolph described as the "talent for turbulence." His mind was never at rest. While not appearing to seek controversies, he possessed a singular power of throwing the House into turmoil and disputation. The stormier the scene, the greater his apparent enjoyment and the more striking the display of his peculiar ability. His readiness of repartee, his great resources of information, his familiarity with all the expedients and subtleties of logical and illogical discussion, contributed to make him not only prominent but formidable in the House for many years. He was distinguished by habits of industry, had the patience and the power required for thorough investigation, and seemed to possess a keen insight into the personal defects, the motives, and the weaknesses of his rivals. He was audacious in assault, apparently reckless in his modes of defense, and in all respects a debater of strong and notable characteristics. Usually merciless in his treatment of an aggressive adversary, he not infrequently displayed generous and even magnanimous traits. He had the faculty of attaching to himself, almost as a personal following, those members of the House who never came in conflict with him, while he regarded his intellectual peers of both political powers as natural foes whom he was destined at some time to meet in combat, and for whose overthrow he seemed to be in constant preparation.[6]

A reporter gazed at the general in action and then wrote:

Make the best of it you can, it is a terrible face, this of Butler's; it looks like a pirate's—the strong, unscrupulous, cruel face, the low wide head, the crossed eyes, the hatchety Roman nose, the thin lips, make a combination powerful and pitiless. Yet we know this man has room in him for large magnanimities, for gentle charities, for good-will and tenderness. Only this is not the nature he faces the world with. He meets that with the brain of a master, the will of a tyrant, and the ambition of a spirit which can brook no superior. "Little children, be not deceived." As a politician, Ben Butler is over-reaching, self-seeking, and will be content with no less than the highest prize in the political game.[7]

A seasoned observer of the Washington political scene declared, "Benjamin F. Butler was another power in the House, who delighted to engage in a debate, with copious invective interlinings, and who was more feared on the Republican side of the House than on the Democratic." [8] Be it remembered that Butler was a Republican at this stage of the game.

When Butler was running against Richard H. Dana, Jr., for the Republican nomination for the Fifth Massachusetts District, a weekly review stated that if Butler should win, "we have no hesitation in saying that it will be the most alarming manifestation ever given in this country of popular indifference to the character of public men." [9] It was a bitter campaign. Dana stumped through the working districts and told the people that he had done dirty work, as they had, while Butler lived like a gentleman and an aristocrat. Butler followed in his footsteps and proclaimed: "As to the averment that it is necessary to be dirty in order to get to be your equal, I assure you I shall not have to get into a manure pit to be fit to associate with you, but simply be a respectable, well-clad, decent American citizen, who knows that one man who behaves well and does his duty to his country and his family is as good as another." [10]

When Dana claimed the support of the Republicans on the ground that he had been a member of that party longer than had Butler, the general triumphantly retorted: "Judas was an older disciple than Paul, and for a time, while Paul persecuted the Christians, might have thought himself a better; but Mr. Dana should remember what happened to Judas." [11]

Butler defeated Dana by 6,000 votes, and the young reporter of *Le Temps* recorded: "The only thing that saved him was his behavior during the trial of the President. The radicals owed it to themselves not to desert the man who had shown himself Mr. Johnson's bitterest enemy." [12]

Perhaps Butler would have won his reelection more handily had he not been devoting his political talents to matters outside his own bailiwick. But he managed to turn up at all sorts of political meetings. At a Loyal Union Convention in Philadelphia, a Johnsonite rejoiced that there "extremes met." "Yes," answered the Massachusetts general, "so they do when a dog chases his own tail, but both extremes belong to the same dog." A Chicago admirer wrote that his observation was worthy of Talleyrand and that if Butler died first he (the admirer) would erect a marble monument at least two hundred feet high, topped with a dog scurrying around after his tail.[13]

Two days before Election Day in 1866, a Republican rally was held in City Hall Park in New York. Addresses were scheduled by such party stalwarts as Horace Greeley, Governor Curtin of Pennsylvania, and General Butler. When it was Butler's turn to speak, there were some cheers, but booing was the predominant sound. "Spoons!" cried someone in the crowd. Other shouts were heard: "General Butler can't make no speech!" "Give us a song, Butler; give us a song!" Someone raised a huge banner (said to have been made in the Common Council) that was shaped like a spoon; in large letters one could read, "Spoons, rally!"

Butler faced the hostile mob for half an hour, waiting to make his prepared speech. Then he was hit with an apple. Butler whipped out a knife, and those in the front row of the crowd drew back in fright. But the general picked up the apple, neatly pared it with his knife, and slowly ate the fruit. "This is a pretty good apple," he said calmly.[14] Then he put on his hat and got down to business. The crowd was out of hand, and the New York *Tribune* reporter declared that he had recognized many mobsters who had participated in the bloody draft riots of 1863. Said the general:

I have hung your betters, and if you do not behave I shall get the chance to do the same to you. I have seen many more than you with arms in their hands, with minie rifles and muskets and bayonets, and I did not flinch from them. Do you suppose I shall flinch from onion-stinking breaths? A man who has smelt gunpowder can stand garlic. You, the hooters here, think you are the equal of the negro, oh! no! The negro is as much, as immeasurably your superior, as heaven is above the hell where you are going. I do not respect you, and I certainly do not want your respect. You may be quite sure I do not fear you.[15]

An awed but respectful crowd then listened to Butler's political speech.

The general's correspondence was huge; the demands upon him were tremendous. In a single week he received letters such as a request for a pension, an inquiry about prize money on vessels captured during the war, a poem from a colored woman ("The Charge of the Black Brigade"), questions about points of law, requests for funds, invitations to patriotic meetings, invitations to political gatherings, offers of new inventions, notification of his election to a literary society, plans for a hospital in which he might be interested. One correspondent asked the date on which the general had arrived at Ship Island. A colored preacher wanted to know to where he should look for his income.[16]

From a baronet in England came a challenge to "meet me in mortal combat. . . . If you fail to attend your fate will be destined to be that of President Lincoln's." On this letter Butler penned a note to his secretary, "An. Bah!"[17] Another British request (for the "lovely wife of the Earl of Clarendon") was couched in more diplomatic language: "I have boldly undertaken the perilous task of asking the terrible Bluebeard of New Orleans for a fac-simile of his awful signature."[18]

Butler generally tried to obtain action upon soldiers' requests, but when one man wrote from the National Asylum for Disabled Volunteer Soldiers to seek a job as customs inspector, the general replied:

"You have a good home and provision for life. Why should you desire to get a good place away from a good soldier who cannot come to the Asylum— Be contented with enough." [19]

But not everything was a volunteer service. There were those whose interests he had to protect, and the Secretary of the Navy noted that "Major-General Benjamin F. Butler is exercising a great and dangerous influence at the Treasury Department." [20] He had to protect himself from many confiscation suits brought against him as a result of his wartime administration, primarily at New Orleans; he engaged his old political mentor, Caleb Cushing, to vacate service against him (Butler) on the ground that as a member of the House he was constitutionally guaranteed full freedom from arrest while going and coming from his duties. [21] Suits and accusations against him he tried to avoid, not answer; and a contemporary magazine said pointedly of him: "The man who, with the means of vindication within his reach, refuses to use them, and not only sits down in hardened indifference to the opinion of his fellows, but asks them to clothe him with official rank, is a moral monster." [22]

Accusations about stolen spoons seemed to nettle the general, even if greater charges went unanswered. "If," he declared, "any person chooses to believe that the commanding General of a department would steal spoons, when, by a simple order, he could control millions of money, he will so believe, because his own mind is so constituted that he knows *he* would have stolen spoons if he had the opportunity." [23] Yet the general was never to divorce himself from the spoons allegation, despite a well documented defense. [24]

Butler felt obliged to keep a sharp eye upon the South. When a Southern newspaper charged the North with having treated its war prisoners brutally, the Massachusetts general replied: "We are poor illiterate men, mere jailers. We were not educated at the peoples' expense at West Point as President Davis and General Lee were." [25] It was not often that one had the opportunity of making a single slur apply to the Confederacy *and* to West Point.

As the guiding spirit of the powerful Committee on Reconstruction of the House of Representatives in the Fortieth Congress, Butler saw to it that the South remembered who had won the war.²⁶ His theory of reconstruction was simple, as he explained it. "With the radical Republicans of my party I held the proposition . . . that the rebel States should be held as territories under military government until all possibility of a race war or race dissensions between white and black should be obliterated, and that then these Territories might be admitted into the Union as States when the negro had learned how to be a citizen, and the white man had learned how to be a loyal one." ²⁷ In 1867 a Southern newspaper printed this topical verse:

> High diddle, diddle,
> The Radical fiddle—
>> The War closed a little too soon.
> The little dogs laugh
> While Butler and staff
>> Ran away with another teaspoon.²⁸

"I would have confiscated the real estate of all those who had voluntarily taken an active part in the Rebellion," Butler declared. "I would have permitted all to run away who desired to and expatriate themselves as they had tried to do by bloody war,—and some of them by so going away justified the propriety of my suggestion. Their lands so forfeited I would have divided among the private soldiers of the army to be theirs at the end of five years of occupation." ²⁹ He would have had Jefferson Davis tried by a military commission of major generals, to be presided over by the senior major general of the army (one Benjamin F. Butler).³⁰ As to the impartiality of such a commission, "I assumed that the result would be, that we should come to the conclusion to advise the President that he was guilty of the acts alleged against him." Butler even imagined himself saying: " 'After considering your case the commission will advise the President and Commander-in-Chief that you are guilty of the treasonable acts alleged against you in the manner and form in which they are set forth, and will advise that he should proceed with your execution by hanging on a day to be by him fixed.' " ³¹ The Secretary of the Navy at first thought that Butler would be an excellent addition to counsel for the prosecution of the Confederate President; ³² but he later concluded that he "might be an unpleasant associate, and there is danger that he would think more of Benjamin F. Butler than [of] the case at hand." [33]

Butler was determined to punish the Confederate war leaders, and he even went as far down in the hierarchy as General Pickett, whose small army had outwitted Butler's at Petersburg; he declared that Pickett should be found guilty of treason, for he had joined the Southern army before his resignation from the United States Army had been formally accepted in Washington. After Appomattox, Federal Generals Ingalls and Pitcher advised Pickett to get out of the country before Butler's vengeance caught up with him; [34] if he did not do so he would be tried by a military commission "organized to convict." [35]

When a riot broke out in New Orleans in August, 1866, Butler warned the South that "we will march once more, and woe to him who opposes us." [36] After an Ohio-born carpetbagger (who got to be a tax collector) was flogged in Mississippi, his blood-stained shirt was sent to Washington as an exhibit. Butler carried it to the floor of Congress and waved the garment above his head as he warned of punishment to the South; and from this incident all Reconstruction ranting became known as "waving the bloody-shirt." [37]

The once-proud Southern states should not be allowed to rise again, said Butler.

The governments of these states were part and parcel of the Confederacy and should, in my view, have been entirely obliterated. . . . I advised that those territories should be given specific names. For instance, Virginia should be the territory of Potomac; North Carolina, the territory of Cape Fear; South Carolina, Georgia, and Florida, the territory of Jackson; Louisiana, the territory of Jefferson; Texas, the territory of Houston and Arkansas, the territory of Lincoln. I believed that the lines of those territories should be so drawn as to cut up the boundaries of the original States so that there should be nothing of State pride left. By their proceedings the people of these States had forfeited all honorable mention, and when they should be fit to come back into the Union . . . they should come in with the boundaries and names given, and that would have blotted out forever all brotherhood of Confederate against the United States.[38]

McDowell, the army general commanding the military district in which Mississippi was located, removed Governor Humphreys and replaced him with Butler's son-in-law, Adelbert Ames. When Humphreys refused to yield except to superior force, Ames said in a conciliatory manner, "If you want military pantomime, it shall be carried out with all the appearance of reality without actual indignity."[39] But Ames's carpetbag government was so corrupt even for that day that he was impeached for bribery. Butler knew just the lawyer to defend him: Roger A. Pryor, the former Confederate hothead who had done so much to push Virginia into the war early in 1861. Pryor was now a struggling attorney in New York City, but he was still well regarded in the South. Butler was one of his first clients, to defend Ames.[40] It was a brilliant if sly choice, and soon Pryor was able to write Butler: "I opened negotiations with the leading men against us, with many of whom I had old and intimate associations, and, after a strenuous struggle, it was arranged that they should dismiss the charges, and then the Governor should resign."[41] Ames wrote to his father-in-law: "Conviction was certain. . . . A conflict could have resulted in no good to any one."[42] Therefore the deal was accepted: Congress dropped the articles of impeachment and Ames resigned.[43]

Butler took an active part in the setting up and maintenance of carpetbag governments in a number of Southern states: the idea, he said, was to exhibit "the power that Congress had to protect all its citizens . . . against wrong, rapine, and murder."[44] He even tried to have elections postponed for two years in Georgia on the ground that there had been intervention by a military government.[45]

Butler was an outspoken critic of the Ku-Klux Klan, and he advocated strong measures against this secret society. In Congress he explained in 1871: "Gentlemen on the other side of the House threaten us that if we pass this bill we shall destroy the Republican party; that an outraged and indignant people will drive us from our seats. If they believe what they say, then why not get out of the way and let us pass it? Why filibuster to prevent enactment of this, or, as they declare, a worse one from being offered?"[46]

Representative Swann of Maryland endeavored to object to the severity of the bill against Klan activities, but Butler turned upon him with such vehemence that Swann had to run off the floor of the House. When the Marylander dared return, Butler turned upon him again. "Has the gentleman got back?" he asked. "The last I saw of the gentleman was a dissolving view of him going out of the other side of the House." The general added that he had not even been able to see Swann during his military occupancy of Baltimore in 1861, for the cattle had been driven off the streets before his arrival.[47] "Congress has adjourned," noted a New York attorney in his diary, "after passing the Ku-Klux Bill, from which little good is to be expected, and after a disgraceful interchange of Billingsgate between the Hon. B. F. Butler and certain other 'honorable' blackguards." [48]

The Massachusetts general was not afraid to make speeches in the South. A Scotch visitor to Richmond learned that Butler was coming to make an address in that city, and he was amazed to find out that the general was going to stop at the Ballard House. "Why shouldn't they?" a friend asked. "Ain't they bound to give entertainment to man and Beast?" [49] The hotel itself contained numerous pictures of Butler, adorned with horns and hooves; and when the visitor asked whether the pictures would be left in view when the general arrived he was told, "O yes. Butler don't care a curse, if we don't lock up the spoons." [50]

Butler's speech upon that occasion was to a colored audience in the First African Church. The Scotch visitor decided to go and report his reactions:

A short, stout man, with large bald head, a round body, and short spindle legs, stood at the front of the platform, speaking in a somewhat harsh but very fluent and articulate voice. It was easy, even at a glance, to see how this man had the power to make himself an object of such deadly hate to a whole people. There was power in the big bald head, in the massive brow, in the vulture nose, in the combatively bullying face, in the heavy eyelids, and in the keen, scrutinizing eye. . . . His speech, as far as I heard it, was clear, logical, and full of practical wisdom, but was delivered with an audacity of manner that made one reluctant to admire even what deserved admiration.[51]

CHAPTER XV

POLITICS AND
FINANCE, I

AS the 1868 elections approached, Butler's availability for the Republican nomination became manifest. His services in the war and in the Washington arena had made him one of the best known persons in the land. Who had a better claim to the Republican nomination: Greeley, Stanton, Colfax, Phillips, Seymour, Sumner, Wade, Stevens? None could match Butler's war record, such as it was. Grant was the man to be watched.

When it became apparent that Grant's star was rising, the Massachusetts general (it was said) had detectives on the trail of his former commander; [1] and Butler kept himself well posted on the progress of Grant's efforts to stay sober.[2] There were tips about Grant to be investigated. George Suckley wrote to Butler about the possibility of an alliance with "Baldy" Smith against Grant. "I suggested that you and he had better 'hitch horses,' because I am convinced that Genl. G. is possessed of important information on certain matters, and it might be well for you to obtain the same." Smith had intended to make a singlehanded fight, continued Suckley, but he stated that he "was willing (as far as no sacrifice of dignity is concerned) *to enter into an alliance 'offensive and defensive' with you to beat a common enemy*." [3] This was indeed an odd combination, for Butler had engineered General Smith's disgrace; and Suckley, Grant's staff surgeon,[4] had helped another of Butler's enemies, the Confederate General Pickett, to escape from Richmond.[5]

Butler could not have forgotten that Grant had dismissed him from the Army of the James after the Fort Fisher fiasco; and Grant's earlier remark about Butler's being bottled up at Bermuda Hundred still rankled. But the final rupture came when Grant sent an extremely belated invitation to a reception to the Butlers. The Massachusetts general answered with icy formality: "General Butler has the honor to decline the invitation of Lieutenant General Grant. General Butler has now no desire for further acquaintance." [6] According to a New York newspaper, Butler had told Grant, "In no event would I be willing to hold personal intercourse with yourself or any member of your family." [7]

Butler had better things to do than to sulk in his tent, but he and Grant remained strictly aloof. The Massachusetts general did have time to start a book that would give the people some hitherto unaired intelligence about Grant,[8] but for some reason the volume never was published. Butler made no effort to hide his own feelings about the lieutenant general. To the wife of his biographer he wrote: "I think Grant will stagger into the White House. To this complexion have we come at last!" [9]

Yet the good of the party required that there be a reconciliation before Election Day; and perhaps a broker who could bring the parties together would find the reward worth the effort. The challenge was accepted by George Wilkes, publisher of sporting and political papers, co-founder of the *National Police Gazette,* and early proponent of pari-mutuel betting.[10] Wilkes had been closely associated with Butler in a land-exploitation scheme, and he felt that the post of minister to Mexico would be a fair compensation for effecting the reconciliation.[11] The adventurer saw Grant, who was now willing to explain that the obnoxious phrase "bottled up" was only a figure of speech; furthermore, the invitation had not been sent earlier because Grant had not known that the Butlers were in Washington.[12]

Butler vouchsafed that Grant's position "would seem to render it convenient at least, that no impediment should exist to social recognition each of the other even if supposed or real grievances to either, unexplained or unredressed, should forbid more." Butler agreed to withdraw his answer to the invitation to Grant's reception, and he accepted the explanation that Grant never "intended any offense in the use of the phrase 'bottled up' in relation to my entrenched command at Bermuda Hundreds. . . . When General Grant makes known to me his desires to give opportunity for explanation of other matters of difference I will promptly point out to him such topics in his report wherein I think he has done me injustice and if he agrees with me as I believe he will upon reflection I see no difficulty in mutually satisfactory explanations which however I cannot even seem to seek from him." [13]

Grant was not willing to make a complete surrender. He was willing to accept Butler's withdrawal of his reply to the invitation, but he would not apologize for the phrase "bottled up." Butler could explain this in any manner that he saw fit.[14]

But even if Wilkes did not earn his brokerage fee, the Grant-Butler feud began to peter out. When one man congratulated Butler upon the reconciliation, the latter replied:

Gen Grant thinks his great name & deeds will carry him into the Presidency without the aid of lesser men like myself. He forgets the fable of the mouse and the lion. . . . If the republicans elect Grant then Conservatism, West Pointism, regular Navyism, a General in the War dept., and an Admiral in the Navy dept. will change the Civil form of our Government to one of military orders. He is too weak to prevent it. He will be the victim if not the tool of his Army and family associates who are anything but republican. . . . What then is there for me, for you or any other true radical republican to labor for in the coming election. Simply to "win a loss." [15]

When a reporter asked if it were true that Butler would not act in harmony with a Grant administration, the general replied: "I say that charge is a slander on Gen. Grant, for I shall be entirely in harmony with true progressive Republican principles, upon which, I assume, his administration will be conducted. Of this I have no doubt, and so his administration will have no more ardent supporter than myself." [16]

Butler wrote to a constituent on Christmas Day, "I may mention it as a piece of news that General Grant left his card with me today by his private secretary." [17] When a political club's members expressed their pleasure in reading that Butler had not used his influence to keep the soldiers from voting for Grant, the Massachusetts general replied, "Never believe any thing you see of me in the Newspapers good or bad, either will be false." [18]

On February 10, 1869, the electoral vote was counted. It was by then a certainty that the Republican slate of Grant and Colfax would be elected, but Butler objected to Georgia's answering the roll call. His objections took so much time to express that it began to appear that the time set by the Constitution for the count could not be observed, and the presiding officer had to call the sergeant at arms to keep Butler from making further motions.[19] Butler distinguished himself by the violence of his language, and some of his remarks had to be omitted from the *Congressional Globe*. Meanwhile some of the Senators came into the House chambers to watch the goings on, and Butler moved that they be ejected. "We certainly have the right to clear the hall of interlopers." [20]

By the time of Grant's inaugural, a complete reconciliation was effected between the President and Butler, since the former "asked if our former kindly relations might not be restored." [21] Butler showed what his friendship could do instantly. On March 9th, just five days after Johnson had relinquished the Presidency, the Massachusetts general introduced a bill of two lines' length which absolutely repealed the Tenure of Office Act, for a constructive violation of which he had urged impeachment barely ten months previously.[22]

Butler did not think well of Grant, who, he stated, "is stupidly dull and ignorant and no more comprehends his duty or his power under the Constitution than that dog." [23] The dog was not identified. But his frank appraisal of the President did not deter Butler from achieving a complete degree of intimacy, and he later wrote, "I can say without fear of contradiction, that few men possessed a greater share of his confidence, or had more personal influence with General Grant upon public questions than I had." [24] He openly boasted that he ran the Grant administration.[25] This soon became obvious to others, and General Sherman wrote to his brother: "I have observed with great concern that General Grant is moved by the urgent demands or remonstrances of men who care no more for him, and would as gladly sacrifice him . . . Ben Butler, Logan and men of that stripe."[26] Butler had more influence with Grant than had anyone else in the House, and he became the President's champion in that chamber.[27] In return, he became Grant's chief spoilsman[28] and office-broker.[29]

Because of Grant's favors, Butler also became an autocrat in the Massachusetts political sphere.[30] As Butler's influence with the President increased, the Massachusetts general even got his wartime superior to "correct" the Butler war record. President Grant told a correspondent of the New York *Herald:* "I believe now, that if General Butler had had two corps commanders such as I might have selected, had I known the material of the entire army as well as I did afterwards, he would have" captured all south of Richmond to Petersburg.[31] But it was General Grant who had selected the two corps commanders that President Grant later repudiated.[32] When Grant eventually got around to writing his account of the war, he could at least give his postwar spoilsman an "E" for effort: "General Butler certainly gave his very earnest support to the war; and he gave his own best efforts personally to the suppression of the rebellion."[33]

Another Massachusetts Congressman went to the President and told him angrily that Butler openly had boasted that the President would not refuse any of *his* requests. The best defense that the President could give was that "I have refused his requests several times."[34] Grant did not seem to consider that Butler might even be his rival for the chief executive's chair, although an Ohio politician had written that the Massachusetts general "is in training for the presidency."[35] Another politician-general, Nathaniel P. Banks, confidently said to a friend that Butler's tremendous popularity would never gain presidential votes: "[W]hen I came down to the House this morning, there was a fight between two monkeys on Pennsylvania Avenue. There was an enormous crowd, shouting and laughing and cheering. They would have paid little attention to you or me. But when they come to elect a President of the United States, they won't take either monkey."[36]

Butler did not have too high a regard for his superior. He sent to one of the Massachusetts Senators "A Confidential Report from

Washington," headed "State Secret," which contained such choice
morsels as: "The ex-President and the President for the time being
have no cordial regard for each other; and the supporters of each
constantly vilify and reproach each other. So, it happens that in the
popular meetings got up by their respective proteges, one is called
the 'drunken tailor' and the other the 'drunken tanner.' The two
high contending persons entertain the same sentiments toward each
other." [37] Yet Butler could see that the President had his good points.
"Grant evidently did not get enough of West Point into him to hurt
him any; he was less a West Point man than any officer I ever
knew." [38]

Because of the ample patronage that the Grant regime put at his
disposal, Butler was able to keep his state organization in fine condition. Through Federal appointments he kept his political fences in-
tact; [39] and he had an army of Federal marshals and postal clerks
helping the cause of the Republican party in Massachusetts.[40] Thus
the domestic scene acquired an almost routine aspect for the time,
and Butler turned his vast energies to foreign affairs.

Cuba was undergoing an insurrection when, on April 10, 1869, the
House of Representatives unexpectedly passed a resolution of sympathy for the rebels. Under the leadership of Butler and Banks, the
Congressmen offered to support President Grant if belligerent rights
were proclaimed.[41] Nothing happened just then, but by the following June 15th it was discovered that Butler had started his own inquiry into Cuban conditions. A stormy scene followed, during which
General Logan accused Butler of having interested himself in the
matter because of certain Cuban bonds. Butler replied that what he
had done was with the approval of his fellow Representatives, whereupon Logan charged that the Massachusetts general had acquired a
hold over many of the members by having detectives hound them
through the hovels and dens of Washington. "Butler seemed to be
the only one perfectly at his ease," declared Logan's biographer.[42]

Butler could not do very much about matters in Cuba, but the
Alabama claims offered better possibilities, for the party of the second
part was the general's old enemy, England. The damage caused by
the *Alabama, Sumter, Rappahannock,* and other vessels equipped in

England in defiance of the laws of neutrality had to be settled; more-over, Butler was still smarting over the rebukes that had been ad-ministered to him by the Secretary of State at the instance of the British prime minister and the minister in Washington. England must pay. He demanded that a portion of Canada be ceded to the United States in settlement of these claims.[43] Grant raised no objec-tions,[44] but Butler's "Cede Canada or Fight" speeches aroused little enthusiasm in Congress.[45] Butler made this proposal: The United States should say to England: " 'You have done more against our country than you can ever repay. To settle those injuries we want you to remove yourself as far as possible from being our neighbor, and give up the province of Canada. You have been an exceedingly bad neighbor from the beginning, and we want you near us no more. Cede Canada to us and we will settle all difficulties and give you a clean release of all claims.' " [46]

But the Massachusetts general had to carry on his fight virtually without assistance. Naturally his belligerent tones aroused answer-ing echoes in England. "Jackson was placarded in the streets of Lon-don as a tyrant and a beast," exclaimed the general in a speech on April 4, 1871, "because he stood for the rights of his country. I am the only American beside him that has been so honored." [47] He declared that an open break with Great Britain would be the best means of revitalizing the Republican party for the 1872 elections.[48] When the treaty of settlement was being drafted by American and English diplomats, certain language was inserted with the understanding that its inclusion was purely formal. These portions "had been advanced by Senator Sumner and advocated by General B. F. Butler,—both factors in Washington not to be disregarded." But the British com-missioners understood the situation of their American opposite num-bers and tacitly "forgot" these passages.[49]

The Treaty of Washington, as concluded on May 8, 1871, settled not only the *Alabama* claims but also the rights of American fisher-men in Canadian waters and the San Juan boundary dispute in Puget Sound. On May 21st Butler denounced the agreement, which, he said, had been accepted because of fear that the United States could no longer borrow money in England if the treaty failed of acceptance.

"But is it necessary for us to sacrifice our national honor in order that we may borrow money at usury?" he demanded. Our credit would not really be destroyed. "Let neither the seduction of money, the menaces of England, nor any other motive but the just preservation and care of American honor and American rights determine the decision of an American Executive and an American Senate." [50] But three days later the United States ratified the treaty. [51]

When the United States purchased Alaska, it was suggested that that "icebox" had only been acquired so that Butler could be got rid of by sending him off as governor of the new territory. [52] But he roundly opposed the purchase, saying: "If we are to pay this price as usury on the friendship of Russia, we are paying for it very dear indeed. If we are to pay for her friendship, I desire to give her the seven million two hundred thousand dollars in cash and let her keep Alaska, because I think it may be a small sum to give for the friendship if we could only get rid of the land, or rather the ice, which we are to get by paying for it." [53] And if we wanted territory detached from the body of our national domain, he demanded, why should we not buy Crete and free it from the Turks? [54]

But as was so often the case with Butler, he seemed to have profited from a transaction that he so vehemently had opposed. An American named Benjamin Perkins claimed that in 1855 he had made an agreement with the Russian minister Stoeckl to deliver ammunition to Russia. Stoeckl denied that there was such an arrangement, and the New York State Supreme Court dismissed Perkins's suit. Perkins took $200 to drop the case. After Alaska was acquired, Perkins's heirs made contact with various Congressmen, and an $800,000 appropriation was tacked to the Alaska purchase bill, to be withheld from the purchase price. The Russian Foreign Office archives mentioned among those whose aid had been enlisted by the heirs *"Butler [qui] est interessé pour 30,000 dollars dans l'escroquerie Perkins."* [55]

In the same year, 1868, the New York *World* observed, "Now this Butler was more Sutler than any other Beast in the field!" [56]

Some American businessmen had sizable investments in San Domingo, and it seemed finally desirable to have the island brought under the American flag. In return for a tract of land on Samana

Bay, Butler agreed to introduce a resolution authorizing an American protectorate over the area, and he recommended to Grant that immediate action be taken.[57] Grant "proceeded like a cavalry officer on a raid" and sent General Babcock to negotiate a secret treaty, leading to annexation.[58] One of the promoters wrote to an associate in New York: "General Butler spoke of his share of the scheme. I told him that you would arrange that in a satisfactory manner." [59] In April, 1870, Butler proposed annexation by joint resolution, but his motion was defeated in the House.[60] On June 27, 1870, Simon Cameron and Butler went to see Secretary of State Fish with a proposition. They could get the San Domingo annexation treaty passed, they said, if they could line up a few more votes. If the Collector of the Port at New Orleans, Casey, were removed, the proper appointment would win favorable response from the Louisiana Senators and possibly others, for a potential gain of six votes. Fish declined, for had the men forgotten that Casey was Grant's brother-in-law? Butler then suggested that Motley, the minister to the Court of St. James's, be recalled, with Senator Sumner to be appointed in his place. That would create a vacancy in the Massachusetts Senators, which Butler would contrive to fill himself; and with this replacement of the obdurate Sumner the treaty could be forced through the Senate. But Fish was not agreeable to these changes, and the Senate ultimately defeated the annexation bill on June 30th.[61] The president of Cornell University, who had been appointed by Grant to be a member of the commission that visited San Domingo, wrote of Butler that he was

a man of amazing abilities, but with a certain recklessness in the use of them which has brought him into nearly universal discredit. His ideas regarding the annexation of Santo Domingo seemed to resolve themselves, after all, into a feeling of utter indifference,—his main effort being to secure positions for one or two of his friends as attaches of the commission.[62]

Foreign affairs did not keep Butler's agile mind from domestic matters, and fiscal policies were of great concern to him. When he sponsored a bill that would tax Federal bond interest to the extent of 10 per cent, he was accused of repudiation; [63] United States issues always had been considered as tax-exempt so that the Government could successfully sell its bonds in competition with private issues not equipped with this feature. And if people had purchased Government bonds with the expectation that their interest would not be taxed, would not a tax repudiate the conditions of purchase?

But the Massachusetts general soon was to become known as a really large-scale advocate of repudiation of Government obligations. After the nation had become accustomed to a paper-money currency during and after the Civil War, the "hard money" advocates insisted that there should be a return to specie payments as quickly as possible. The inflationists, however, argued just as strongly that the Government should continue to use paper money, even in paying off bonds that had been issued originally for "hard money." "We want a money," declared Butler, "based not only upon the gold in the country, but upon every other source and element of the national prosperity, emancipated from the control of all other nations." [64] He wanted Congress to authorize the issuance of paper money that would not even be a promise to pay.[65] To the House of Representatives he said: "I stand here . . . for inconvertible paper money, the greenback, which has been held by us as a just equivalent for the blood of our soldiers, the lives of our sons, the widowhood of our daughters, and the orphanage of their children." [66] In a word, he was opposed to the promised resumption of specie payment.

Butler said that the greenbacks would be money—not hard money but *fiat* money, from the Latin word meaning "let there be." He illustrated the use of the word: God has said *Fiat lux*—Let there be light. A Massachusetts rival of Butler seized upon this explanation. "That, Fellow-citizens, is precisely the difference between Omnipotence and Humbug, between the Almighty and General Butler. God said let there be light and there was light. General Butler says let there be money and there is—rags. This is the first time in our history that the American workingman has been gravely asked to take for his wages money it costs nothing to make, that it is no loss to lose, that it is no gain to get, and that even a Chinamen won't touch." [67] The Secretary of the Navy was just as skeptical, and he noted, "No one but a knave or a fool would take the position he does, and Butler is not a fool." [68]

A national weekly jumped into the fray. "The value of every man's property, and the amount of his debts, may at present, as one of the effects of the Legal Tender Act, be altered arbitrarily and suddenly from day to day, every time . . . a Butler can get forty or fifty demagogues to join him in an assault on the public credit." [69]

Butler did not win many adherents in Congress in 1868, for the legislators were more responsive to the cause of the bondholders than to the demands of the debtor classes, who preferred to pay back their debts in depreciated currency. But he did win the support of widows and veterans. [70]

The Panic of 1872 and the resultant depression brought the issue of greenbackism to the fore again, for now the farmers and many businessmen wanted a more plentiful form of money than specie provided. In April, 1874, Congress raised the authorized total circulation of greenbacks, thanks in large measure to Butler's active work toward the achieving of inflationism. Prior to this time, new notes were only reissues of paper that had been authorized and paid out during the Civil War; there had been no increase as a new proposition in time of peace. The proposed bill provided that there should be a permanent increase in legal-tender notes from $382,000,000 to $400,000,000. [71] After some indecision Grant vetoed the bill. [72] The great cartoonist Nast celebrated the event with a cover picture for a national weekly, on which he depicted Grant's veto as effectively bottling up Butler again. [73] But Butler had won new sympathizers in the South and West by his efforts to help the debt-ridden people pay off their obligations in inflationary paper. [74]

The Redemption Act of 1875 provided that beginning on January 1, 1879, the Treasury would redeem in gold any greenbacks that were presented for redemption. As the Republicans had lost control of Congress in the November, 1874, elections, the Democrats had the burden of enforcing this legislation. [75] Because redemption of greenbacks would mean a contraction of the currency, the advocates of inflationary paper money formed the Greenback party, which nominated Peter Cooper for President of the United States. The party's

platform included a demand for repeal of the Resumption Act, an
issue of legal-tender notes that would be convertible into Government
bonds, discontinuance of all bank notes, and abolition of the sale
of gold in foreign markets.[76] Butler became one of the leading figures
in the party. Whether he was willing to take his pay in greenbacks
is conjectural, for during the height of the controversy an attorney

*Nast drawing of Grant "bottling up" Butler
by vetoing the money bill. 1874.*

wrote him from New York that "there is a matter I wish to present for your consideration which promises *gold*—your share of which shall be paid in such other money as you may prefer." [77]

Since the debtor classes could not obtain a more plentiful and therefore cheaper form of money by means of greenbacks, the proponents of inflation turned to silver. In 1878 the Bland-Allison bill came before Congress. "The bill was pushed and passed by the efforts, principally, of the greenback inflationists and the representatives of the silver States." [78] "It is scarcely too much to say that the demand for the coinage of silver dollars began where the cry for unlimited paper money left off. . . . The debtor class was catered to, and the prejudices of class feeling invoked in favor of the Bland bill as they had been in earlier years in favor of worthless paper." [79] Butler was consistent in his desire to side with the inflation-seeking groups. Suppose the metal in a silver dollar were only worth 90 cents or 92 cents, would it be any more dishonest to pay off debts in 90-cent dollars than to continue tolerating a subsidiary coinage which had an even lower value relatively? [80]

The bill itself provided for the purchase by the Government of silver bullion for monetary purposes at the rate of not less than $2,000,000 worth per month, and not more than $4,000,000, the ratio of the coinage to be $412\frac{1}{2}$ grains of standard silver per dollar.[81] The bill was regarded as highly inflationary, for the Government would be pumping sizable amounts of money into the economy each month.[82]

Butler spoke vigorously for the bill in the House, but stanch opposition was voiced by Senator Ben Hill of Georgia; and Nast depicted the Massachusetts general tripping over a "Hill," thereby losing his hold on bricks labeled "90 cent silver." [83] But when President Hayes vetoed the bill on the ground that a cheaper dollar would constitute a repudiation of existing Government obligations, Hill voted against the veto. Nast was obliged to present a new drawing to depict Butler looking for the slippery Hill from Georgia, who meanwhile had disappeared into the earth.[84] The soft-money advocates had won their fight.

Public finance was scarcely more important to Butler than private finance. The financiers of the Union Pacific Railroad Company made use of an organization known as the Crédit Mobilier to aid in the construction and financing of the railroad. Representative Oakes Ames, the directing genius of the Crédit Mobilier, had at his disposal certain shares to distribute to members of Congress for unspecified purposes.[85] In 1870 the financier Jay Cooke tried to get the railroad company some concessions from Congress. The Senate agreed readily enough, but the House was not so sure. Butler at first voted against the bill, declaring that "Jay has said nothing to me of this." Then Cooke authorized Butler's employment as counsel for the company "if such a step were necessary to secure his support";[86] and the Massachusetts general reconsidered his previous position.

In time the entire Crédit Mobilier acquired a noisome stench, and a congressional committee made a thorough investigation, as a result of which Ames and several other Congressmen were named as having been participants of a bribery scheme in 1868. On February 7, 1873, Butler made a speech in the House before the committee's report had been completed. The House had no jurisdiction over a crime said to have been committed five years previously, he declared.[87] Furthermore, Congress was about to adjourn, so why bother to expel the miscreants now? "They are no worse now than five years ago, upon the finding of the committee. If we are not contaminated up to this time, we are very likely to escape as well during four days more." [88] He cited another Congressman who was tainted. "Now, then," he cried, "by the grace of God and the Republican party, that man having all of his disabilities removed at his own request and brought here among us by his own constituents, to sit with us, if we can stand that contamination, cannot we stand Oakes Ames, the honest man?" [89]

Butler was not shown to have received any of the shares that Ames had distributed so freely around Congress; but how about counsel fees that he had received from the stockholders, plus $1,000 for expenses unspecified? Butler appeared before the Wilson Crédit Mobilier Committee to answer the charge. "There is nothing that I desire to palliate, to excuse, or to defend," announced the general. "I should just do so again and will do so again when I please, where I please, and how I please—all the world to the contrary notwithstanding." [90]

When Oakes Ames was drastically disciplined for his part in the scandal, Butler again rose to defend the accused in a witty speech marked for its cynicism.[91] Butler even refused to permit Ames to be criticized after his enforced departure, stating, *"De mortuis nihil sine bonum"* (Say of the dead nothing but good).[92]

When Representative Whittemore was charged with selling a West Point cadetship for $300, he begged Butler to defend him on the floor. Logan, as chairman of the Military Affairs Committee, presented the case; and when Butler interrupted him Logan asked whether the Massachusetts general wished to be considered as Whittemore's attorney. Butler vouchsafed that that was so. The chairman reminded him that one Congressman could not act as attorney for another in any case before the House. Butler replied that it was only a matter of sympathy on his part. Then Logan launched a fierce attack upon Butler for apologizing for a criminal who had violated the law. Whittemore was expelled.[93]

Yet Butler's qualities of sympathy and forgiveness had their limits. When Admiral Farragut died on August 14, 1870, Porter was nominated to succeed him; but Butler organized a strong opposition in the House to his Civil War enemy.[94] When he could not get the President to withdraw the nomination, Butler endeavored to have the grade of admiral eliminated entirely, so that none could get it. He spoke touchingly of Farragut's admiral's flag: "[T]he brave, frank, open-hearted sailor who has just died had with his dying lips said to his attendant, 'Never raise that flag over me, nor carry it before my coffin—that flag which has been imposed upon me by the man who expects to become my successor!'" Two ineffectual Senate floor discussions followed, while Porter explained that "the best proof that he made use of no such expression is to be found in Butler's statement that he did." Ultimately the Senate did confirm Porter's nomination as admiral.[95]

CHAPTER XVI

POLITICS AND FINANCE, II

IN 1871 Butler sought the Republican nomination for the governorship of Massachusetts. So well had he built up the Republican state organization through patronage from Grant that the nomination would be tantamount to election; but within the party there was strenuous opposition to the general. He therefore set out for a series of personal talks. In one speech he declared that he could buy certain newspapers for fifty dollars. At a speech in Springfield, on August 24th, a representative from one paper got up and challenged Butler to prove his statement. The general was prepared. The only way in which his backers could get news of their meetings published in this opposition newspaper, he declared, was to buy space. Waving a receipt, he continued: "I once said I could buy some newspapers for $50 apiece. I take it all back. I can buy them for much less than half-price—$12." [1]

On September 13th Wendell Phillips spoke for Butler at a political meeting at Salisbury Beach. He had known Butler since boyhood, he declared:

And I came here to say that I hope Gen. Butler will be governor, because he represents that element of disturbance in the Republican party; and, the moment he doesn't represent it, the great labor element that clasps hands from Moscow to San Francisco will trample him under its feet. . . . If I were Pope to-day, there is not a man among all the candidates, Butler included, that I would make a saint of,—not one. . . . [2] I don't believe, that if you could import a saint, brand-new and spotless, from heaven, that he could get a majority in the State of Massachusetts for any office that has a salary.[3]

Butler was obliged to stress his party regularity, for his Republican foes were reminding the people that the general had been a Democrat for many years. He said to an audience at Worcester, "I see no man but President Grant with whom we can go into the coming contest with any hope of success." [4] At Woburn he declared, "But if General Grant were my dearest foe, and Horace Greeley my warmest friend, I would vote for Grant because he is the nominee of the Republican party." And regularity should be taken seriously. "A party," continued the general, "should be managed like an army, where they welcome recruits and shoot deserters." [5]

Butler learned that Senators Sumner and Wilson, his old friends, were now opposing him as the Republican nominee. He angrily confronted them at the Coolidge House in Boston and said: "This all comes of your hostility to Grant. I am for him, and you are against him." Sumner then asked, "But, general, to be frank, do you think any better of Grant than I do?" There was no answer. "I know you do not," declared Sumner.[6] The Senators would not give Butler their support.

The party managers defeated Butler at the nominating convention in Worcester, and a New York diarist noted, "Butler did great service at New Orleans, but his subsequent career has been more curious than useful." [7] The disappointed candidate then turned his attention to the law; he formed a partnership with Edwin L. Barney that was soon to obtain what was believed to be the largest damage award yet made in an American court.[8] He also interested himself actively in the so-called McGarrahan Claim, which was based upon a dubious Mexican land grant covering mineral lands in California. The Massachusetts general pushed the claim actively before the Department of the Interior, until Grant intervened and said that it was a matter for Congress to settle.[9]

When Congress created a Territorial Government for the District of Columbia in that year, 1871, Butler took an active part in the management of the District. When the District was on the verge of bankruptcy as a result of too much patronage, the general was instrumental in getting the United States to assume its debts.[10]

Butler was certainly not bored with being a Congressman, and his extracurricular activities did not prevent him from being active in the House. The Massachusetts general became angry at Blaine for not making him chairman of the Ways and Means Committee, and he challenged Blaine's authority. The Maine Congressman replied that the general henceforth could make his demands to a party caucus. "I will ask God, and not you," exclaimed Butler. "I am glad the gentleman will," replied Blaine. "I have no favors to ask of the devil," continued Butler.[11]

Butler then asked Blaine to put him on the Committee on Appropriations. Because Blaine did not dare to say a point-blank refusal, when Butler went to the Maine representative's office for the known purpose of making his demand Blaine jumped out of the window. Then he quickly rounded up a full committee and returned to tell the general that, honestly, there were no vacancies to be filled.[12]

The general did serve on the Judiciary Committee. To this committee was referred a bill, introduced by Representative Julian of Indiana, which would have authorized woman suffrage. Victoria Woodhull, representing the National Women Suffrage Association, delivered a memorial to the committee on December 21, 1870. It appeared that she made particular efforts to win Butler's active support. "I wish, General Butler, you would say 'contraband' for us," she said sweetly.[13] A contemporary newspaper observed that "the youth, beauty, and wealth of Mrs. Woodhull carried the day, and the grave legislators, 'e'en Ben Butler,' bowed before these combined attractions."[14] There is small wonder that Butler admired Mrs. Woodhull's well documented speech, for he had written it for her to present to his committee.[15]

Susan B. Anthony wrote to Victoria Woodhull: "Glorious old Ben! He is surely going to pronounce the word that will settle the woman question, just as he did the word 'contraband' that so summarily settled the Negro question."[16] But that was not enough. The Judiciary Committee reported adversely, saying that Congress had no power to act. Butler and William Loughbridge of Iowa submitted a minority report, in which they offered this resolution: *"Resolved, by the House of Representatives,* That the right of suffrage is one of the inalienable rights of citizens of the United States, subject to regulations by the States, through equal and just laws." [17] That minority report, declared a prominent suffragette, "is perhaps the strongest and most exhaustive ever written on women's right to vote under the Constitution." [18] Butler was definitely on the side of woman suffrage, as, for example, his Worcester speech of August 30, 1871, made clear. [19] On December 12, 1872, Butler wrote to Susan B. Anthony that the Constitution certainly authorizes the right of women to vote. "But," he continued, "the difficulty is, the courts long since decided that the constitutional provisions do not act upon the citizens, except as guarantees, ex proprio vigore, and in order to give practical force to them there must be legislation." [20]

Butler was not forgotten by Victoria Woodhull. She was angered by attacks on her by the sisters of Henry Ward Beecher, whereupon she published in her weekly newspaper the story of an alleged intimacy between the clergyman and Mrs. Theodore Tilton. She was arrested for publishing obscene literature and sending it through the mails. [21] She wrote to Butler for help, but he pleaded the press of other duties. "I cannot believe," he wrote, "that in . . . the prosecution of yourself and sister for sending obscene literature through the mails, in the Courts of the United States, there is the slightest need of my services or my counsel. I feel as certain as I can upon any question, that the action of the United States Prosecuting Attorney was based wholly upon a misconstruction and misconception of that statute." [22] And such was the case, for she was acquitted.

Butler did have time, however, to aid in the passage of the bill for the incorporation of the Brotherhood of Locomotive Engineers. [23] He was able to find time to look after his loyal followers. Richardson, who managed the treasury's funding operations in England, wrote to him that "you never forget your friends." [24]

Butler's position in Congress was high, but as to Congress itself the same could not be said. Thurlow Weed wrote: "Statesmanship in Congress is now so low that it will take years to build it up to a higher tone. Probably the most influential man in Congress to-day is Benjamin F. Butler,—as he is the worst. Massachusetts never served the country so badly as when she sent General Butler to Congress. It is an alarming sign of the times that a man of his astuteness thinks that the course he chooses to adopt is one which will give him a large following." [25] But in a day of brilliant Congressmen, wrote General H. V. Boynton, "there were few on the floor who ever cared to encounter him in debate." [26] When he made some charges against Representative Bingham, the latter replied, "Such a charge is only fit to come from a man who lives in a bottle and is fed with a spoon." [27] This reference to his New Orleans days did not sit well with the Massachusetts general, and he turned on his tormenter with such vigor that Bingham completely lost control of himself and could only talk in gibberish.[28] When Representative S. S. Cox was debating (as he thought) an issue with Butler, the Massachusetts general replied: "There is no need for me to answer the gentleman from New York. Every negro minstrel just now is singing the answer, and the hand organs are playing the tune, 'Shoo Fly, don't bodder me.' " [29]

James Russell Lowell thus wrote about his state's legislators: "Of our representatives, George Hoar is an able and respectable man, but of the others nobody ever heard, or, if he did, it was to their disadvantage. The two best known are Butler and a vendor of patent medicines. *Non tali auxilo!*" [30] An observer of the Washington scene in 1873 has left this portrait:

BENJAMIN F. BUTLER, of Massachusetts, is a burly, heavy man, who waddles as he walks, and carries his head slightly bent forward. He is the best abused, best hated man in the House. It suits some persons to imagine that Ben Butler, as he is popularly called, is simply a blustering, swaggering politician without much ability of any kind. The truth is that Butler's big head contains a good share of the brains of the House, and he possesses qualities that would make him a leader in any cause he might espouse. . . . Butler is much of a philosopher. He is a man of strong feelings, but he has learned to control them, and, when it suits him, he can pocket his grievances, and work with a smiling face by the side of the men whom he hates with all the intensity of his nature. Giving him credit for patriotism, it cannot be denied that he has a thorough appreciation of the interests of Benjamin F. Butler, and those who know him feel sure that his acts, which sometimes seem inexplicable to the outside public, are all directed to the permanent advancement of these same interests.[31]

Butler knew how to gain popularity in Congress. He declared in a speech in the House that "if I desired to 'bring down the house' in a storm of applause, I would utter some biting sarcasm upon the intellect, or some attack upon the character, of some member of the House." [32] He made continuous reference to his war record, with the result that non-military men were embarrassed by their lack of an army career.[33] But when Butler taunted Representative Hoar of Massachusetts for not having been in the war, the latter turned upon him with unexpected venom:

Those persons who did not go to the war may, perhaps, possess at least this advantage, that they can form an impartial opinion of the merits of those who did. It is the pride and the honor of this noble Commonwealth of ours, that of the hundred thousand brave soldiers and sailors she sent to the war, there was but one notorious braggart, there was but one capable of parading up and down the Commonwealth, vaunting that he had hung a man; exhibiting himself as the Jack Ketch of the rebellion. I bow reverently to the brave, modest, patriotic soldier, who, without thought of personal gain, gave youth, health, limb, life to save the country which he loved. I am willing to abide by his opinion, and to yield to him every place of honor and of office. But to you, General Butler, whose military career is made up of the plunder and slaughter of Big Bethel; of the powder explosion at Fort Fisher; of the engineering at Dutch Gap; of the "bottling-up" at Bermuda Hundred; of the trading with the rebels through the lines in North Carolina; of the scandals of New Orleans; to you, who were ordered by General Grant to go home in disgrace; to you whose best service had been, if you, too, had stayed at home, I have no such tribute to offer. When Benedict Arnold taunts Jefferson that he did not go into battle in the Revolution, when Aaron Burr taunts John Adams for his want of patriotism, then it will be time for you to boast yourself over the men who performed the duties of civil life during the Rebellion.[34]

But Butler got his revenge, of a sort. When his attacker's brother, Ebenezer Rockwood Hoar, the Attorney General of the United States, was nominated for the Supreme Court by President Grant, Butler got his friends in the Senate to refuse to confirm the appointment.[35]

If Butler was disliked by his fellow Congressmen, there unquestionably was sound financial reason why he *should* have been liked. Representative James A. Garfield submitted a General Appropriations bill toward the end of the term of the Forty-second Congress; and late one night Butler added a rider, without which, he threatened, the bill could not possibly pass.[36] Salaries of the President, Vice President, Cabinet members, Justices of the Supreme Court, and Congressmen would be raised. As to Congressmen, there would be a 50 per cent increase, retroactive to the beginning of the term two years previously; [37] accordingly, each Congressman got an extra five thousand dollars to take home with him, courtesy B. F. Butler. In the confusion of the last days of the term, no effective opposition could be marshaled; and when Representative Upson of Ohio tried to strike out the retroactive clause Butler called out: "I can suggest a remedy to any gentleman who does not think this increase of salary is right and proper; let him come up and sign a pledge that he will not take the increase. Virtuous men and true, come up and sign it!" [38] Butler said that any man not worth the increase should not be in Congress. "He ought to resign!" [39] The bill was passed on the night of March 3, 1873.[40]

Butler's biographer wrote to the general of "your ever glorious salary grab—only defective, perhaps, in the method. In the substance, most wise, most just." [41] But public indignation was so great at this "Back Pay Steal" that many legislators wondered how they could purge themselves of tainted money. To one such Congressman F. E. Spinner, the Treasurer of the United States, wrote, "It is possible that you might divest yourself by a last will and testament, stating as a consideration the love and affection you bore your native land." [42] Butler alone seemed unmoved, and when a remonstrating constituent protested about the salary grab the general sent him a three-cent piece for his share in the increased taxation to pay for the raises.[43] In the face of this storm, members literally fell over themselves at the next session of Congress to see who could lead the movement to reverse the grab. Butler won the distinction. First he urged lawsuits to force the recipients (including himself) to disgorge; this was not approved. So, ten months after the increases, they were legislated back to the old level, except in so far as the President and the Supreme Court Justices were concerned.[44]

Butler had not lost his hold on the underprivileged. His appeal to the debtor classes through monetary inflation has been related in the previous chapter. He was so popular with the Labor Reform parties in Massachusetts that they decided to nominate no candidate of their own in 1873 for the governorship of Massachusetts; instead, they would select the choice of Big Business, Butler.[45] Butler then went to a temperance meeting in South Farmington and rather surprisingly announced that the two main planks in his forthcoming gubernatorial campaign were public ownership of the railroads and prohibition.[46] Wrote a New York attorney: "That disinterested patriot, Ben Butler, is trying to be Governor of Massachusetts and is backed by Grant's influence, which I regret for Grant's sake." [47] Nast produced a drawing of the general escaping from a flagon entitled "Bottled Butler," to menace a cradled baby identified as Massachusetts.[48]

Butler and Boss Tweed were the two primary targets of the powerful cartoonist Nast, although Butler did not try to retaliate by means of a smear campaign as Tweed did.[49] Nast had supplied the heroic portrait frontispiece for Parton's biography, but almost immediately he turned his talents to a *carte de visite* entitled "Bluebeard of New Orleans," which showed Butler holding a huge bloody sword in one hand and a helpless woman in the other.[50] At the time of Butler's abortive campaign for the governorship in 1874, Nast had taken to lecturing, during which he illustrated contemporary persons on a large easel. Butler was one of his most appreciated caricatures.[51]

But when his other ambitions were snuffed, Butler could always keep himself occupied in Washington. As a Congressman, he had the privilege of making an appointment to West Point. His first two candidates failed scholastically; his third choice, a colored man, was not allowed to enter. Therefore the general appointed his son, Ben Israel Butler, to the military academy. The father did not think well of West Point training ("That big-mouthed bastard Smith won't wipe his nose till he finds the right chapter in Jomini to tell him how" [52]) ; hence when his son was graduated Butler had him serve for a year with a colored regiment on the Western Plains.[53] When the first Negro Congressmen were met with cold courtesies on every hand, Butler was quick to be on familiar terms with them.[54] His solicitude for Negroes was so great that at a colored banquet in New Orleans, the master of ceremonies offered this well intended toast : "Here's to General Butler. He has a white face, but he has a black heart." [55]

Butler's congressional duties were not allowed to interfere with a job that he had got as a private citizen. Federal legislation set up a National Asylum for Disabled Volunteer Soldiers, the board of managers of which was to consist of the President of the United States, the Secretary of War, the Chief Justice of the United States, and nine other citizens, "not members of Congress ; . . . to be selected by joint resolution of the Senate and the House of Representatives." [56] On April 21, 1866, a joint resolution designated Butler, who was not yet a Congressman ; and he was subsequently elected president and treasurer of the board of managers.[57] Jay Cooke was a vice president. When Butler entered Congress, the disability about his being a manager *and* a Congressman was waived. It was not a minor undertaking; thus from June 2, 1866, to January 7, 1871, $4,684,235.65 was drawn on the War Department on vouchers payable to Butler.[58] Substantially all of this money was deposited in his personal bank account. When an investigating committee asked, "Have you any objection to exhibiting to the committee your bank account, showing the deposit of those funds?" he replied, "I cannot exhibit my bank-account, showing the deposit of this fund, without exhibiting my private bank-account." This he refused to do, on the grounds that it would expose his private business ; [59] unquestionably it would have. Who actually got the interest on these moneys in his account never has been established.[60] He also sold property to the asylum at a modest profit; the Chesapeake Female College property grossed 25 per cent.[61] The actual "seller" in that transaction was Butler's brother-in-law, Hildreth; but Butler had purchased the property originally, receiving from Hildreth only $12,000 of the $38,000 cost. Each said that the *other* had gotten the $50,000 paid by the asylum.[62]

The 1870's found Butler doing quite well financially. In addition to his congressional and business income, there was a thriving law practice. His partner at that time, Edwin L. Barney, was to say admiringly: "He was, to my mind, the greatest lawyer, the greatest man the country ever produced. Starting from nothing, unknown and most abjectly poor, he battled constantly uphill, till at the bar he had no equal as an all-round advocate. In admiralty, before a jury, before courts, in common practice, in equity, or in private practice he had no superiors." [63] His fees were extremely respectable in the dollars of that period. When he represented Admiral Farragut in a ship-condemnation proceeding that went to the Supreme Court, his fee was $75,000.[64]

Since so much of his time was spent in Washington, Butler built a huge granite house on the southern edge of the Capitol grounds, which, when it had served its purpose, he was to sell to the government.[65] Then he acquired the famous yacht *America,* which won the International Trophy Cup.[66] Butler enjoyed cruises as a respite from his governmental duties; but even after his government service had ended an investigating committee discovered that his yacht was being remodeled at the Boston Navy Yard.[67]

As Butler became more prosperous, doubtless he rejoiced to see that certain of his friends also were doing very nicely. There was John D. Sanborn, of Massachusetts, who entered Butler's service as a detective. Subsequently he was appointed a provost messenger on the Baltimore to Fortress Monroe boat, to maintain law and order. Prior to his employment by the Treasury Department, he was known as Butler's man for dirty work.[68] After some Treasury experience he was awarded a contract to assist in the discovery and collection of moneys owed to the government, his fee to be 50 per cent of the take. His original contract called for the investigation of thirty-nine distillers and purchasers of whisky; but subsequently he prevailed upon the Secretary of the Treasury to add the names of 760 persons suspected of deficiencies in income and inheritance taxes. Later, 592 railroads were added to his list.[69]

Sanborn's method of operation was simple. In the case of inheritances, he obtained lists from the local surrogate, and these he turned over to the nearest Collector of Internal Revenue for audit.[70]

In the case of railroads, he copied corporate names from *Appleton's Guide* [71] and then claimed his 50 per cent on the taxes paid by these companies, pointing out the undoubted fact that their names were on his list; actually the Collectors of Internal Revenue did all the work.[72] In two years' time Sanborn received fees from the government in excess of $200,000, in addition to the blackmail he picked up along the way.[73] Butler was accused of having got Sanborn his post by violating a committee rule of secrecy, but the general sarcastically answered that it was impossible to violate the rules of that committee.[74] Therefore the Ways and Means Committee turned its attention to Sanborn and asked, "Did you not contribute a sum to the expenses of a certain gubernatorial campaign in Massachusetts?" "Yes, sir," was the reply; "I always do." "That had nothing to do with the contract?" asked a committeeman. "Not in any shape." [75]

Butler modestly started to withdraw at that point, but a committeeman called, "You had better remain, General, and attend the sessions of the committee, because, as your name keeps constantly dropping out, it would be a matter of some difficulty to send for you every time." [76] But nothing could be proved against the general, except that he had introduced Sanborn to the Secretary of the Treasury, William A. Richardson; and it was Richardson who lost his job.[77] When the special agent stood trial, "It was anticipated by many that Benjamin F. Butler would appear for his partner, Sanborn, but he was represented only by his shadow, United States Commissioner John I. Davenport, who frequently consulted with the counsel for the defense." [78]

The people of Massachusetts were further outraged when a Butler henchman, William A. Simmons, was nominated as Collector of the Port of Boston.[79] George Boutwell, a lifelong friend of Butler's in Massachusetts, was a member of the Committee on Commerce, which reported adversely upon Simmons's nomination, whereupon Butler announced furiously that he would spend half a million dollars to defeat Boutwell when he came up for reelection.[80] Simmons was rammed through despite the objections of many Massachusetts politicians; and as a rebuke the voters of the commonwealth failed to return the general to Congress in the elections of that year (1874).[81] Butler did not admit that he had been defeated at the polls; he recorded that "in the meantime my district had been stolen from me." [82] Grant had now lost interest in the Massachusetts general, and he gleefully showed a telegram from the Bay State: "Butler defeated, everything else lost." [83]

Before his term expired, Butler shoved through Congress a so-called Amnesty bill, the largest portion of which actually provided relief from litigation for those who had committed abuses in suppressing the secessionist cause. "Amnesty for the conqueror!" observed one Congressman sardonically.[84] But the Senate would not cooperate in passing Butler's "Force bill," which would have given the President the right to suspend the habeas corpus for two years in certain of the Southern states.[85]

Former Congressman Butler was not really out of employment, for his services were greatly in demand. When Phelps, Dodge & Company became involved in a tariff difficulty, Butler teamed up with Senator Roscoe Conkling and quickly earned a $50,000 fee.[86] The governor of Ohio noted in his diary, "I hate the corruptionists of whom Butler is the leader." [87]

The general's fame had spread widely. An orator declared in 1874, "It is often the surprise of travelers in our distant States and in the farthest country to find that the life and speeches of General Butler furnish the only international theme upon which they can converse with the people, with a mutual interest." [88] His name had even become a part of the national vocabulary. Congressman John Young Brown of Kentucky said in a speech in the House, "If I was to desire to express all that was pusillanimous in war, inhuman in peace, forbidding in morals, and infamous in politics, I should call it 'Butlerizing.' " [89] A Scotch traveler to the Southwest heard a boy say to his sister, who was taking more than her share of a pie, "Now, don't you Butlerize all that pie." [90]

On April 8, 1876, Butler's wife died in the Massachusetts General Hospital of a thyroid tumor of ten years' duration.[91] He was deprived of the constant companionship of the woman who had shared his turbulent life. "In the highest sense," wrote one of Butler's enemies of the moment, "she was an excellent woman, and her death touches many beyond her own household." [92]

Butler had lost his reelection to Congress in 1874 as candidate from the Essex district; for the 1876 elections he sought the Republican nomination from the Middlesex district, which embraced his real home in Lowell. "Harvard College was called upon to do missionary work in my district to push Mr. Hoar, who was one of its fellows," recorded the general.[93] It was a year of uncertain political fortunes. A Congressman from New York wrote to Butler: "That we are in a precarious predicament party-wise and otherwise is obvious. For one I am ready to stand and act on the truth be it great or small, and nothing will try me personally so severely as to see on our side anything closely resembling fraud or tricky devices." [94]

Butler was reelected to Congress, and one editorial declared: "It is very pleasant to listen to an intellectual athlete like Butler while he is 'chawing up' a rebel like Ben. Hill, but we lose in strength, power, and the good opinion of mankind whenever we put into office wretches of this sort, no matter how 'smart' they may be." [95]

President Hayes, who came into office in the 1876 elections, wrote in his diary: "If there are any two men in the country whose opposition and hatred are a certificate of good character and sound statesmanship, they are Conkling and Butler. I enjoy the satisfaction of being fully endorsed by the hatred and opposition of both of these men." [96] Yet the President might have had some anxious moments over these words; for after the disputed Hayes-Tilden presidential contest a congressional committee was formed to look into the Democrats' charge of fraud, and Butler was one of eleven on that committee.[97]

Most of Butler's legislative efforts in this congressional term were devoted to his work in the interests of the greenback and silver movements, as has been related in the previous chapter. There were always political chores to be done, however. He tried to get for a soldier-constituent the postmastership at Methuen, Massachusetts. It so happened that the soldier had an artificial leg which was so excellent a fit that many people in his own shop did not know about it. When the postal office was being considered, Butler had the ex-soldier appear before the Senate Committee on Post Offices on crutches, without the artificial limb, to elicit sympathy.[98]

A newspaperman sketched this picture of Congressman Butler in his office in the year of his reelection, upon the occasion of a visit in the evening. "The summit of his extremely bald brow glowed in the gas-light. He received me kindly and as we talked twisted around and around the unlighted cigar he held between his teeth. The cigar was always there and generally in active rotation, but then or afterward I never saw it inflamed." [99]

It was Butler who saved the priceless negative collection of Mathew Brady, the distinguished Civil War photographer. Brady had tried in vain to get the Government to purchase his two thousand negatives of the war and its principal participants, which creditors otherwise would have seized. Butler had the sum of $25,000 inserted in the Sundry Appropriations bill for the purchase of this material.[100]

Butler's interest in scientific matters was great. Ever since he had been a public figure, the general's correspondence had been huge; now he tried to find a modern device for keeping up with his mail. Perhaps he had seen Edison's first announcement of his phonograph in 1878: "The apparatus now being perfected in mechanical details will be the standard phonograph. . . . The main utility of the phonograph, however, being for the purpose of letter-writing and other forms of dictation, the design is made with a view to its utility for that purpose." [101] Butler wrote to the inventor, who replied: "I shall probably come to Washington in a few days with the Phonograph and will show it to the C.S.O. as you request. It talks clear and distinct, and I will give one of your stenographers a chance to take down 500 clearly articulated words in a minute." [102] Actually Edison did not perfect this device for another ten years, for it remained in a "period of arrested development" while the inventor was perfecting the incandescent lamp.[103]

As the 1878 election drew near, many of Butler's constituents felt that their "sound money" ideals were being threatened by his greenback agitation. The following resolution was published:

Resolved, That we warn the people of the Commonwealth, whose votes General Butler is now soliciting by promises to serve them faithfully, that his professions when seeking office have been found in our experience to be easily made and as easily repudiated when the time for redeeming them came.

That they are neither gold nor good paper, but are a kind of fiat currency, having no intrinsic character, being cheap, delusive, irredeemable and worthless.[104]

Butler was defeated for reelection, and the President of the United States noted in his diary: "The crushing defeat of Butler was one of the best events that has happened since the war. Unscrupulous, able, rich, untiring, he was the most dangerous and wicked demagogue we have ever had." [105]

Butler had some accounts to settle before leaving Congress again. There was Richard H. Dana, who had had the temerity to run against the general for the House. Dana was nominated by the President to be minister to the Court of St. James's, whereupon Butler brought charges of dishonesty against him, alleging that the nominee had pirated some notes of an edition of Wheaton's treatise on international law.[106] The Senate forthwith rejected the nomination.[107] Then there was Judge Hoar, "whom I destroyed utterly by a kindly open letter to him describing his political acts and character." [108]

In the same year Butler vainly sought the governorship of Massachusetts on the Greenback party ticket; the party platform espoused payment of public and private debts with paper, the paper not being based on anything.[109] Nast recognized the fact with a drawing of Butler's being crowned with the symbol of inflation by Peter Cooper,[110] who two years previously had been nominated for the Presidency by the National Independent party (greenbackers) at Indianapolis.[111] Running against the Republican and Democratic candidates, the general made a hundred speeches in cities and villages. The campaign was very spirited, and the Boston *Herald* editorialized: "The laborers employed by Gen. Butler in his various enterprises —mills, quarries, etc.,—will be expected to vote for him, or give up their situations. The same rule will hold good on the other side. There will be no shotguns or threats. Every thing will be managed with

*Nast drawing of Peter Cooper's placing upon Butler
the Inflation Crown. 1878.*

decorum, adorned with noble sentiments." [112] Thomas Talbot, candidate of the Democratic and Independent tickets, won the election.[113]
One of Talbot's most effective campaign devices was the publication of
a comparative wage scale of his mills and Butler's:

	TALBOT MILLS	MIDDLESEX MILLS (BUTLER'S)
Card-strippers	$1.25 per day	.86–$1.00 per day
Picker-men	1.25	.85– .90
Jack-spinners	1.70	$1.00
Wool-sorters	1.50	1.35
Yard-men	1.25	.95–$1.00 [114]

That wage scale lost Butler much of the labor vote. The millowners, in turn, were antagonized when the general became sympathetic to Denis Kearney, a radical labor leader who sought to exclude the Chinese from this country. Butler felt that this was a local as well as a national issue, for no state could, as long as it was "independent and sovereign, be made the lazar house of the world." [115] And to the lost votes of labor and capital there were added those of Boston's solid citizenry, "whose staid respectability was shuddering at the audacious financial heresies with which Benjamin F. Butler was infecting the people." [116]

The year 1878 was one of Butler's most unsuccessful, for in addition to his defeats in his campaigns for Congress and for the governorship he lost his position as major general in the state militia when that body was reorganized.[117] To complete the picture, his henchman William S. Simmons was ejected as Boston's Collector of the Port.[118]

But the Massachusetts general persisted in the political arena. He endeavored to make some sort of alliance through the Greenback party, and Nast sketched a cartoon entitled "In The Matrimonial Market Again," in which the widow Butler was shown hopefully with the rag doll which the artist used to symbolize greenbackism.[119] In 1879 Butler again ran for the governorship as the Greenback party candidate, although he was really an independent to such a degree that Nast drew a lone fisherman from Massachusetts.[120] Butler was defeated by John D. Long, the Democratic and Independent party nominee.[121] Nast sketched an appropriate scene of the widow Butler mourning.[122]

In 1880, at the Democratic State Convention at Worcester, Butler solemnly withdrew from the Republican party and made his confession of faith as a Democrat.[123] This reversal of form might have confused the American electorate; but eleven years earlier the correspondent of *Le Temps* had written that "Mr. Butler would be returning to his old ways before long and would once more set himself up as a champion of the Democratic party." [124] Butler supported General Hancock for the Presidency, the first Democrat he had so favored since the outbreak of the Civil War.[125]

Butler then made one of his perennial returns to his law practice, which he never had left in fact. In September, 1881, the day before

Nast drawing of "The Widow" Butler with the rag baby symbol of greenbackism. 1878.

he was to have entered into partnership with the general, his second son, Ben Israel, died.[126] A month later Butler was asked to serve as defense counsel for Charles Guiteau, the assassin of President Garfield.[127] Guiteau's brother-in-law declared that he had written to the Massachusetts general at the murderer's own request, "but the letter addressed to him must have miscarried." [128]

Nast drawing of Butler after his
defeat in Massachusetts. 1879.

CHAPTER XVII

GOVERNOR BUTLER

IN 1881, running as a Democrat, Butler became the governor of Massachusetts. Inasmuch as the balance of his ticket was defeated, the election was regarded as a personal triumph for him; [1] but perhaps the victory could have been attributed in part to the fact that many Massachusetts Republicans were voting for Butler through sheer force of habit over the years. Doubtless he also gleaned the votes of many still hopeful greenback apostles.

His biographer sent congratulations, hoping that the general might "be as good a governor as you were a candidate!!" [2] Among the very large number of felicitations were the greetings of Clara Barton, president of the American Association of the Red Cross,[3] who had been Superintendent of the Department of Nurses in the Army of the James under General Butler.[4] The new governor reciprocated and appointed her to the superintendency of the women's reformatory at Sherborn, Massachusetts.[5]

As governor, Butler had little real power, for no executive steps could be undertaken without the approval of the Governor's Council, which was Republican in composition, as were both houses of the legislature.[6] As a result of this dichotomy, forty bills became law during the Butler administration without the general's signature, and four additional bills were signed by the lieutenant governor during Butler's absence from Massachusetts.[7]

But the new executive had determined to be more than an official figurehead. Because his drive and inquisitorial powers had to have an outlet, Butler turned his eye on the commonwealth almshouse at

Tewksbury, which had a population of some eight hundred paupers.[8] He promptly charged that the administration (Republican) of the almshouse had been making unsavory dollars through the sale of paupers' bodies and that "the selling and tanning of human skins was an established industry in Massachusetts." [9] A full-fledged investigation was made, without substantiation of the allegations, although

*Nast drawing of Butler the
Lone Fisherman. 1879.*

some bodies were laid before the committee, with the supposition that these were some of the persons who had died at Tewksbury. During the examination the governor outraged some of his constituents by ordering audibly, "Give me the skin that came off the nigger." Congressman William P. Frye of Maine claimed that Butler's charges were made in order to gain the favor of the Southern states by catering to their wartime prejudices against Massachusetts.[10]

Ultimately the investigation petered out. But Harvard University, which had been accused of being a purchaser of Tewksbury corpses for its medical school, never forgave Butler. Nor did the general think well of the medical school, and of it he said: "Every institution has bad men in it and every institution has good ones. When Christ, aided by Omniscience, too, chose twelve disciples, he chose one who had a devil. I don't believe the Harvard Medical School averages better than that." [11]

Shortly afterward, Governor Butler and President Eliot of Harvard met on a speakers' platform. Both dignitaries appeared at the celebration of Exeter Academy's hundredth anniversary on June 21, 1883. George Bancroft, the eminent historian, first introduced the general. "And I request you,—Exeter makes nothing of turning out a Governor to a State,—I request you to listen to what may be said by the gentleman whom the great majority of the people of Massachusetts have raised to the executive chair of that State—Benjamin Franklin Butler." [12]

Butler completely captured most of his auditors with his wry speech:

In my judgment, while I do not underrate classical learning, having but very little of it, and what little I have I shall not undertake to exploit here, for I have not studied a book of quotations day before yesterday in order to have some here; and if I had, so far as the Latin language is concerned, I should not know how to pronounce it. For instance, when you and I were boys we were told that Caesar said "Veni, vidi, vici," and we read with admiration the orations of Cicero, but now we are told by the highest and best authority that what Caesar said was, "Wane, wede, witche," and that no such man as Cicero exists, and that he has left behind him one "Kikero." Even the dead languages change.[13]

But when the general launched into a eulogy to the machine age and told his listeners that surely they would rather have built the Brooklyn Bridge than have been the greatest poets of any age, that was too much for Harvard's president. He ignored his prepared speech and told the audience earnestly that, "believe me, the supreme powers of this universe are not mechanical or material; they are hope and fear and love." [14]

Six days later Butler and Harvard University had more of a showdown. Ever since Harvard had the authority to confer degrees of honorary Doctor of Laws, this distinction had been conferred upon the governor of the commonwealth. But now the university hesitated to show its recognition of the questionable character of Butler; all too recent were the charges of body snatching.[15] When the anticipated degree was not listed among Harvard's commencement awards, the governor professed to be disturbed not at all; for already he had received this degree from colleges in three New England states, "and I can read my diploma in the Latin tongue, as perhaps one half of my predecessors in the executive office who got the degree could not do." [16] But he attended the commencement exercises anyway, to the great embarrassment of the university officials; and as Butler brought with him his full military staff and escort in the panoply of the state militia, he furnished a most colorful display even without academic robes.[17] The president of the Harvard Alumni Association resigned his post so that he would not have to receive the governor upon this occasion.[18]

At the commencement banquet that night, Governor Butler and President Eliot were the guests of honor, separated only by the toastmaster, Joseph Choate. With his long training in the courtroom, Choate was able to keep the proceedings orderly. During the entire dinner, he told the audience, he had been seated between the two horns of a veritable dilemma, for no ordinary alumnus could contend with Charles Eliot, an athlete of renown. "And as to his Excellency, a long professional observation and some experience of him have taught me that he, too, like the President, is a safe man to let alone." [19]

But to his wife Choate wrote that "Butler appeared to great advantage and quite turned the tables upon the College overseers." [20] The press split its verdict. "That the people of Massachusetts have elected General BUTLER to be the Governor of the State," thought a national weekly, "is no more reason that the University should make him an LL.D. than that Andover Seminary should make him a D.D."[21] "This reminds us," commented a newspaper, "of the big booby who makes faces at a little girl because her brother Jack punched his head behind the school house. The action of the 'H.I.F.'s' of Harvard cannot fail to add to Gen. Butler's popularity with the people."[22]

Butler, of course, enjoyed himself hugely in his controversy with Harvard. To his daughter he wrote:

I suppose you have got the papers I sent you about the Harvard pother. It was only a little game of skill between Self and brother Hoar. . . . I hope you liked the speech. It was a poor one not by any means up to concert pitch. But had a real good speech carefully prepared because I supposed I should have a row, and then you know one must be prepared and say on the *spur of the moment* the worst possible things. . . . Alas! there was a good speech . . . lost to the world.[23]

Butler had surprised many persons when he sent his son Paul to Harvard, "not because I deemed it the best school in the country," the general explained, "but because I could not foretell what might be his future, and I chose that he should not be hindered, as his father had been, by the fact that he was not a graduate of Harvard."[24] Paul Butler was graduated from Harvard and immediately entered the service of the U.S. Cartridge Company, one of the general's enterprises.[25] Because of his personal friction, Butler placed Harvard as second only to West Point in his black book of contempt. "The less of West Point a man has the more successful he will be."[26] But curiously enough, he sent one of his sons to each of the despised institutions.

Butler, as governor, appointed a Negro judge, George L. Ruffin, to the consternation of many.[27] He also appointed the first Irish Catholic to be given a judicial office in the commonwealth, M. J. McCafferty.[28] A very large proportion of his executive appointments was rejected by the council, however. But Butler always managed to capitalize his misfortunes, and he professed not to mind at all the rejection of his appointments; by having made the appointment, he explained, he discharged an obligation or made a friend, and when he was given the opportunity of making a second appointment to the same position he could repay a second favor with one office.[29] There was scarcely a limitation to the potentialities of this.

The governor invited the Lord Chief Justice of England to visit him at Lowell. The British dignitary later said that many of his American friends had treated him coldly after this invitation, and Richard Dana, a highly esteemed friend, even refused to call upon his lordship for that reason.[30] But the governor made efforts to take a more conciliatory attitude toward the British. At a banquet at the Parker House to representatives of the Foreign and Domestic Exhibition, he declared that the United States owed much to England. "For years and years, until it was debauched by the newspapers, we spoke better English in Massachusetts than was spoken on earth." [31]

Butler's Fast Day Proclamation, a traditional observance in Massachusetts, created a scandal by advising the clergy to refrain from political discussions.[32] The proclamation concluded with these words: "I do specifically exhort the ministers of the Gospel on that day to feed their flocks the divine word, and not discourse upon political and other secular topics which divert the serious thoughts of the people from the humble worship of the Father." The final words of the proclamation were, "God save the Commonwealth of Massachusetts," [33] which many ministers echoed with undue reverence.

Because of the Massachusetts system of checks and balances, Butler's year as governor of the commonwealth was uneventful legislatively; it was a political stand-off. But he thought he could do better in his second term. As the 1882 elections neared, the general believed that the Republicans were importing "repeaters" from New York, Philadelphia, and Chicago. He considered that the Board of Police Commissioners were hostile to him, so he determined to have the state militia guard the polls; the 9th Massachusetts, an Irish regiment, was the one he most trusted for this kind of duty. At the last moment, his political advisers talked him out of the step, lest it be misunderstood (*sic*) to be an effort to control a civil election with the military.[34]

Butler confidently expected reelection for a second term. He had his grounds prepared for a magnificent illumination in honor of the contemplated victory; [35] but to his surprise the electorate turned him down. The general thought he knew why: "My defeat was wholly due to the opposition headed by the rum element of the Democratic party in Boston. . . . I was informed and believe that the inducement for their so doing was the payment of money by the Republican party to that end. One thing happened: the press in Boston upon which were being printed my ballots the night before election fortunately for them broke down, so that there was a great scarcity of my ballots at the polling-places." [36] The fact is indisputable that a scarcity of ballots for Butler was noticeable when the boxes were opened after Election Day.

CHAPTER XVIII

THE END OF AN ERA

WHEN former Governor Butler returned to private life (if such his could ever be called) in 1883, he was sixty-five years of age. But he still had all his vigor and drive, and his health was as robust as ever. Thus at the Evacuation Day celebration that year, he stood bareheaded in the rain on lower Broadway in New York City for more than an hour. He always enjoyed a reminder of British humiliations, but, more importantly, the passing veterans could see that the general was still available.[1]

Butler continued to make his presence noted as often as possible. He was very much in demand as a speaker upon all occasions. On November 26, 1883, he attended a dinner of the Chamber of Commerce of the State of New York, where he sat next to the celebrated attorney Joseph H. Choate. It was Choate's assignment to speak first, and he began, "I came here tonight with some notes for a speech in my pocket, but I have been sitting next to General Butler and in the course of the evening they have mysteriously disappeared." Choate was interrupted by loud laughter, in which the general joined. "The consequence is, gentlemen," the speaker continued, "that you may expect a very good speech from him and a very poor one from me."[2] Of course, the audience knew better than to expect a poor speech from either man.

What could he do next with that portion of his time not required for his law practice? His past defeats were behind him; Butler always looked ahead, and ahead of Congress and governorship there could only be the Presidency.

The Presidency was indeed a possibility despite his baffling party affiliations, for at no time since Monroe had party names carried less meaning; in the House, members rarely voted along party lines.[3] Butler was one of the most logical choices for the Democratic nomination, as he had been one of the three "tidal wave" governors that the party had got into office in the last gubernatorial elections; and of his two rivals, Pattison of Pennsylvania and Cleveland of New York, the former had not yet attained his thirty-fifth birthday as required by the Constitution.[4] And if things worked out ill with his Democratic aspirations, why must one assume that this had to be a two-party nation? For example, there was the Greenback party.

The general had not lost his interest in greenbackism, the principles of which he stated in a letter:

The greenback is money, and is within the control of the Government as all money is within its control. . . . There is a practical difficulty with making the greenback nominally receivable for duties at the Custom House, because customs dues have been pledged by law to be received in gold as security for the interest on the national debt. That pledge of course cannot be broken. But gold certificates are received instead of gold, because they are the same thing. And the greenback, as long as it is equal to gold, or as now at a premium above it, will be received in the same way. . . .

I believe all thoughtful men are Greenbackers, and that the people will rise up *en masse* at any attempt to destroy the greenback. National Bankbills are subject to the greenback because they are redeemed by it.[5]

At the Greenback Convention at Indianapolis in 1884, Butler was asked if he would accept the party's nomination for President of the United States on a satisfactory platform.[6] He coyly endeavored to withhold acceptance until he could see whether he would get the nomination of the Democratic National Convention,[7] and his answer was another question: "Is not my record as a Greenbacker for twenty years sufficient without a formal pledge to you which would cause me to be pointed at as a man who bids for the nomination?"[8]

The Republican party's platform called for maintenance of the tariff, a sound currency based if possible on an international gold and silver agreement, higher pensions, and denunciation of fraud by

Southern Democrats in recent elections.[9] James G. Blaine was the presidential nominee. But many independent Republicans could not accept him, and they invited the Democrats to put up an acceptable candidate that the dissident "Mugwumps" could support.[10]

Butler determined that he should be that man. He was a Massachusetts delegate at large at the Democratic National Convention in Chicago, where it was quickly recognized that the big fight would be Butler and John Kelly (the head of Tammany Hall) against Cleveland. The South, unforgiving, would have none of its old enemy, and a Georgia delegate said of the Massachusetts general, "We may be willing to eat crow, but we'll be d——d if we'll eat turkey buzzard." [11]

The platform committee proposed a program of hard money, civil service reform, supremacy of the Federal Government within the Constitution, and equality of all citizens before the law.[12] But Butler gave a minority report (he was the minority), in which he offered most of the inflationary features of the Greenback platform.[13] He spoke out against civil service.

You start off in your platform at one point and say that you are for an honest Civil Service reform. Now I will venture to say that there is not a man now in this Convention that is in favor of Civil Service reform unless he is a schoolmaster. . . . What is this Civil Service reform? It is to give the man the preference who shall appear to have the most learning. . . . Now, what I want is that men from the people, honest and earnest men, men of purity and integrity, shall have the offices; and you cannot learn that by any schoolmaster examination.

Oh, what is this above my head? The portrait of George Washington! And he could not have passed examinations for a clerkship. Let me repeat. George Washington could not have passed a Civil Service examination in the capital named for him for a $1200 clerkship.[14]

Then Butler antagonized the Democrats by arguing for a high, Republican-style tariff:

I object to the tariff plank of your platform adopted by your Committee, for it took them 36 hours to frame it; and if it took those able gentlemen that time to frame it and get it in form there must be some reason for it. . . . I am here about no boys' play. . . . If you do not say to the workingmen of New York, New Jersey, Connecticut, New Hampshire and Massachusetts that you mean protection to their interests when you can and say it with no uncertain sound, God help you, for I cannot.[15]

As a result, he could not find a spokesman to put his name in nomination.[16]

But if Butler could not win the nomination, he was determined that Cleveland should not have it. The general selected Governor Hendricks of Indiana as a possible dark horse to stampede the convention if the stage could be properly set. Butler, Hendricks, and Kelly bribed the gallery ticket taker at the convention hall to recognize no tickets except counterfeits which they quickly had printed; then the spurious tickets were distributed to Chicago loafers, who, for a modest fee, were to whoop it up for Hendricks at the proper signal. The plan almost succeeded, for the deafening din raised by the hired gentry in the gallery upon every mention of Hendricks's name was exceedingly persuasive.[17] Yet Grover Cleveland did win the nomination, and at that point Butler ceased to be a Democrat.

Somewhat belatedly he accepted the nomination of the Greenback party. On the first ballot at the convention in Indianapolis, Butler received 323 votes as against 98 for Jesse Harper of Illinois, whereupon the vote was recorded as unanimous despite loud cries of "No!"[18] For good measure the Massachusetts general also accepted the nomination of the Anti-Monopoly party, which had a platform demanding an interstate commerce act, direct election of Senators, a graduated income tax, government aid to agriculture, and certain other features with a strangely modern look.[19]

Although the Greenback party had been largely a farmers' organization, Butler devoted most of his attention to the labor vote. Yet when General W. H. Parsons, chairman of the Greenback-Labor Committee of Maryland, went to New York to get Butler to make speeches in Maryland, Butler's manager referred him to the Republican National Committee, which, the manager said, was directing Butler's campaign.[20] And despite his sponsorship, Butler devoted most of his time to wooing Democrats. He fought desperately to engineer a revolt in Tammany Hall, and it was not until a few weeks before Election Day that Tammany decided to stick to the party ticket.[21]

Forcefully the general appealed to the registered Democrats to vote for him instead of for Cleveland; Butler was not a party Democrat, of course, but a special kind, a Butler Democrat.[22] He was encouraged in his quasi-Democratic candidacy by the Republicans, and an important Republican meeting was held at Portsmouth, New Hampshire, in July, where such party stalwarts as William F. Chandler, the Secretary of the Navy; Young, Collector of the Port of Portsmouth; and Senator Rollins made pleas to the willing Butler that he run as a Democrat despite Cleveland's nomination. The Republican National Committee agreed to pay a large part of Butler's campaign expenses.[23] The deal further provided that Butler should take to the stump against Cleveland in New York, New Jersey, and Connecticut, with the understanding that if the Republican candidate, Blaine, were elected, Butler would have a say in the bestowing of Massachusetts political patronage.[24]

Butler worked strenuously to fulfill his part of the bargain. Nast jeered at the general's labor support by sketching Butler's being carried into the White House by a procession of Irishmen and convicts;[25] but as the nominee of the Anti-Monopoly party, Butler was supposed to be the workingman's candidate. He none the less toured the countryside in a new private railroad car, gaily painted, which cost $150 per day to rent, and a well furnished liquor pantry was part of the equipment.[26] Butler told large groups of workingmen that if Cleveland were elected, they would starve.[27] His speeches were in deadly earnest, but the unhumorous Cleveland was amused. After one harangue the Democratic nominee wrote to Daniel S. Lamont: "I have just read Butler's address and think that it is very funny. It ought not to be dangerous, but in these days 'you can't most always tell.' I am glad that it is out this early so that it and its author can be well sifted."[28]

Perhaps Cleveland could have outbid the Republicans but he carefully refrained from having anything to do with the general, and he wrote to his own secretary: "I had rather be beaten in this race than to buckle down to Butler. . . . I don't want any pledge made for me that will violate my professions or betray and deceive the good people that believe in me."[29] Yet the Republicans later claimed that

Butler had made a secret agreement with the Democrats after the Portsmouth affair. The campaign has been regarded generally as the dirtiest in the history of the United States.[30] A national weekly depicted Butler as a jester in a turbulent scene entitled "Vulgarity A Campaign Novel." [31]

It was the opinion of many that Butler, despite the sponsorship of the Greenback and Anti-Monopoly parties, was merely serving as a stalking-horse for Blaine, the Republican candidate, whom Nast had sketched as making up to the general and his rag doll (greenbackism).[32] Henry George concluded that the Massachusetts general was insincere and was a mere "decoy duck for the Republican party." [33] A McDougall cartoon showed Butler as "Only a 'blind' for Blaine," [34] and Nast portrayed the same idea with a picture of Blaine using a mask of Butler to dupe the workers.[35] Yet the great labor leader Samuel Gompers admitted that he was going to vote for the general. "I am not a Butler man," he explained. "I am no man's man. Butler is my man." [36]

It did not go unnoticed that Butler and Blaine used the identical campaign tactics of appealing to patriots by insulting England, a device known as "twisting the lion's tail." [37]

The New York *Sun* would not support Cleveland and could not support Blaine, so Dana, the editor, announced for Butler, thinking that as President the general "would shake things up in Washington." [38] As a result of supporting Butler, the *Sun* lost half of its circulation.[39]

Cleveland won the Presidency, his victory being assured when, on the eve of the election, a Blaine supporter (a clergyman) declared that the Republican canvass was directed against Rum, Romanism, and Rebellion; and the huge Irish vote was thus driven back to the Democratic party.[40] How many Cleveland votes Butler was able to swing to Blaine is not known; but Butler polled only 175,000 votes in his own name, whereas the Greenback party candidate in the previous election, James B. Weaver, had collected 300,000 votes.[41] Butler's Greenback party polled 15,000 fewer votes than did the Prohibition party.[42] But the general insisted that large numbers of his votes in New York had been miscounted for Cleveland.[43]

This decisive defeat marked the end of Butler's personal campaigning for office. His law practice saw him regularly again. With Frank L. Washburn and Prentiss Webster, he maintained offices at 6 Ashburton Place, Boston, while his New York office was on the

*Nast drawing of Blaine hiding behind
the mask of Butler. 1884.*

sixth floor of the Mutual Life Insurance Building, 32 Nassau Street.[44] His only venture back into politics was in the 1888 campaign, when he stumped Michigan for Harrison; but the veteran campaigner had lost none of his magic. On one occasion he spoke under a tall tree, from which someone lowered a bunch of spoons on a rope. The general

Nast drawing of Butler and Blaine twisting
the British lion's tail. 1884.

looked at the tableware critically and observed, "Those are some of the spoons that I did not get at New Orleans." From then on the crowd was his.[45]

Butler's association with spoons never was to be forgotten. Twenty years after the New Orleans occupation, a former member of the 12th Mississippi Infantry sent the general a postal card which stated, in its entirety, "I am satisfied now that you did not get those spoons." [46] But others remained unconvinced, and Nast frequently managed to get a spoon into his Butler caricatures.

In 1889 was Admiral Porter's golden anniversary, which brought forth eulogies and glamorous references to his Civil War services. Porter's adulation not unnaturally depicted Butler in a questionable light; honoring one meant dishonoring the other. That revived the Butler-Porter feud, which had been smoldering for twenty-six years; and the war records of the two men were trotted out again. Butler claimed that Porter had run away from the New Orleans forts; to prove the allegation he had an agent search the Navy Department archives for the log of the admiral's flagship, the *Harriet Lane,* and when the book could not be found Butler happily concluded that this was *proof* that Porter had had the log spirited away before it could be scrutinized. Only then did the admiral reply that the ship had been captured by the Confederates at Galveston seven months after the fall of New Orleans, for which reason the Navy Department never did receive the *Harriet Lane*'s log.[47]

But that was only the beginning of a bitter newspaper battle between the two aging commanders. One paper observed, "This row betwixt the porter and the butler is a real kitchen shindy." [48] The billingsgate and invective got so heated that Porter, unused to this kind of combat, was stricken with a heart attack, from which he died early in 1891.[49] Butler, however, throve in any kind of battle condition, and the Boston *Globe* thus described him: "The general looked well and was apparently not worried by the fight. He had a sprig of mignonette and a big rose in his buttonhole, and he chewed on his gum with great zest. Age had not blunted his combative qualities." [50]

In 1892 the general's long-awaited autobiography, *Butler's Book,* was published. In his preface he wrote:

I admit frankly that this book should have been written before, so as to reap the advantage of being able to apply to my compatriots in their lifetime, and to verify the facts, as far as necessary, herein described. But being still in active business in the ardent pursuit of my profession, which has always been the pleasantest occupation of my life, I could not find the time in which it could well be done. But the delay has one advantage: I have outlived most of my compatriots having to do with the events treated of, and my mind is free from almost every possible prejudice, and in a position where the temptation is strong to obey the maxim, *de mortuis nil nisi bonum,* so that I trust nothing will be said save where it is necessary to the cause of truth.[51]

No one ever suggested that Butler used a ghost writer; the style and sentiments of the volume were too characteristically his. One writer has declared, "Probably no serious book ever written by a person of equal prominence contains so much bitter abuse and unmeasured invective as his autobiography."[52] General O. O. Howard spoke for many when he said, "I have found it more intriguing than any novel."[53] General H. V. Boynton observed, "His book is crowded with facts which afford full explanations to his credit of numerous lines of attack upon him with which the public was regaled during and after the war."[54]

Butler's characterizations of his contemporaries were devastating. Of General in Chief Halleck he wrote, "I surmised what the trouble with Hallock was: inconsistency, vanity, cowardice."[55] That worthy also was described as "a lying, treacherous, hypocritical scoundrel with no moral sense."[56] General Badeau, whose book had spoken ill of Butler, was dismissed in a footnote about "the criticisms of Badeau—which I take to be the French for 'dirty-water' . . . I have no objection to being slandered by such a man, and therefore allow the criticisms of this unassigned lieutenant upon me to remain unanswered except by showing what sort of creature made them."[57] He referred to a book by Major General Humphreys, which neglected to give Butler credit for a forward movement, "simply because he was, and I was not, a captain in the regular army. I hope what I say may not give too great a sale to his book, which can be bought anywhere for a dollar." [58] Porter was described as "a reckless, conscienceless, and impudent liar." [59] That admiral's admission "that he was so afraid that [the Fort Fisher powder boat] would explode the boilers of his steamers twenty-five miles away unless their steam was run down, shows him as ridiculous in his cowardice as he was false in his statements." [60] He spoke well of his client Admiral Farragut, who was "far too busy fighting during the war to go around with a marking pot,—as Porter did, stencil-marking bales of cotton on shore in the Red River campaign: 'Captured by the U.S. Navy. D. D. Porter.' " [61] When the Secretary of the Navy reduced the sentence of an officer accused by Butler of running away from the enemy, the general scornfully noted that Welles "thought cowardice excusable." [62] Butler sneered at the ten-volume opus of John Hay, Lincoln's secretary, who had questioned the general's originating the phrase "contraband" as applied to slaves: "If it is all written like this specimen,—for I have not read it all because I know more about Abraham Lincoln than you ever did,—God help poor Lincoln's memory thus to go down to posterity. You can't weigh a load of hay with fish scales, you know." [63] The only soldier whose reputation escaped unscratched was "General Grant, whom I cheerfully acknowledge to be a great general in very many respects." [64] That was more magnanimous than his critique of President Grant, who "is a moral coward." [65]

Butler did not mind printing the revilings that had been directed at him, such as a quotation from the Richmond *Examiner* that he was "the beastliest, bloodiest poltroon and pickpocket the world ever saw." [66] He distributed his book to numerous libraries, including the British Museum.[67]

In addition to his memoirs, Butler enjoyed that other hobby of the aging man: reminiscences of the past. One of his faithful correspondents was George W. Nesmith, late Justice of the Supreme Court of Judicature in New Hampshire,[68] to whom Butler wrote a typical letter:

When I wrote you I did not know but you could give me some knowledge of General Wilson's ancestors, who I know to have been gypsies, or Judge

Clifford's ancestors who I know to be gypsies on one side. Whether Mrs. Webster the mother of Daniel Webster was not one of that family, as I know the mother of William Fitzfessenden was, and believe the mother of General Caleb Cushing was. The family seems to have produced only horse thieves and counterfeiters when they married in and in, but when the children came on the wrong side of the sheets, they made statesmen and lawyers, which is an interesting psychological fact that I desired further to discuss.[69]

The general's law practice was heavy and profitable. He represented the Irish relatives of A. T. Stewart in one of the great will cases,[70] and he was counsel in one of the Edison patent litigation suits.[71] He observed, "I am called in largely in desperate cases." [72] Wendell Phillips wrote to Butler about the general's getting a claim paid: "I doubt if any one but yourself could have got it paid and I am sure no one but yourself could have frightened a bold scamp into so full and prompt a payment." [73] Phillips said of Butler's sizable fee, "If those interested in the award had been offered Davies's services for five thousand dollars, or Butler's at a hundred thousand, they would have eagerly clutched at Butler's." [74]

A type of difficulty that had plagued Butler in the Civil War took place again. In litigation regarding the New York Novelty Company, the general made an unqualified statement about Jews, to which exception was taken. The general replied as follows:

There are, and there always have been, good Jews and bad Jews, as there are of every other people. The earlier examples in Jewish history are Enoch, who "walked with God" for so many years, and Esau who cheated his brother out of his birthright for a mess of potage. Subsequently we had the Son of David, and Judas Iscariot. . . . I did not speak of Jews in general, but I spoke of these particular Jews and if you knew the case that I was talking about as well as I do you would as soon take me to task for abusing Judas Iscariot or the Penitent thief on the Cross.[75]

Butler was a lawyer's lawyer; the most accomplished attorneys bowed to his knowledge. One of the leading lights of the New York bar wrote about a brief: "I have framed it in conformity with my conception of the case. But undoubtedly you will reinforce the argument by many cogent considerations." [76] Another attorney telegraphed to the general, "Were you here I think you could accomplish the matter in a day & save months in court." [77]

Butler was called in to help other lawyers when the going got tough. In one such case the issue involved was the general's pet subject of whether greenbacks were as good as other forms of money. Augustus D. Juilliard, a New York citizen, sold 100 bales of cotton to Thomas S. Greenman of Connecticut, who offered to pay in legal-tender greenbacks. The seller maintained that he was not obliged to accept that form of payment. The buyer's attorneys engaged Butler to assist in the defense, that good money had been offered and what more could a buyer do? The actual question before the Supreme Court was whether notes of the United States, emitted under an Act of Congress declaring the issue to be legal tender for payment of private debts, had to be accepted as valid payment, even if the notes had been reissued by the Government under the Act of 1878. On March 3, 1884, Mr. Justice Gray delivered the Court's opinion, holding that greenbacks were legal tender in payment of private debts. Mr. Justice Field, dissenting, expressed the case against greenbackism: "And why should there be any restraint upon unlimited appropriations for the government for all imaginary purposes of public improvement, if the printing press can furnish the money that is needed for them?" [78]

There is an old legal adage to the effect that an attorney who handles his own case has a fool for a client, but when the general was involved in litigation he could take care of his own affairs. The National Home for Disabled Volunteer Soldiers brought an action against the general for misappropriation of funds during the time that he had served as treasurer, and a trial court found against Butler. But he won himself a remand of the case for a new trial, even though the Court recognized that the Butler finance techniques were "a bookkeeper's puzzle or problem." [79]

"General Butler is unquestionably a believer in the doctrine that it is the duty of counsel to try his client's side of the case and not the other, and to win victory for that side." [80] In later life his reputation won victories. Butler told one impoverished client, "They will settle on your terms when you tell them I have the case." As the client reported back, "They trembled at the sound of his name; and, after a brief conference with his client, the attorney told me they would settle on my terms." [81]

On one occasion Butler appeared before the Supreme Court to ask leave to file a motion for a rehearing, after the Court unanimously had denied such a motion. In amazement, the Chief Justice of the United States asked how many rehearings should be permitted in a given case. The general replied: "I am aware of the rule, Your Honor, but I should say in answer to that question, in the abstract, as many hearings as are necessary to establish the truth and justice of the case; in the concrete, as many as any gentleman fit to practice at your bar will peril his reputation by moving for. And I take leave to assure the court with all solemnity that a great error has been unfortunately committed in this case, which the court, if you will grant me a rehearing, will thank me for having brought to their attention." He was given leave to prepare an argument ("in the heroic vein, I am bound to say"), as a result of which the motion of denial of rehearing was vacated. On the rehearing he won his client a reversal. Mr. Justice Swayne later thanked Butler for permitting the correction of an injustice, attributable to the Court's haste. [82]

But all of his cases were not so harmonious. On April 10, 1891, he was arguing the perjury case of Mrs. Clarietta E. Johnson before Judge Carpenter of the United States District Court. The general had occasion to say, "I hope that this is the last criminal case with which during my life I shall trouble a jury, and," he added, looking straight at the judge, "it is certainly the last in this court." At a hearing the following day, the judge declared, "You are forbidden to address me at any time, Mr. Butler." The general was told that he could file any motions with the clerk; he could not address them to the judge. Butler began, "May it please your honor . . ." Instantly Judge Carpenter called: "Mr. Marshal, Mr. Butler is in disorder. You will kindly remove him from the room." "I yield to force," the general answered, as he was ushered out. [83]

"The old man . . . was capable of more hard work and prepared himself more thoroughly for each suit than does the average graduate from lawyers' offices or college about to argue his first case," observed one newspaper. [84] He shuttled about constantly between Boston, New York, and Washington. In New York he lived at the Fifth Avenue Hotel, where he had a suite on the ground floor near the 23rd Street side. He breakfasted at the Lawyers Club. For lunch he had a sandwich.[85] "Legend hath it that this doughty warrior lunched midnightly on doughnuts and whiskey."[86] Every Monday he was a familiar figure at the session of the United States Supreme Court, when its decisions were handed down.[87] His marked features and broad-brimmed hat were conspicuous at that Court; in the winter he would wear a fur cap and great fur overcoat.

His faculties remained unimpaired throughout his days; it was not until 1891 that he wore spectacles. Toward the end he did not readily recognize his acquaintances, and it was noted that he had gotten awkwardly stout.[88]

On Friday, January 6, 1893, Butler left Lowell for New York by Fall River steamship.[89] That day, in discussing the sudden death of vice president Dubarry of the Pennsylvania Railroad, the general stated: "And that is the way I wish to die when my time comes. I am in no haste to leave this world. I shall be well content to stay here some years longer; but when my time shall come that is the way I wish to go. I want to do my day's work and die."[90] On Monday the 9th, he argued a case in Washington before the Supreme Court.[91] Later he consulted with O. D. Barrett about the Soldiers' Home case in Massachusetts, for the trial of which he was preparing. At three o'clock that afternoon he went to the War Department to see Secretary Elkins about a Moore-Grant suit. When that business was completed, the elevators had stopped running, so Butler had to walk down two long flights of stairs; then he had to wait for his carriage in the cold.[92] The next day he had a cold, but he went down to the War Department in the afternoon to transact some business. He had dinner in his own home at 220 New Jersey Avenue, when he made reference to the illness of his old political rival James G. Blaine; he said that Blaine would outlive them all and he repeated his own preference for instant death "like a flash."[93] With death thus on his mind, he might have recalled an epitaph that he had written for himself just a year previously: "Here lies the general who saved the lives of his soldiers at Big Bethel and Fort Fisher, and who never commanded the Army of the Potomac." [94] Even after dinner there was business to discuss with Judge Barrett. At 11:00 P.M. the general retired.[95]

Shortly after 1:00 A.M. on the 11th, his coughing awakened his Negro valet, West, who helped the general into the bathroom. It was noticed that Butler's expectoration was discolored with blood. At length the valet helped him back to bed, and Butler said: "That's all, West. You need not do anything more." He apparently went to sleep, but his heavy breathing caused the valet to arouse Butler's nephew by marriage, Lanier Dunn, who lived in the same house. A call was sent at once to Dr. Bayne, the family physician; and his assistant, Dr. Luce, answered the summons. He saw that nothing could be done.[96] At half past one in the morning, the general died, the immediate cause being the bursting of a small blood vessel as the result of a violent fit of coughing.[97] At his bedside were the relatives with whom he lived, his nieces Miss Stevens and Mrs. Dunn, and the latter's husband.[98]

At 3:00 P.M. the following day, Butler's body was removed from his Washington residence and taken back to Lowell, with an escort supplied by the B. F. Butler Post of the Grand Army of the Republic, Lowell. Requests were made by Grand Army of the Republic posts all over the country to delay the funeral until delegations could be sent there.[99] Private funeral services were held at Butler's home by the Reverend Dr. A. St. John Chambre of St. Anne's Episcopal Church. Then the general was borne to Huntington Hall, where the body lay in state. On his coffin were the sword and epaulettes he had worn from Lowell to New Orleans and back. President Harrison sent a wreath, and flowers were sent by the convicts in the state prison. One whole side of the building was banked with floral tributes from all over the country. On Sunday, January 16th, the crowd of persons who wished to see the remains was so great that the door was almost burst from its hinges. The police were bowled over by the swarm of visitors, and screams filled the air. Glass in a window was shattered; a woman suffered a broken leg. The doors had to be forced shut to give the police an hour's rest.[100] Later the doors were opened again, with forty firemen on hand to help the police, and, said a reporter, "This time the people were beaten into lines." [101] The following day, almost as many people wished to view the body; an estimated 30,000 persons were there each day. Seventy people per minute were allowed to pass the coffin; no one could pause.[102]

As the body was taken on its last journey, the fire-alarm bells of the city tolled seventy-five strokes for the general's age. For a mile the slow cortege went: down Merrimack Street to Bridge, to Hildreth, and thence to the cemetery. There was a cold wind at the cemetery, "and it was only by violent exercise that the little knot of ushers . . . could keep warm." A platform was laid around the hole in the earth, the edges of which were completely covered by branches of savin and ground ivy. At the foot was placed the image of a white dove, resting preparatory to flight. Hundreds of persons scrambled in knee-deep snow for places of vantage, but police charged vigorously to drive the people back. Cannon were fired; there were three volleys of musketry; there was the roll of muffled drums. Then a bugler sounded taps [103] for the last volunteer general who had served in the Union army.[104]

No eulogy was spoken at Butler's funeral,[105] but the press was to make up for that. The general's death and funeral were Page One news all over the country, and the leading journals devoted their principal editorials to the career of Benjamin F. Butler. Most of the accounts were complimentary; even the unfriendly articles were tinged with awe. Perhaps the best of all the eulogies was an editorial in the New York *Herald:* "He will be remembered as a remarkable American." [106]

CHAPTER XIX

BENJAMIN F. BUTLER
—AN APPRECIATION

BEN BUTLER had the attributes that should have made him one of the great American heroes of all time. He had most of the characteristics that spell out the American credo of successful distinction. Here was a poor boy who, without relatives or influence, became wealthy and important. He was no dull, one-tracked man who carved out limited success in some narrow field; he was a conspicuous success at law, business, politics, and everything else he essayed except the battlefield; and as a military administrator even such acrid critics as Welles thought he was unsurpassed.[1] He did not succeed just because of his physical attractiveness; he was unprepossessing, even repulsive to many, with his squint eyes, heavy paunch, and bald pate. He was no silver-tongued orator who captured auditors by the magnificence of his voice; contemporary accounts indicate that he was a poor speaker.[2] And—so important among American virtues—he was a dauntless fighter, usually against tremendous odds.

Other of his doings might have been expected to endear him to his countrymen. When the Civil War broke out, he had one of the most lucrative law practices in the nation; but he threw aside a vast income to enter military service. It was a war that he personally had tried to avert, one that was identified wholly as the machination of the other political party, yet he was the first prominent civilian to rush to the colors. That he personally profited seems obvious; but when he donned uniform he had no way of knowing this, for the possibilities of gain were not even suspected at that time.

He was not a political hack who blindly stuck to his party right or wrong; he switched his political allegiance whenever it seemed to be to the country's interest (or his own, for he sometimes could not see the distinction). He was a progressive, and many of his social and economic objectives have been adopted nationally. That his progressivism also extended into army matters was his military undoing, but at least he was not a general who fought by the rule books of bygone days.

Why, then, has not Butler survived as a truly great American, if he had all the ingredients of popular success? The answer is that with all of his merits, he likewise had more than his share of demerits. He was a remarkably compound man.

It is an oversimplification to say that Butler was, first and last, a politician. That is true, of course; but in between he was much else. "Politician" was no slurring epithet to him, who believed that American greatness was attributable to our political system; Butler said that he was personally conversant "with the political management which has established the American Republic in power, prosperity, glory, and stability unequalled by that of any nation of the earth." [3] But he felt that politics was not for any lawyer who had not made money elsewhere; a man should not have to live on politics. [4]

He followed that rule himself, with tremendous success. One attorney stated, "I believe him to be as able a member of the profession as the country contains, and certainly the most remarkable one." [5] An obituary declared that "Gen. BUTLER would unquestionably have been numbered among noted Americans were it only for his triumphs at the bar." [6] "The Tiger," who knew both well, wrote that Butler "is as fine a lawyer as he is a poor general," [7] which was lavish praise. To the general, law was more than a profession; it was a way of life, and "Butler had all his life been on the side of law and order." [8]

He was a businessman as well as a lawyer; and just as he saw everything in terms of law he also saw everything (including the battlefield) in terms of business. "Leaving out any sentiment in the matter," he said, "every man I have in my command has cost the government on the average more than three thousand dollars in his preparation to save the Union. If I gain what I am to undertake, shall I not lose to the country more than its worth toward the termination of the war?" [9]

His prodigious memory helped his manner of operating. "Whatever enters his mind remains there forever." [10] More particularly, he remembered those accounts that were to be settled (he was a businessman), and he once declared, "I never forgot a friend or forgave an enemy." [11] Similarly, "he never turned his back upon a friend or showed it to an enemy." [12] As General Howard recalled: "There was a principle discoverable in Gen. Butler, especially throughout the most vigorous portion of his public career. It was this: If a man goes out of his way to do me an injury I will punish him." [13]

It was fortunate (for Butler) that his memory was good, for he had many enemies to remember. Thirty-seven years after his death, it was stated: "The mention of Benjamin F. Butler and his activities is still apt to start controversy in Massachusetts; but whatever his faults, he was a man of ability." [14] "In all the war no man was so severely criticized by his enemies," wrote a not overly friendly team, "or more warmly defended by his friends." [15] But that was Butler's nature, to do nothing by halves and to do nothing in the easy, conciliatory way. "He was radical by nature, in the etymological sense of the term." [16] He was styled as one of the "ultraists." [17] In politics, too, he espoused the radical side of whatever party interested him at the moment, and a rival stated that "he naturally affiliated with that side because it never was General Butler's habit to be moderate in the advocacy of any public policy." [18] He was never a neutral or lukewarm about anything; that is why he so quickly and readily understood the significance of the Civil War, which "was the harsh conflict of two antagonistic civilizations. . . . Somebody must be hurt." [19]

In addition to his strong personal position on every question, Butler oppugned people readily. He "always carried a devil-may-care air about him." [20] "Butler antagonized by his manner; he laid himself open to attack by his disregard of red tape." [21] "His whole person breathed contention and effrontery." [22] As a newspaperman wrote, "It may be said of him that he loved fighting." [23] "He was a vindic-

tive fighter." [24] He admitted that "I have so lived as to defy my enemies." [25] As he vouchsafed, he was "somewhat thick-skinned to newspaper attacks." [26] He was appraised as being "tough-minded." [27] He
did not wilt under the fiercest criticism ; thus during the Fort Fisher
turmoil he wrote to a fellow general of "the delightful stream of
obloquy which is pouring upon me." [28] All this he tolerated as a necessity, for he wrote that "sufferance is the badge of all of our tribe." [29]

Through an extraordinary knowledge of human weaknesses, he exerted a mastery over others. As the Boston *Traveller* noted, "If
there is any one among the opponents of General Butler who has a
weak place in his armor, the general may be trusted to find it out,
and to use his advantage in a way that will be most annoying to his
opponent." [30] As other Congressmen of his day understood a horse,
Butler understood "the plebian mind." [31] "It is only when they cannot imitate it," observed the general, "that they complain of my sharp-
ness." [32]

"Butler . . . was . . . not apt to be long cast down," reported one
of his critics. "He was always ready to adapt himself to the situation,
no matter how disagreeable, when once it was inevitable." [33] A contemporary writer recognized that "a man of such immense vitality
as Butler can never be put down in this country without his own
consent." [34] It was noted: "In everything he was an opportunist.
. . . He always went to the extreme limit of the logic of his position.
. . . He was one of the most resourceful men of his time, and in his
way one of the most successful." [35] His originality greatly impressed
those who encountered him. "The most original, unique, audacious
and resourceful general taking part in the war of the rebellion was
Benjamin Franklin Butler." [36] When the general died, Charles A.
Dana said of him, "For the last quarter of a century at least Benjamin
Franklin Butler has stood out as the most original, the most American, and the most picturesque character in our public life." [37]

He did not tie himself to permanent principles, nor was he bound
by issues. "Butler was the free lance, riding, unencumbered, hither
and thither, heedless of corselet and helm." [38] The senior member
of the House of Representatives, Charles O'Neill of Pennsylvania,
said of him: "He was a big man ; one of the big men in the war, and

the thing that impressed me most in his career in Congress was his independence. He had self-leadership." [39] The course of a deviationist is fraught with perils, but the general felt that "nothing was ever greatly gained without something was *greatly risked*." [40]

Butler was not lacking in bravery. His physical courage was manifested in New Orleans, when he exposed himself to an embittered enemy with a coolness that was insolent in itself. His moral courage was shown at the very start of his career when, in an overwhelming Whig community, he espoused the Democratic party; it could not have been to get popularity, office, or personal advantage, for his party then had nothing to give or even to promise. And he took pains to make himself understood, regardless of the consequences. "Right or wrong, there is not the slightest difficulty in knowing where he has stood or stands," declared one of his admirers who knew the general personally.[41] An observer who was not an admirer similarly said that "Butler was, in truth, one of the sincerest among the leaders of the Impeachment. He may be said to have been the representative of its coarsest phase. But he knew exactly what he wanted and was not ashamed to own it." [42] Wendell Phillips stated that Butler "has been charged with about every sin that can be imagined, except of not doing what he said he would do." [43]

He was ever a realist. Except for political rights, the doctrine of "all men are created equal" is "an utter absurdity so far as it is made to describe other mutual relations of people. He would not be considered sane who should solemnly declare that all individuals of any other of the larger species of animals are created equal. Take the horse, for example." [44] Knowing mankind as he did in his cynical way, the general was certain that "this country is to have a war in each generation." [45] Thus he sent a son to West Point, "so that his efforts for his country might not be thwarted by the officers of the regular army because he was not of their nobility." [46]

Was he personally honest? Here the writer must pause. There is no scintilla of *evidence* that Butler profited personally, and yet . . . He never took an oath of poverty, and his wealth when he died was estimated to be $7,000,000; [47] but no one could *prove* that Butler had earned his money dishonestly. The result is no technical Scotch verdict of "Not proven," for the general's enemies were legion and they included the most powerful, the most determined, and the most vindictive persons of that day (except for himself); but the result of numerous investigations, spies, and sundry probings was nothing. "In so far as Gen. Butler is concerned the historian must be content to recognize that if he were guilty, he was certainly too clever to leave proofs behind him; a cleverness somewhat unfortunate for him, if he were indeed not guilty." [48] All around him there was corruption; but that it touched him personally none can say with *certainty*.

He was a man characterized by the greatest vigor, down to the very end. While he strove to get shorter workdays for labor, he never spared himself; and he toiled far more hours per day than the schedules he labeled inhumane for others. In his seventy-third year he was thrown out of court.

Perhaps the greatest of Butler's accomplishments was the ability to get things done. He was a *doer*. As Gurowski wrote to him, "You speak deeds not words." [49] A moralist might shudder at some of the general's methods; and, from a distance, one could denounce his stratagems if not actual tactics. But he got results, and that was the greatest secret of his success. He had such a tremendous hold over people because *he delivered*. In Congress, "His appearance on the floor meant business"; [50] and on the battlefield, too, "he did expedite business." [51] When something *had* to be done, Butler was the man to do it. If one's country is engaged in a great war, it is comforting to know that a Butler might be found, who would fight to win and no questions asked. To a lesser degree, a client might wish to see some of that quality in his attorney. And on a more personal plane, what woman will not be honest enough to admit that she wished her husband had more of this Butlerian ingredient—for the children's sake?

NOTES

FOREWORD

[1] Jan. 12, 1893.   [2] Jan. 12, 1893.   [3] Jan. 11, 1893.
[4] Jan. 12, 1893.
[5] George Fort Milton, *Conflict* (New York, 1941), p. 54.
[6] Jan. 11, 1893.
[7] *Dictionary of American Biography* (New York, 1929), III, 357.
[8] Jan. 11, 1893.
[9] Maunsell B. Field, *Memories of Many Men* (New York, 1874), p. 285.
[10] Fletcher Pratt, *Ordeal by Fire* (New York, 1935), p. 9.
[11] Jan. 12, 1893.   [12] Jan. 11, 1893.
[13] Robert R. McCormick, *Ulysses S. Grant, The Great Soldier of America* (New York, 1934), p. 133.
[14] Thomas Ewing Dabney, "The Butler Regime in Louisiana," *Louisiana Historical Quarterly*, Baton Rouge (April, 1944), XVIII, 487.
[15] John Russell Young, *Around the World with General Grant* (New York, 1879), II, 304.
[16] Jan. 13, 1893.

CHAPTER I

[1] Blanche Butler Ames, *The Butler Ancestry of Gen. Benjamin Franklin Butler in America* (Lowell, 1895), p. 7.
[2] Elliott C. Cogswell, *History of Nottingham, Deerfield, and Northwood* (Manchester, 1878), p. 100.
[3] Ames, *op. cit.*, p. 7.
[4] James Parton, *General Butler in New Orleans* (New York, 1864), p. 13.
[5] Benjamin F. Butler, *Butler's Book* (Boston, 1892), p. 44. The factual accuracy of *Butler's Book* appears to be high, for throughout his public career he seemed to feel that his actions should be justified rather than excused. Although he did not rely extensively upon authorities for his statements, accuracy to the greatest degree possible was virtually guaranteed by his awareness that his many enemies would be quick to pounce upon his slightest misstatement. As to that portion of his book which was frankly opinion rather than fact, the statement may reasonably be made that Butler believed what he said.
[6] *Ibid.*, p. 40.   [7] Boston *Globe*, Jan. 11, 1893.   [8] *Butler's Book*, p. 40.
[9] *Ibid.*, p. 41.   [10] *Ibid.*, p. 42.
[11] William McFee, *The Law of the Sea* (Philadelphia, 1950), p. 105.
[12] *Butler's Book*, p. 43.
[13] M. M. Pomeroy, *Life and Public Services of Benjamin F. Butler* (New York, 1868), p. 5.

[14] Horace Greeley, *The American Conflict* (Hartford, 1864), I, 508 n.

[15] B. M. Stevens to B. F. Butler, Butler Manuscript, March 18, 1872.

[16] *Butler's Book*, p. 43.   [17] *Ibid.*, p. 44.   [18] *Ibid.*, p. 45.

[19] Cogswell, *op. cit.*, p. 259.   [20] *Butler's Book*, p. 46.   [21] *Ibid.*

[22] *Ibid.*, p. 57.   [23] *Ibid.*, p. 49.

[24] Charles H. Bell, *History of the Town of Exeter* (Exeter, N.H., 1888), p. 293.

[25] *Exercises at the Centennial Celebration of the Founding of Phillips Exeter Academy* (Exeter, 1884), p. 59.

[26] T. A. Bland, *Life of Benjamin F. Butler* (Boston, 1879), p. 8.

[27] Benjamin F. Butler, *Private and Official Correspondence* (Norwood, Mass., 1917), V, 137. Butler's granddaughter, Jessie Ames Marshall, served as editor. "So far as my examination goes, she has performed this duty with impartiality" (Gamaliel Bradford, *Damaged Souls* [Boston, 1923], p. 235). "It has been a bitterness that unjust criticism has made such a publication as this a necessity . . ." (Jessie Ames Marshall to Mrs. Anderson in an undated letter now owned by the author).

[28] Parton, *op. cit.*, p. 14.   [29] *Butler's Book*, p. 81.

[30] Pomeroy, *op. cit.*, p. 8.   [31] New York *World*, Jan. 12, 1893.

[32] *Butler's Book*, p. 48.   [33] Pomeroy, *op. cit.*, p. 9.

[34] *Butler's Book*, p. 52.   [35] Bland, *op. cit.*, p. 9.

[36] Margaret Terrell Parker, *Lowell: A Study of Industrial Development* (New York, 1940), p. 1.

[37] Charles Cowley, *A Hand Book of Business in Lowell* (Lowell, 1856), p. 8.

[38] Parker, *op. cit.*, p. 59.

[39] Nathan Appleton, *Introduction of the Power Loom and Origin of Lowell* (Lowell, 1858), p. 20.

[40] Parker, *op. cit.*, pp. 63, 67.

[41] Marshall B. Davidson, *Life in America* (Boston, 1951), I, 500.

[42] Henry A. Miles, *Lowell, As It Was, and As It Is* (Lowell, 1845), p. 64.

[43] *Ibid.*, p. 69.

[44] Harriet H. Robinson, *Loom and Spindle, or, Life Among the Early Mill Girls* (New York, 1898), p. 89.

[45] Charles Cowley, *A History of Lowell* (Boston, 1868), p. 111.

[46] *Ibid.*, p. 173.   [47] *Butler's Book*, p. 152.

[48] Isaac Hill to Charlotte Butler, Butler Manuscript, Sept. 30, 1835.

[49] S. R. Hanscom, unaddressed, Butler Manuscript, Jan. 23, 1836.

[50] William Graves, unaddressed, Butler Manuscript, Jan. 22, 1836.

[51] Theodore Edron, unaddressed, Butler Manuscript, Jan. 25, 1836.

[52] Caleb Cushing to Charlotte Butler, Butler Manuscript, Feb. 17, 1836.

[53] *Butler's Book*, p. 57.   [54] Parton, *op. cit.*, p. 18.

[55] Edwin Carey Whittemore, *Colby College, 1820–1925* (Waterville, 1927), p. 9.

[56] Henry S. Burrage, "The Beginnings of Waterville College," *Collections and Proceedings of the Maine Historical Society*, IV, 128.

[57] Parton, *op. cit.*, p. 19.   [58] *Butler's Book*, p. 58.

[59] Parton, *op. cit.*, p. 18.   [60] Whittemore, *op. cit.*, p. 66.

[61] Parton, *op. cit.*, p. 19.   [62] *Butler's Book*, p. 59.   [63] *Ibid.*, p. 69.

[64] Parton, *op. cit.*, p. 20.   [65] *Butler's Book*, p. 60.

[66] Parton, *op. cit.*, p. 21.   [67] *Butler's Book*, p. 65.   [68] *Ibid.*, p. 63.

[69] *Ibid.*, p. 64.   [70] Whittemore, *op. cit.*, p. 41.   [71] *Ibid.*, p. 49.

[72] Bland, *op. cit.*, p. 9.   [73] *Butler's Book*, p. 66.   [74] *Ibid.*, p. 69.

[75] *Butler's Book*, p. 71.

[76] *Reed* v. *Batchelder*, 1 Metcalf 559 (1840). It was held that a negotiable note made by an infant is voidable and not void, and if he, coming of age, promises the

payee that the note will be paid, the payee may negotiate it, so that the holder may maintain an action in his own name against the maker. The defendant at the trial in the Court of Common Pleas objected to the admission of evidence as to the maker's repeated promise to pay, but Judge Warren (at Butler's suggestion) admitted the evidence, and a verdict was returned for the plaintiff. The defendant alleged error, but Chief Justice Shaw of the Supreme Judicial Court overruled the exception.

[77] Bland, *op. cit.*, p. 13.

[78] B. F. Butler to W. P. Webster, Butler Manuscript, Feb. 27, 1854.

[79] New York *Post*, Jan. 11, 1893.   [80] Bland, *op. cit.*, p. 12.

[81] *Butler's Book*, p. 89.   [82] Harriet H. Robinson, *op. cit.*, p. 31.

[83] Bland, *op. cit.*, p. 14.   [84] Boston *Globe*, Jan. 11, 1893.

[85] *Butler's Book*, p. 91.   [86] Parker, *op. cit.*, p. 102.

[87] Miles, *op. cit.*, p. 59.

[88] Caroline F. Ware, *The Early New England Cotton Manufacture* (Boston, 1931), p. 279.

[89] John R. Commons and others, *History of Labour in the United States* (New York, 1918), III, 461.

[90] Davidson, *op. cit.*, II, 501.   [91] Harriet H. Robinson, *op. cit.*, p. 12.

[92] John Coolidge, *Mill and Mansion: A Study of Architecture and Society in Lowell, Massachusetts, 1820–1865* (New York, 1942), p. 105.

[93] *Butler's Book*, p. 92.   [94] *Ibid.*, p. 98.   [95] *Ibid.*, p. 101.

[96] *Ibid.*   [97] *Ibid.*, p. 104.   [98] Bland, *op. cit.*, p. 21.

[99] *Butler's Book*, p. 104.   [100] *Ibid.*, p. 105.   [101] *Ibid.*, p. 106.

[102] *Ibid.*, p. 109.   [103] *Ibid.*, p. 107.   [104] *Ibid.*, p. 108.

[105] *Ibid.*, p. 109.

[106] George F. Hoar, *Autobiography of Seventy Years* (New York, 1905), I, 354.

[107] Bland, *op. cit.*, p. 13.

[108] John G. Nicolay and John Hay, *Abraham Lincoln: A History* (New York, 1890), IV, 133.

[109] Hoar, *op. cit.*, I, 330.   [110] *Butler's Book*, p. 988.   [111] *Ibid.*, p. 989.

[112] Boston *Globe*, Jan. 12, 1893.   [113] Cowley, *A History of Lowell*, p. 157.

[114] Don C. Seitz, *The "Also Rans"* (New York, 1928), p. 301.

[115] New York *Times*, Jan. 12, 1893.   [116] Hoar, *op. cit.*, I, 330.

[117] *Ibid.*, I, 178.   [118] *Butler's Book*, p. 987.   [119] *Ibid.*, p. 989.

[120] Parton, *op. cit.*, p. 25.   [121] New York *Times*, Jan. 12, 1893.

[122] *Butler's Book*, p. 986.   [123] Boston *Globe*, Jan. 11, 1893.

[124] *Butler's Book*, p. 989.   [125] *Ibid.*, p. 1019.

[126] New York *Times*, Jan. 12, 1893.   [127] *Butler's Book*, p. 1007.

[128] *Ibid.*   [129] 21 Howard 170 (1859).   [130] *Butler's Book*, p. 1021.

[131] *Ibid.*, p. 1001.   [132] Hoar, *op. cit.*, I, 334.   [133] *Butler's Book*, p. 1000.

[134] Parton, *op. cit.*, p. 34.   [135] *Nation*, Sept. 3, 1868, p. 186.

[136] New York *Post*, Jan. 11, 1893.

[137] Moorfield Storey, *The Record of Benjamin F. Butler* (Boston, 1883), p. 23.

[138] Parton, *op. cit.*, p. 35.   [139] Robinson Scrapbook, III, 238.

[140] *Butler's Book*, p. 78.

[141] Gamaliel Bradford, *Wives* (New York, 1925), p. 201.

[142] Bill of sale, Butler Manuscript, Nov. 8, 1842.

[143] *Butler's Book*, p. 79.   [144] Bradford, *Wives*, p. 211.

[145] *Dictionary of American Biography*, III, 357.

[146] Parton, *op. cit.*, p. 35.   [147] Coolidge, *op. cit.*, p. 246.

[148] *Butler's Book*, p. 79.   [149] *Ibid.*, p. 77.

[150] Cowley, *A History of Lowell*, p. 173.   [151] *Butler's Book*, p. 77.

[152] Cowley, *A History of Lowell*, p. 158.

[153] Allan Nevins, *Ordeal of the Union* (New York, 1947), I, 190.

[154] *Butler's Book*, p. 125.   [155] Milton, *Conflict*, p. 309.

[156] Claude M. Fuess, *The Life of Caleb Cushing* (New York, 1923), II, 108.

[157] Seitz, *The "Also Rans,"* p. 303.

[158] Boston *Globe*, Jan. 11, 1893.   [159] Cowley, *A History of Lowell*, p. 144.

[160] Hoar, *op. cit.*, I, 331.   [161] Boston *Globe*, January 11, 1893.

[162] Humphrey J. Desmond, *The Know Nothing Party* (Washington, 1904), p. 88.

[163] Ray Allen Billington, *The Protestant Crusade, 1800–1860: A Study of the Origins of American Nativism* (New York, 1938), p. 381.

[164] *Ibid.*, p. 388.   [165] *Butler's Book*, p. 125.

[166] Cowley, *A History of Lowell*, p. 159.

[167] Rufus Choate to B. F. Butler, Butler Manuscript, April 24, 1845.

[168] Caleb Cushing to B. F. Butler, Butler Manuscript, Nov. 20, 1851.

[169] Nathaniel Banks to B. F. Butler, Butler Manuscript, March 16, 1853.

[170] Charles Sumner to B. F. Butler, Butler Manuscript, Dec. 22, 1853.

[171] George S. Boutwell to B. F. Butler, Butler Manuscript, Oct. 31, 1853.

[172] Ben: Perley Poore, *Reminiscences of Sixty Years in the National Metropolis* (Philadelphia, 1886), I, 499.

[173] Cowley, *A History of Lowell*, p. 159.   [174] Hoar, *op. cit.*, I, 335.

[175] Albert Bushnell Hart, ed., *Commonwealth History of Massachusetts* (New York, 1900), IV, 66.

[176] William T. Davis, *History of the Judiciary of Massachusetts* (Boston, 1900), p. 252.

[177] Robinson Scrapbook, III, 151.

CHAPTER II

[1] William B. Hesseltine, *Lincoln and the War Governors* (New York, 1948), p. 83.

[2] Stewart Mitchell, *Horatio Seymour of New York* (Cambridge, Mass., 1938), p. 213.

[3] Avery Craven, *The Coming of the Civil War* (New York, 1950), p. 415.

[4] Parton, *General Butler in New Orleans*, p. 28.

[5] Bland, *Life of Benjamin F. Butler*, p. 30.   [6] *Ibid.*, p. 27.

[7] *Butler's Book*, p. 134.   [8] Parton, *op. cit.*, p. 29.

[9] Dwight Dumond, *The Secession Movement, 1860–1861* (New York, 1931), p. 88.

[10] Roy Franklin Nichols, *The Disruption of American Democracy* (New York, 1948), p. 299; Lillian Adele Kibler, *Benjamin F. Perry, South Carolina Unionist* (Durham, N.C., 1946), p. 3.

[11] Boston *Weekly Journal*, Jan. 13, 1893.

[12] Hoar, *Autobiography of Seventy Years*, I, 332.

[13] *Butler's Book*, p. 996.   [14] Storey, *The Record of Benjamin F. Butler*, p. 7.

[15] Robinson Scrapbook, III, 165.

[16] J. G. Randall, *Lincoln the President* (New York, 1945), I, 140.

[17] Bland, *op. cit.*, p. 34.

[18] Fuess, *The Life of Caleb Cushing*, II, 267.   [19] *Butler's Book*, p. 149.

[20] *Ibid.*, p. 150.   [21] Bland, *op. cit.*, p. 32.

[22] *Butler's Book*, p. 151. But the statute appeared to state that when an insurrection is too large for ordinary Federal officers to overcome, the President may take steps to suppress it (Andrew C. McLaughlin, *A Constitutional History of the United States* [New York, 1935], p. 600).

²³ *Butler's Book,* p. 155.   ²⁴ *Ibid.,* p. 156.   ²⁵ *Ibid.,* p. 159.
²⁶ Butler, *Correspondence,* I, 10.   ²⁷ Parton, *op. cit.,* p. 66.
²⁸ Storey, *op. cit.,* p. 4.   ²⁹ *Butler's Book,* p. 180.
³⁰ *Ibid.,* p. 171.   ³¹ Parton, *op. cit.,* p. 69.   ³² *Butler's Book,* p. 172.
³³ Carl Sandburg, *Abraham Lincoln: The War Years* (New York, 1939), I, 277.
³⁴ *Butler's Book,* p. 127.   ³⁵ *Ibid.*   ³⁶ Milton, *Conflict,* p. 309.
³⁷ Bland, *op. cit.,* p. 199.   ³⁸ *Butler's Book,* p. 174.
³⁹ Bland, *op. cit.,* p. 37.   ⁴⁰ *Ibid.*   ⁴¹ *Boston Globe,* Jan. 11, 1893.
⁴² *Butler's Book,* p. 183.   ⁴³ Bland, *op. cit.,* p. 37.
⁴⁴ *Butler's Book,* p. 175.   ⁴⁵ *Ibid.,* p. 174.   ⁴⁶ Bland, *op. cit.,* p. 37.
⁴⁷ *Butler's Book,* p. 184.

CHAPTER III

¹ Bland, *Life of Benjamin F. Butler,* p. 38.   ² *Butler's Book,* p. 192.
³ Bland, *op. cit.,* p. 39.   ⁴ *Butler's Book,* p. 169.
⁵ Hoar, *Autobiography of Seventy Years,* I, 333.
⁶ *Butler's Book,* p. 199.   ⁷ Greeley, *The American Conflict,* I, 468.
⁸ Bland, *op. cit.,* p. 40.
⁹ Clarence Edward Macartney, *Lincoln and His Generals* (Philadelphia, 1925),
p. 49.
¹⁰ *Butler's Book,* p. 207.   ¹¹ Butler, *Correspondence,* I, 52.
¹² William Howard Russell, *My Diary North and South* (Boston, 1863), p. 406.
¹³ Edward Conrad Smith, *The Borderland in the Civil War* (New York, 1927),
p. 6.
¹⁴ Butler, *Correspondence,* I, 32.
¹⁵ Letters included in the Butler Manuscript, May, 1861.
¹⁶ Butler, *Correspondence,* I, 49.   ¹⁷ *Ibid.,* I, 52.
¹⁸ E. D. Keyes, *Fifty Years' Observation of Men and Events, Civil and Military*
(New York, 1884), p. 402.
¹⁹ *Butler's Book,* p. 222.
²⁰ Rutherford Birchard Hayes, *Diary and Letters* (Columbus, 1922), III, 483.
²¹ Sandburg, *Abraham Lincoln: The War Years,* I, 275.
²² Parton, *General Butler in New Orleans,* p. 113.   ²³ *Butler's Book,* p. 232.
²⁴ *Ibid.,* p. 234.   ²⁵ Parton, *op. cit.,* p. 115.
²⁶ Carl Schurz, *Reminiscences* (New York, 1907), II, 225.
²⁷ J. G. Randall, *The Civil War and Reconstruction* (Boston, 1937), p. 324.
²⁸ Bland, *op. cit.,* p. 41.   ²⁹ Pratt, *Ordeal by Fire,* p. 68.
³⁰ Parton, *op. cit.,* p. 110.   ³¹ *Butler's Book,* p. 228.   ³² *Ibid.,* p. 234.
³³ Gideon Welles, *Diary* (Boston, 1911), II, 270.
³⁴ Clara Hay, ed., *Letters of John Hay and Extracts From His Diary* (Washington,
1908), I, 25.
³⁵ Parton, *op. cit.,* p. 325.   ³⁶ Butler, *Correspondence,* I, 64.
³⁷ Sandburg, *op. cit.,* I, 275.   ³⁸ *Ibid.*
³⁹ *Official Records of the War of the Rebellion* (Washington, 1880–1901), Ser.
I, Vol. II, p. 28.
⁴⁰ *Butler's Book,* p. 235.   ⁴¹ *Ibid.,* p. 236.
⁴² *Ibid.,* p. 235. A violent controversy arose as to whether Butler was really the
senior major-general in the army. Those who denied his claim had accepted at face
value a statement published in the *Official Records* that several other generals' commissions antedated Butler's. Actually, Butler was right and the published order
was wrong. Butler was appointed on May 16, 1861; and *subsequently* commissions

were given to McClellan as of May 14th, Frémont as of May 14th, Banks as of May 16th, and Dix as of May 16th. But whereas Butler's appointment was actually on May 16th, Banks was appointed on June 5th, Dix on June 14th, McClellan on July 24th, and Frémont on July 24th. On May 16th, the Secretary of War wrote to Butler that "You are hereby informed that the President of the United States has appointed you Major General . . . to rank as such from the sixteenth of May. . . ." Butler, *Correspondence*, I, 93. Possibly Lincoln or his advisors later regretted that Butler's commission had a date before which no other commission could be issued and hence certain later appointments were *retroactively* dated; but the fact remains that Butler was in active service when he was commissioned (he was actually promoted for services already performed); and as of that time, McClellan and Banks were still in private employment with railroad companies and Frémont was in Europe on personal business. A Government order may have said that these commissions were earlier than Butler's, but that was only because of somebody's ignoring the calendar. As Butler declared, "there is no act of congress which has or can settle seniority of rank otherwise than as the almanac, taking note of the lapse of time, has settled it." Parton, *op. cit.*, p. 614.

43 Parton, *op. cit.*, p. 117.

CHAPTER IV

1 Randall, *The Civil War and Reconstruction*, p. 425.

2 *Butler's Book*, p. 241.   3 *Ibid.*, p. 242.

4 Wayne Whipple, *The Story-Life of Lincoln* (n.p., 1908), p . 411.

5 *Butler's Book*, p. 245.   6 Parton, *General Butler in New Orleans*, p. 121.

7 *Ibid.*, p. 122.   8 *Butler's Book*, p. 173.   9 *Ibid.*, p. 243.

10 *Ibid.*, p. 264.

11 Henry Warren Howe, *Passages From the Life of* (Lowell, 1899), p. 28.

12 Robinson Scrapbook, III, 151.   13 Parton, *op. cit.*, p. 126.

14 Sandburg, *Abraham Lincoln: The War Years*, I, 278.

15 Butler, *Correspondence*, I, 96.   16 *Nation*, Sept. 3, 1868.

17 William Russell, *My Diary North and South*, p. 409.

18 Joseph B. Carr, "Operations of 1861 About Fort Monroe," *Battles and Leaders of the Civil War* (New York, 1888), II, 146.

19 Russell, *op. cit.*, p. 410.   20 *Ibid.*, p. 412.   21 Parton, *op. cit.*, p. 160.

22 *Ibid.*, p. 161.

23 Bessie L. Andrew to B. F. Butler, Butler Manuscript, June 11, 1861.

24 Parton, *op. cit.*, p. 128.   25 Bland, *Life of Benjamin F. Butler*, p. 50.

26 Parton, *op. cit.*, p. 127.

27 James G. Blaine, *Twenty Years of Congress* (Norwich, Conn., 1884), I, 369.

28 Burton J. Hendricks, *Lincoln's War Cabinet* (Boston, 1946), p. 229.

29 John Bigelow, *Retrospections of an Active Life* (New York, 1909), I, 509.

30 Scott had won the Battle of Lundy's Lane in the War of 1812.

31 Butler, *Correspondence*, I, 117.   32 *Ibid.*, I, 119.

33 Milton, *Conflict*, p. 222.

34 B. F. Butler to John Magruder, Butler Manuscript, June 18, 1861.

35 Russell, *op. cit.*, p. 413.   36 Butler, *Correspondence*, I, 162.

37 B. F. Butler to Edward Pierce, Butler Manuscript, June 6, 1861.

38 F. Stansbury Haydon, *Aeronautics in the Union and Confederate Armies* (Baltimore, 1941), p. 82.

39 John La Mountain to B. F. Butler, Butler Manuscript, June 10, 1861.

40 O. A. Gager to B. F. Butler, Butler Manuscript, June 22, 1861.

41 John La Mountain to B. F. Butler, Butler Manuscript, June 25, 1861.

42 B. F. Butler to Simon Cameron, Butler Manuscript, July 1, 1861.

43 John La Mountain to B. F. Butler, Butler Manuscript, July 2, 1861.

44 *Ibid.,* July 15, 1861.   45 Haydon, *op. cit.,* p. 92.   46 *Ibid.,* p. 95.

47 John La Mountain to B. F. Butler, Butler Manuscript, July 31, 1861.

48 *Ibid.,* Aug. 10, 1861.

49 B. F. Butler to Thomas A. Scott, Butler Manuscript, Aug. 13, 1861.

50 Fred Albert Shannon, *The Organization and Administration of the Union Army, 1861–1865* (Cleveland, 1928), I, 147.

51 William Ernest Smith, *The Francis Preston Blair Family in Politics* (New York, 1933), II, 97.

52 Milton, *The Age of Hate* (New York, 1930), p. 26.

53 Bland, *op. cit.,* p. 55.   54 *Ibid.,* p. 56.

55 Douglas Southall Freeman, *Lee's Lieutenants* (New York, 1944), I, 17.

56 *Ibid.,* I, 19.

57 Parton, *op. cit.,* p. 139.   58 *Ibid.,* p. 143.   59 *Butler's Book,* p. 269.

60 Parton, *op. cit.,* p. 144.

61 Robert Selph Henry, *The Story of the Confederacy* (Indianapolis, 1931), p. 50.

62 *Butler's Book,* p. 270.   63 Parton, *op. cit.,* p. 144.

64 Butler, *Correspondence,* I, 137.

65 Clifford Dowdey, *Experiment in Rebellion* (Garden City, New York), 1946, p. 78.

66 New York *Herald,* Jan. 12, 1893.   67 Parton, *op. cit.,* p. 153.

68 Montgomery C. Meigs to B. F. Butler, Butler Manuscript, June 11, 1861.

69 Butler, *Correspondence,* I, 142.

70 Lamont Buchanan, *A Pictorial History of the Confederacy* (New York, 1951), p. 39.

71 Russell, *op. cit.,* p. 411.   72 *Butler's Book,* p. 277.

73 Parton, *op. cit.,* p. 175.   74 Butler, *Correspondence,* I, 206.

75 *Ibid.,* I, 215.   76 Bland, *op. cit.,* p. 61.   77 Parton, *op. cit.,* p. 176.

78 Otto Eisenschiml, *Why Was Lincoln Murdered?* (New York, 1939), p. 408.

79 Montgomery Blair to Simon Cameron, Butler Manuscript, June 22, 1861.

80 Lincoln sometimes had thought that Gurowski might kill him (Otto Eisenschiml, *In the Shadow of Lincoln's Death* [New York, 1940], p. 18).

81 Milton, *The Age of Hate,* p. 25.   82 Hendricks, *op. cit.,* p. 391.

83 *Ibid.*   84 Robinson Scrapbook, III, 151.

85 Butler, *Correspondence,* I, 194.   86 *Ibid.,* I, 203.   87 *Ibid.,* I, 208.

88 *Ibid.,* I, 223.   89 *Butler's Book,* p. 282.

90 Butler, *Correspondence,* I, 218.

91 James Rhodes, *History of the United States from the Compromise of 1850 to the Final Restoration of Home Rule in the South* (New York, 1902), III, 489.

92 Nicolay and Hay, *Abraham Lincoln,* V, 12.

93 Butler, *Correspondence,* I, 228.   94 Henry, *op. cit.,* p. 68.

95 Pratt, *Ordeal by Fire,* p. 68.   96 Parton, *op. cit.,* p. 178.

97 Henry, *op. cit.,* p. 68.   98 Howe, *op. cit.,* p. 5.

99 Richard S. West, Jr., *Gideon Welles: Lincoln's Navy Department* (Indianapolis, 1943), p. 126.

100 *Butler's Book,* p. 285.   101 *Ibid.,* p. 287.   102 *Ibid.,* p. 288.

CHAPTER V

[1] West, *Gideon Welles*, p. 126.
[2] Fred Harvey Harrington, *Fighting Politician, Major General N. P. Banks* (Philadelphia, 1948), p. 57.
[3] *Butler's Book*, p. 289.   [4] *Ibid.*   [5] *Ibid.*, p. 294.
[6] Ellis Paxson Oberholtzer, *Jay Cooke, Financier of the Civil War* (Philadelphia, 1907), I, 583.
[7] *Ibid.*, I, 584.
[8] Kenneth Williams, *Lincoln Finds a General* (New York, 1949), I, 104.
[9] *Butler's Book*, p. 295; Butler, *Correspondence*, I, 245.
[10] Parton, *General Butler in New Orleans*, p. 183.
[11] Greeley, *The American Conflict*, II, 81.   [12] Parton, *op. cit.*, p. 585.
[13] Randall, *The Civil War and Reconstruction*, p. 426.
[14] *Butler's Book*, p. 309.   [15] Parton, *op. cit.*, p. 186.   [16] *Ibid.*, p. 187.
[17] Hesseltine, *Lincoln and the War Governors*, p. 189.
[18] *Butler's Book*, p. 310.   [19] Butler, *Correspondence*, I, 253.
[20] *Butler's Book*, p. 392.   [21] *Ibid.*   [22] Butler, *Correspondence*, I, 305.
[23] Parton, *op. cit.*, p. 189.   [24] Butler, *Correspondence*, I, 274.
[25] A. G. Browne, Jr., *Sketch of the Official Life of John A. Andrew* (New York, 1868), p. 69.
[26] Hoar, *Autobiography of Seventy Years*, I, 335.
[27] Butler, *Correspondence*, I, 307.   [28] Hesseltine, *op. cit.*, p. 191.
[29] *Ibid.*, p. 190.
[30] Catherine Drinker Bowen, *Yankee From Olympus* (Boston, 1944), p. 159.
[31] Sandburg, *Abraham Lincoln: The War Years*, I, 471.
[32] Edward Bates, *Diary* (Washington, 1933), p. 208.
[33] Nicolay and Hay, *Abraham Lincoln*, V, 253.
[34] Bland, *Life of Benjamin F. Butler*, p. 64.   [35] *Butler's Book*, p. 314.
[36] Richard S. West, Jr., *The Second Admiral* (New York, 1937), p. 114.
[37] *Dictionary of American Biography*, VI, 568.   [38] *Butler's Book*, p. 325.
[39] George C. Gorham, *Life and Public Services of Edwin M. Stanton* (Boston, 1899), I, 313.
[40] *Butler's Book*, p. 333.   [41] Gorham, *op. cit.*, I, 314.
[42] *Butler's Book*, p. 335.   [43] Macartney, *Lincoln and His Generals*, p. 212.
[44] *Butler's Book*, p. 336.   [45] West, *Gideon Welles*, p. 38.
[46] Alfred T. Mahan, *Admiral Farragut* (New York, 1905), p. 39.
[47] West, *The Second Admiral*, p. 80.   [48] West, *Gideon Welles*, p. 202.
[49] Macartney, *op. cit.*, p. 212.   [50] Butler, *Correspondence*, I, 360.
[51] *Butler's Book*, p. 336.
[52] *Ibid.*   [53] *Ibid.*, p. 340.   [54] *Ibid.*, p. 336.   [55] Parton, *op. cit.*, p. 205.
[56] *Butler's Book*, p. 341.   [57] *Ibid.*, p. 346.   [58] *Ibid.*
[59] Parton, *op. cit.*, p. 208.   [60] *Ibid.*, p. 205.   [61] *Ibid.*, p. 206.

CHAPTER VI

[1] Parton, *General Butler in New Orleans*, p. 207.   [2] Milton, *Conflict*, p. 149.
[3] Parton, *op. cit.*, p. 195.   [4] *Ibid.*, p. 209.
[5] Bland, *Life of Benjamin F. Butler*, p. 66.
[6] Parton, *op. cit.*, p. 193.   [7] Mahan, *Admiral Farragut*, p. 115.
[8] W. T. Sherman, *Memoirs* (New York, 1891), I, 277.
[9] West, *The Second Admiral*, p. 130.   [10] *Butler's Book*, p. 355.

11 Mahan, *op. cit.*, p. 127.   12 Parton, *op. cit.*, p. 223.   13 *Ibid.*, p. 224.
14 *Ibid.*, p. 210.   15 *Butler's Book*, p. 356.   16 Bland, *op. cit.*, p. 68.
17 David Dixon Porter, *The Naval History of the Civil War* (New York, 1886), p. 179.
18 Parton, *op. cit.*, p. 249.   19 Mahan, *op. cit.*, p. 164.
20 Bland, *op. cit.*, p. 71.   21 West, *op. cit.*, p. 139.
22 *Butler's Book*, p. 368.   23 Parton, *op. cit.*, p. 250.
24 West, *op. cit.*, p. 142.   25 *Butler's Book*, p. 368.
26 Butler, *Correspondence*, I, 425.   27 *Butler's Book*, p. 348.
28 *Ibid.*, p. 371.   29 West, *op. cit.*, p. 148.   30 Porter, *op. cit.*, p. 190.
31 Butler, *Correspondence*, I, 428.   32 Mahan, *op. cit.*, p. 177.
33 Parton, *op. cit.*, p. 279.
34 Marion Southwood, *"Beauty and Booty," The Watchword of New Orleans* (New York, 1867), p. 41.
35 West, *op. cit.*, p. 144.   36 Parton, *op. cit.*, p. 279.
37 Bland, *op. cit.*, p. 75.   38 Parton, *op. cit.*, p. 280.
39 Bland, *op. cit.*, p. 75.   40 Greeley, *The American Conflict*, II, 98.
41 Parton, *op. cit.*, p. 279.   42 Southwood, *op. cit.*, p. 43.
43 *Ibid.*, p. 281.   44 West, *op. cit.*, p. 144.   45 Bland, *op. cit.*, p. 77.
46 *Ibid.*, p. 79.   47 Parton, *op. cit.*, p. 283.   48 *Butler's Book*, p. 895.
49 Macartney, *Lincoln and His Generals*, p. 53.   50 *Butler's Book*, p. 376.
51 Bland, *op. cit.*, p. 83.   52 *Ibid.*, p. 82.

CHAPTER VII

1 Rhodes, *History of the United States,* III, 629.
2 Albert Kautz, "Incidents of the Occupation of New Orleans," *Century Illustrated Monthly Magazine,* New York (July, 1886), XXXIII, 455.
3 *Butler's Book,* p. 371.   4 Bland, *Life of Benjamin F. Butler,* p. 102.
5 Parton, *General Butler in New Orleans,* p. 346.   6 Bland, *op. cit.,* p. 103.
7 Parton, *op. cit.,* p. 351.   8 Macartney, *Lincoln and His Generals,* p. 56.
9 Morgan Dix, *Memoirs of John Adams Dix* (New York, 1883), I, 374.
10 Parton, *op. cit.,* p. 441.   11 Macartney, *op. cit.,* p. 54.
12 Southwood, *"Beauty and Booty,"* p. 63.   13 Parton, *op. cit.,* p. 407.
14 Herbert Asbury, *The French Quarter* (New York, 1936), p. 52 n.
15 John Smith Kendall, *History of New Orleans* (Chicago, 1922), I, 283.
16 Butler, *Correspondence,* II, 57.
17 John Rose Ficklen, "History of Reconstruction in Louisiana," *Johns Hopkins University Studies in Historical and Political Science,* 1940, XXVIII, 33.
18 Butler, *Correspondence,* I, 487.   19 Parton, *op. cit.,* p. 417.
20 *Ibid.,* p. 419.   21 *Ibid.,* p. 422.   22 *Ibid.,* p. 424.   23 *Ibid.,* p. 429.
24 West, *The Second Admiral,* p. 152.
25 Sandburg, *Abraham Lincoln: The War Years,* I, 475.
26 Parton, *op. cit.,* p. 307.   27 *Butler's Book,* p. 429.
28 Bland, *op. cit.,* p. 89.   29 Southwood, *op. cit.,* p. 57.
30 Bland, *op. cit.,* p. 125.   31 *Ibid.,* p. 126.
32 E. Merton Coulter, *The Confederate States of America* (Baton Rouge, 1950), p. 95.
33 John Bach McMaster, *A History of the People of the United States During Lincoln's Administration* (New York, 1927), p. 207.
34 Bland, *op. cit.,* p. 128.   35 Parton, *op. cit.,* p. 586.   36 *Ibid.,* p. 583.
37 *Ibid.,* p. 587.   38 *Ibid.*   39 *Ibid.,* p. 589.

[40] William Watson, *Life in the Confederate Army* (New York, 1888), p. 407.

[41] Parton, *op. cit.*, p. 291.   [42] Milton, *Conflict*, p. 309.

[43] Milton, *The Age of Hate*, p. 22.

[44] Asbury, *op. cit.*, p. 225 n. In a biography of Butler's biographer, it was noted that "Only in the volume on General Butler did Parton abandon his usual strong moral convictions regarding his subject" (Milton E. Flower, *James Parton, The Father of Modern Biography* [Durham, North Carolina, 1951], p. 5). Parton himself wrote that "the most gifted and enlightened journalists must of necessity write to order" (*ibid.*, p. 199). When another biographer appeared to do a Butler study, the general offered to buy him off in favor of Parton (*ibid.*, p. 66).

[45] Watson, *op. cit.*, p. 410.

[46] A. F. Puffer, "Our General," *Atlantic Monthly*, Boston (July, 1863), XII, 108.

[47] Butler, *Correspondence*, II, 1.

[48] B. F. Butler to Pierre T. Beauregard, Butler Manuscript, Dec. 5, 1862.

[49] Butler, *Correspondence*, I, 465.   [50] *Ibid.*, I, 625.   [51] *Ibid.*, II, 77.

[52] *Ibid.*   [53] *Ibid.*, II, 93.   [54] *Ibid.*, II, 110.   [55] *Ibid.*, II, 233.

[56] *Ibid.*, II, 232.   [57] *Ibid.*, II, 186.   [58] *Ibid.*, II, 115.   [59] *Ibid.*, II, 272.

[60] *Ibid.*, II, 277.   [61] *Ibid.*, II, 196.   [62] *Ibid.*, II, 393.

[63] Richard B. Irwin, "Military Operations in Louisiana in 1862," *Battles and Leaders of the Civil War* (1888), III, 582.

[64] Parton, *op. cit.*, p. 298.   [65] Bland, *op. cit.*, p. 126.

[66] Parton, *op. cit.*, p. 354.   [67] Bland, *op. cit.*, p. 105.

[68] Parton, *op. cit.*, p. 456.   [69] Bland, *op. cit.*, p. 93.

[70] Parton, *op. cit.*, p. 318.

[71] Ella Lonn, *Foreigners in the Confederacy* (Chapel Hill, N.C., 1940), p. 114.

[72] Bland, *op. cit.*, p. 106.   [73] Parton, *op. cit.*, p. 358.   [74] *Ibid.*, p. 359.

[75] *Ibid.*, p. 568.   [76] *Ibid.*, p. 360.   [77] *Ibid.*, p. 363.

[78] Bland, *op. cit.*, p. 107.   [79] Parton, *op. cit.*, p. 378.

[80] *Butler's Book*, 524 n.   [81] Bland, *op. cit.*, p. 107.

[82] Parton, *op. cit.*, p. 366.   [83] *Ibid.*, p. 369.   [84] *Ibid.*, p. 389.

[85] Butler, *Correspondence*, II, 251.   [86] Parton, *op. cit.*, p. 383.

[87] Butler, *Correspondence*, I, 511.

[88] Thornton Kirkland Lothrop, *William Henry Seward* (Boston, 1898), p. 373.

[89] Bernard C. Steiner, *Life of Reverdy Johnson* (Baltimore, 1914), p. 58.

[90] Parton, *op. cit.*, p. 356.   [91] Butler, *Correspondence*, I, 581.

[92] Bland, *op. cit.*, p. 108.

[93] Willie Malvin Caskey, *Secession and Restoration of Louisiana* (Baton Rouge, 1938), p. 67.

[94] Parton, *op. cit.*, p. 391.   [95] *Ibid.*, p. 471.   [96] *Ibid.*, p. 472.

[97] Bland, *op. cit.*, p. 126.

[98] *United States* v. *Diekelman*, 92 U.S. 520 (1876).

[99] Bland, *op. cit.*, p. 97.   [100] Parton, *op. cit.*, p. 325.

[101] *Butler's Book*, p. 416.

[102] Thomas Williams, "Letters," *American Historical Review*, Washington (Jan., 1909), XIV, 22.

[103] *Butler's Book*, p. 417.   [104] Bland, *op. cit.*, p. 96.   [105] *Ibid.*, p. 98.

[106] *Ibid.*, p. 99.   [107] *Ibid.*, p. 100.   [108] Parton, *op. cit.*, p. 336.

[109] *Ibid.*, p. 339.   [110] Coulter, *op. cit.*, p. 370.

[111] Mary Boykin Chesnut, *A Diary From Dixie* (New York, 1906), p. 183.

[112] Parton, *op. cit.*, p. 341.

[113] Henry Adams, *The Education of Henry Adams* (Boston, 1918), p. 136.

[114] McMaster, *op. cit.*, p. 208.

[115] Sarah Agnes Wallace and Frances Elma Gillespie, eds., *The Journal of Benjamin Moran, 1857–1865* (Chicago, 1942), II, 1028.

[116] McMaster, *op. cit.*, p. 209.

[117] Donaldson Jordan and Edwin J. Pratt, *Europe and the American Civil War* (Boston, 1931), p. 113.

[118] Dowdey, *Experiment in Rebellion*, p. 170.

[119] Frank Lawrence Owsley, *King Cotton Diplomacy* (Chicago, 1931), p. 324.

[120] Asbury, *op. cit.*, p. 227.   [121] Parton, *op. cit.*, p. 343.

[122] Asbury, *op. cit.*, p. 227.   [123] *Butler's Book*, p. 420.

[124] Butler, *Correspondence*, II, 520.

CHAPTER VIII

[1] Parton, *General Butler in New Orleans*, p. 484.

[2] Bland, *Life of Benjamin F. Butler*, p. 129.   [3] *Ibid.*, p. 128.

[4] *Ibid.*, p. 129.   [5] *Ibid.*, p. 130.

[6] Randall, *The Civil War and Reconstruction*, p. 666.

[7] Parton, *op. cit.*, p. 323.   [8] *Ibid.*, p. 484.   [9] Bland, *op. cit.*, p. 130.

[10] Southwood, *"Beauty and Booty,"* p. 114.

[11] Butler, *Correspondence*, II, 178.

[12] *Ibid.*, II, 188.   [13] Bland, *op. cit.*, p. 111.   [14] *Ibid.*, p. 116.

[15] Parton, *op. cit.*, p. 409.

[16] *Official Records of the Rebellion*, Ser. III, Vol. II, p. 173.

[17] Rhodes, *History of the United States*, V, 279.   [18] *Ibid.*

[19] *Butler's Book*, p. 385.   [20] Parton, *op. cit.*, p. 411.   [21] *Ibid.*, p. 303.

[22] Rhodes, *op. cit.*, V, 304.   [23] Butler, *Correspondence*, II, 229.

[24] *Ibid.*, II, 234.   [25] *Ibid.*, II, 236.   [26] *Ibid.*, II, 526.   [27] *Ibid.*, II, 528.

[28] Wilmer C. Harris, *Public Life of Zachariah Chandler, 1851–1875* (Lansing, Mich., 1917), p. 72.

[29] *Ibid.*, p. 106.   [30] Southwood, *op. cit.*, p. 86.   [31] Rhodes, *op. cit.*, V, 304.

[32] *Ibid.*, V, 305.   [33] *Ibid.*, V, 305 n.

[34] W. E. Woodward, *Meet General Grant* (New York, 1928), p. 272.

[35] Sandburg, *Abraham Lincoln: The War Years*, II, 70.

[36] West, *The Second Admiral*, p. 162.   [37] Rhodes, *op. cit.*, V, 310.

[38] J. B. Jones, *A Rebel War Clerk's Diary* (Philadelphia, 1866), I, 185.

[39] *Ibid.*, I, 187.   [40] *Ibid.*, I, 189.   [41] Rhodes, *op. cit.*, V, 308.

[42] *Nation*, Sept. 3, 1868.   [43] Rhodes, *op. cit.*, V, 312.

[44] Parton, *op. cit.*, p. 396.   [45] *Butler's Book*, p. 397.

[46] Parton, *op. cit.*, p. 396.   [47] *Ibid.*, p. 400.   [48] *Butler's Book*, p. 400.

[49] Parton, *op. cit.*, p. 399.   [50] *Butler's Book*, p. 405.   [51] *Ibid.*

[52] Bland, *op. cit.*, p. 109.   [53] Parton, *op. cit.*, p. 401.   [54] *Ibid.*, p. 405.

[55] Butler, *Correspondence*, II, 240.   [56] *Butler's Book*, p. 408.

[57] *Ibid.*, p. 410.   [58] Parton, *op. cit.*, p. 555.   [59] *Butler's Book*, p. 412.

[60] Parton, *op. cit.*, p. 393.   [61] Blaine, *Twenty Years of Congress*, II, 478 n.

[62] Parton, *op. cit.*, p. 394.   [63] *Ibid.*, p. 330.   [64] *Butler's Book*, p. 465.

[65] *Ibid.*, p. 469.   [66] *Ibid.*, p. 490.   [67] Parton, *op. cit.*, p. 566.

[68] W. E. Burghardt Du Bois, *Black Reconstruction* (New York, 1935), p. 94.

[69] Parton, *op. cit.*, p. 466.   [70] *Butler's Book*, p. 510.

[71] Parton, *op. cit.*, p. 473.   [72] *Ibid.*, p. 474.   [73] *Ibid.*, p. 516.

[74] Henry, *The Story of the Confederacy*, p. 181.

[75] Butler, *Correspondence*, II, 465.

[76] William Archibald Dunning, *Reconstruction Political and Economic, 1865–1877* (New York, 1907), p. 87.

[77] *Butler's Book,* p. 1035.   [78] Nicolay and Hay, *Abraham Lincoln,* VI, 450.

[79] Bland, *op. cit.,* p. 134.   [80] Macartney, *Lincoln and His Generals,* p. 47.

[81] Randall, *op. cit.,* p. 666.   [82] Asbury, *The French Quarter,* p. 225.

[83] Coulter, *The Confederate States of America,* p. 368.

[84] Sandburg, *op. cit.,* III, 268.

[85] Jefferson Davis, *The Rise and Fall of the Confederate Government* (New York, 1912), II, 232.

[86] Butler, *Correspondence,* IV, 579.   [87] Randall, *op. cit.,* p. 666.

[88] Parton, *op. cit.,* p. 468.   [89] Butler, *Correspondence,* II, 5.

[90] Bland, *op. cit.,* p. 119.   [91] Milton, *The Age of Hate,* p. 25.

[92] *Butler's Book,* p. 543.   [93] Sandburg, *op. cit.,* II, 150.

[94] Butler, *Correspondence,* II, 149.   [95] Parton, *op. cit.,* p. 599.

[96] *Butler's Book,* p. 526.   [97] Eisenschiml, *Why Was Lincoln Murdered?* p. 409.

[98] Harrington, *Fighting Politician,* p. 85.   [99] Butler, *Correspondence,* II, 512.

[100] *Ibid.,* II, 542.   [101] *Butler's Book,* p. 530.

[102] Lothrop, *William Henry Seward,* p. 373.

[103] Dabney, "The Butler Regime in Louisiana," *Louisiana Historical Quarterly* (April, 1944), XVII, 524.

[104] Boston *Globe,* Jan. 11, 1893.   [105] Sandburg, *op. cit.,* I, 655.

[106] T. Harry Williams, *Lincoln and His Generals* (New York, 1952), p. 222.

[107] Noah A. Plympton, *The Patriotic Service of Gen. Benjamin F. Butler* (Boston, 1896), p. 19.

[108] Butler, *Correspondence,* II, 461 n.

[109] B. F. Butler to Nathaniel Banks, Butler Manuscript, Dec. 16, 1862.

[110] Butler, *Correspondence,* II, 547.   [111] Bland, *op. cit.,* p. 139.

[112] Sandburg, *op. cit.,* II, 213.

[113] Adam Gurowski, *Diary* (New York, 1864), II, 65.

[114] John S. C. Abbott, "Heroic Deeds of Heroic Men," *Harper's New Monthly Magazine,* New York (April, 1865), XXX, 576.

[115] Parton, *op. cit.,* p. 611.

[116] Ficklen, "History of Reconstruction in Louisiana," *Johns Hopkins University Studies in Historical and Political Science,* XXVIII, 36 n.

CHAPTER IX

[1] Abraham Lincoln to B. F. Butler, Butler Manuscript, Dec. 9, 1862.

[2] *Butler's Book,* p. 533.   [3] *Ibid.,* p. 534.   [4] *Ibid.,* p. 551.

[5] *Ibid.,* p. 242.   [6] Sandburg, *Abraham Lincoln: The War Years,* II, 70.

[7] Parton, *General Butler in New Orleans,* p. 615.

[8] Nicolay and Hay, *Abraham Lincoln,* VIII, 316.

[9] Sandburg, *op. cit.,* II, 71.

[10] George S. Denison to B. F. Butler, Butler Manuscript, Feb. 10, 1863.

[11] Welles, *Diary,* I, 209.

[12] John Fiske, *The Mississippi Valley in the Civil War* (Boston, 1900), p. 130.

[13] West, *Gideon Welles,* p. 202.

[14] Rhodes, *History of the United States,* V, 308 n.

[15] B. F. Butler to Andrew Butler, Butler Manuscript, Feb. 18, 1863.

[16] Drafts dated Feb. 17 and Feb. 19, 1863, in the Butler Manuscript.

[17] Draft of Lincoln letter dated Feb. 11th in the Butler Manuscript.

[18] Adam Gurowski to B. F. Butler, Butler Manuscript, Jan. 3, 1863.

¹⁹ Invitations contained in the Butler Manuscript.
²⁰ Parton, *op. cit.*, p. 260.   ²¹ *Ibid.*, p. 625.
²² Thurlow Weed Barnes, *Memoir of Thurlow Weed* (Boston, 1884), II, 383.
²³ Resolutions dated Jan. 8, 1863, contained in the Butler Manuscript.
²⁴ Resolutions dated Jan. 20, 1863, contained in the Butler Manuscript.
²⁵ Resolutions dated Jan. 30, 1863, contained in the Butler Manuscript.
²⁶ Ida Husted Harper, *The Life and Work of Susan B. Anthony* (Indianapolis, 1898), II, 957.
²⁷ January 17, 1863.   ²⁸ Bigelow, *Retrospections of an Active Life,* I, 596.
²⁹ *Butler's Book*, p. 577.
³⁰ T. Harry Williams, *Lincoln and the Radicals* (Madison, Wis., 1941), p. 223.
³¹ B. F. Butler to Andrew Butler, Butler Manuscript, Jan. 19, 1863.
³² Andrew Butler to B. F. Butler, Butler Manuscript, Jan. 24, 1863.
³³ Butler, *Correspondence*, III, 4.
³⁴ Salmon P. Chase to B. F. Butler, Butler Manuscript, Jan. 20, 1863.
³⁵ Daniel Butterfield to B. F. Butler, Butler Manuscript, Jan. 30, 1863.
³⁶ George Butler to B. F. Butler, Butler Manuscript, Jan. 16, 1863.
³⁷ Butler, *Correspondence*, III, 37.
³⁸ B. F. Butler to William H. Seward, Butler Manuscript, Feb. (?), 1863.
³⁹ Butler, *Correspondence*, III, 50.
⁴⁰ B. F. Butler to James Parton, Butler Manuscript, Jan. 27, 1863.
⁴¹ Williams, *op. cit.*, p. 277.
⁴² Hesseltine, *Lincoln and the War Governors*, p. 358.
⁴³ Butler, *Correspondence*, III, 61.
⁴⁴ William Osborn Stoddard, *The Volcano Under the City* (New York, 1887), p. 288.
⁴⁵ Sandburg, *op. cit.*, II, 369.   ⁴⁶ Welles, *op. cit.*, I, 373.
⁴⁷ Edward Conrad Smith, *The Borderland in the Civil War*, p. 385.
⁴⁸ Sandburg, *op. cit.*, II, 402.   ⁴⁹ *Butler's Book*, p. 577.
⁵⁰ W. J. Cash, *The Mind of the South* (New York, 1941), p. 139.
⁵¹ Bland, *Life of Benjamin F. Butler*, p. 145.
⁵² Eisenschiml, *In the Shadow of Lincoln's Death*, p. 6.
⁵³ *Butler's Book*, p. 584.   ⁵⁴ Bland, *op. cit.*, p. 146.
⁵⁵ Sandburg, *op. cit.*, II, 526.   ⁵⁶ Bates, *Diary*, p. 337.

CHAPTER X

¹ Ulysses S. Grant, *Personal Memoirs* (New York, 1886), II, 132.
² Charles A. Dana, *The Life of Ulysses S. Grant* (Springfield, Mass., 1868), p. 184.
³ Adam Badeau, *Military History of Ulysses S. Grant* (New York, 1885), II, 44.
⁴ James Harrison Wilson, *The Life of John A. Rawlins* (New York, 1916), p. 250.
⁵ Porter, *The Naval History of the Civil War*, p. 692.
⁶ B. H. Liddell Hart, *Sherman: Soldier, Realist, Statesman, American* (New York, 1929), p. 273.
⁷ Charles Francis Adams, *An Autobiography* (Boston, 1916), p. 159.
⁸ Badeau, *op. cit.*, II, 247.   ⁹ *Butler's Book*, p. 649.   ¹⁰ *Ibid.*, p. 678.
¹¹ *Ibid.*, p. 690.   ¹² Butler, *Correspondence*, IV, 157.
¹³ Kenneth Williams, *Lincoln Finds a General*, I, 1.
¹⁴ Douglas Southall Freeman, *R. E. Lee* (New York, 1935), III, 275.
¹⁵ Randall, *The Civil War and Reconstruction*, p. 541.
¹⁶ Bland, *Life of Benjamin F. Butler*, p. 149.
¹⁷ Coulter, *The Confederate States of America*, p. 92.

18 Dana, *op. cit.*, p. 184.   19 *Ibid.*, p. 220.

20 Rhodes, *History of the United States*, IV, 445.

21 Charles Francis Adams, *Studies Military and Diplomatic, 1775–1865* (New York, 1911), p. 270.

22 David E. Johnston, *The Story of a Confederate Boy in the Civil War* (Portland, Ore., 1914), p. 244.

23 George E. Pickett, *The Heart of a Soldier* (New York, 1913), p. 138.

24 Henry, *The Story of the Confederacy*, p. 359.   25 Freeman, *op. cit.*, III, 335.

26 Dowdey, *Experiment in Rebellion*, p. 348.   27 Freeman, *op. cit.*, III, 335.

28 Grant, *op. cit.*, II, 152.

29 *Official Records of the Rebellion*, Ser. I, Vol. XXXVI, Pt. I, p. 20.

30 During this same campaign Butler likewise was to refer to the French general whose slowness might have caused Napoleon's defeat. In reprimanding Smith, the Massachusetts general noted, "The delay of Grouchy, for three hours, lost to Napoleon Waterloo and an empire, and we all remember the bitterness with which the Emperor exclaimed as he waited for his tardy general, 'Il s'amuse à Gembloux' " (Butler, *Correspondence*, IV, 426). Was he reminding Smith that even non-West Pointers had studied the Napoleonic campaigns?

31 Adams, *Studies Military and Diplomatic*, p. 281.

32 J. F. C. Fuller, *The Generalship of Ulysses S. Grant* (London, 1929), p. 294.

33 Butler, *Correspondence*, IV, 245.

34 Freeman, *Lee's Lieutenants*, III, 500.   35 Dana, *op. cit.*, p. 219.

36 *Butler's Book*, p. 694.

37 William Farrar Smith, *From Chattanooga to Petersburg Under Generals Grant and Butler* (Boston, 1893), p. 28.

38 *Official Records of the Rebellion*, Ser. I, Vol. XL, Pt. I, p. 28.

39 William Farrar Smith, *op. cit.*, p. 176.   40 Woodward, *Meet General Grant*, p. 347.

41 William Farrar Smith, *op. cit.*, p. 178.   42 *Ibid.*, p. 175.

43 Wilson, *Rawlins*, p. 249.   44 Rhodes, *op. cit.*, IV, 493.

45 Butler, *Correspondence*, IV, 594.   46 *Butler's Book*, p. 694.

47 William Farrar Smith, *op. cit.*, p. 189.   48 *Ibid.*, p. 41.

49 Woodward, *op. cit.*, p. 346.   50 Butler, *Correspondence*, IV, 481.

51 *Ibid.*, IV, 482.   52 William Farrar Smith, *op. cit.*, p. 43.

53 Confederate General Jubal A. Early's raiders were then threatening Washington (Randall, *The Civil War and Reconstruction*, p. 568).

54 Butler, *Correspondence*, IV, 484.

55 *Official Records of the Rebellion*, Ser. I, Vol. XL, Pt. III, p. 334.

56 William Farrar Smith, *op. cit.*, p. 52.   57 *Butler's Book*, p. 697.

58 Butler, *Correspondence*, IV, 411.

59 *Official Records of the Rebellion*, Ser. I, Vol. XXXVI, Pt. II, p. 274.

60 Margaret Leech, *Reveille in Washington* (New York, 1941), p. 440.

61 Butler, *Correspondence*, IV, 171.   62 *Ibid.*, IV, 269.

63 *Official Records of the Rebellion*, Ser. I, Vol. XXXVI, Pt. II, p. 283.

64 *The Gatling Gun. Official Reports of Trials, Description, General Directions, Targets, &c.* (Hartford, 1878), p. 14.

65 Butler, *Correspondence*, IV, 303.

66 *Official Records of the Rebellion*, Ser. I, Vol. XL, Pt. 2, p. 559.

67 *Ibid.*, p. 598.   68 Macartney, *op. cit.*, p. 199.

69 James Fairfax McLaughlin, *The American Cyclops* (Baltimore, 1868), p. 3.

70 Edwards Pierrepont, *A Review of General Butler's Defense, Before the House of Representatives in Relation to the New Orleans Gold* (New York, 1865), p. 5.

[71] *Ibid.*, p. 9.   [72] *Ibid.*, p. 15.

[73] *Ibid.*, p. 22. The records are vague as to the ultimate disposition of the gold.

[74] J. G. Randall, *Constitutional Problems Under Lincoln* (New York, 1926), p. 467.

[75] Charles H. Ambler, *Francis H. Pierpont, Union War Governor of Virginia and Father of West Virginia* (Chapel Hill, N.C., 1937), p. 245.

[76] Milton, *The Age of Hate*, p. 129.   [77] Ambler, *op. cit.*, p. 232.

[78] *Ibid.*, p. 233.   [79] *Ibid.*, p. 234.

[80] Nicolay and Hay, *Abraham Lincoln*, IX, 440.   [81] Macartney, *op. cit.*, p. 62.

[82] Sandburg, *Abraham Lincoln: The War Years*, III, 208.

[83] Welles, *Diary*, II, 81.   [84] Sandburg, *op. cit.*, III, 66.

[85] Bates, *Diary*, p. 359.   [86] Sandburg, *op. cit.*, III, 208.

CHAPTER XI

[1] Randall, *The Civil War and Reconstruction*, p. 497.

[2] Butler, *Correspondence*, III, 174.

[3] Ambler, *Francis H. Pierpont*, p. 247. Butler believed that the Negro should be given full citizenship status, regardless of whether conditions or environment had prepared him for this responsibility (Butler, *Correspondence*, V, 679).

[4] Butler, *Correspondence*, III, 182.   [5] *Ibid.*, III, 204.

[6] Sandburg, *Abraham Lincoln: The War Years*, III, 150.

[7] *Official Records of the Rebellion*, Ser. I, Vol. LI, Pt. II, p. 900.

[8] George E. Pickett, *The Heart of a Soldier*, p. 136.

[9] Arthur Cole, *The Irrepressible Conflict, 1850–1865* (New York, 1934), p. 329.

[10] Freeman, *Lee's Lieutenants*, III, 532.   [11] Butler, *Correspondence*, IV, 28.

[12] *Ibid.*, IV, 138.   [13] *Ibid.*, IV, 120.   [14] *Ibid.*, IV, 136.

[15] *Ibid.*, IV, 567.   [16] Nicolay and Hay, *Abraham Lincoln*, VI, 334.

[17] *Butler's Book*, p. 833.   [18] *Ibid.*, p. 835.

[19] Simon Wolf, *The Presidents I Have Known From 1860–1918* (Washington, 1918), p. 8.

[20] Max J. Kohler, "The Board of Delegates of American Israelites," *Publications of the American Jewish Historical Society*, No. 29, 1925, p. 117.

[21] *Ibid.*, p. 120.

[22] *Official Records of the Rebellion*, Ser. I, Vol. LI, Pt. II, p. 874.

[23] Butler, *Correspondence*, III, 276.   [24] *Ibid.*, III, 153.

[25] Leech, *Reveille in Washington*, p. 320.   [26] *Butler's Book*, p. 864.

[27] Pratt, *Ordeal by Fire*, p. 355.

[28] Parton, *General Butler in New Orleans*, p. 614.

[29] Butler, *Correspondence*, IV, 220.

[30] *Official Records of the Rebellion*, Ser. I, Vol. XXXVI, Pt. II, p. 858.

[31] Butler, *Correspondence*, IV, 231.   [32] *Butler's Book*, p. 841.

[33] *Ibid.*, p. 842.

[34] Lew Wallace, *An Autobiography* (New York, 1906), II, 674.

[35] *Official Records of the Rebellion*, Ser. I, Vol. XL, Pt. II, p. 595.

[36] Pratt, *op. cit.*, p. 354.

[37] Coulter, *The Confederate States of America*, p. 370.

[38] *Butler's Book*, p. 729.   [39] *Ibid.*, p. 495.

[40] Whipple, *The Story-Life of Lincoln*, p. 498.   [41] *Butler's Book*, p. 410.

[42] *Ibid.*, p. 847.   [43] Butler, *Correspondence*, IV, 262.   [44] *Ibid.*, IV, 342.

[45] *Ibid.*, I, 75.

[46] *Official Records of the Rebellion*, Ser. I, Vol. XL, Pt. III, p. 676.

47 Butler, *Correspondence*, IV, 417.   48 *Ibid.*, V, 30.   49 *Ibid.*, V, 72.
50 *Ibid.*, V, 85.   51 *Ibid.*, V, 119 n.   52 West, *Gideon Welles*, p. 292.
53 Nicolay and Hay, *op. cit.*, VII, 460.
54 *Official Records of the Rebellion*, Ser. II, Vol. VI, p. 768.
55 Dowdey, *Experiment in Rebellion*, p. 334.
56 West, *Gideon Welles*, p. 292.
57 Alfred Hoyt Bill, *The Beleaguered City* (New York, 1946), p. 196.
58 *Butler's Book*, p. 584.   59 West, *Gideon Welles*, p. 295.
60 Macartney, *Lincoln and His Generals*, p. 52. Butler had reason to be sensitive on the subject of deserters, one of whom had informed Beauregard that the Massachusetts general secretly had been reinforced by a complete army corps (Ella Lonn, *Desertion During the Civil War* [New York, 1928], p. 194).
61 *Official Records of the Rebellion*, Ser. II, Vol. VI, p. 683.
62 Whipple, *op. cit.*, p. 564.   63 Pratt, *op. cit.*, p. 354.
64 George Alfred Townsend, *Rustics in Rebellion* (Chapel Hill, N.C., 1950), p. 265.
65 Bland, *Life of Benjamin F. Butler*, p. 154.   66 *Butler's Book*, p. 751.
67 *John Dooley, Confederate Soldier, His War Journal* (Washington, 1945), p. 98.
68 Freeman, *Lee's Lieutenants*, I, 251.   69 Bill, *op. cit.*, p. 121.
70 Coulter, *op. cit.*, p. 370.   71 Bill, *op. cit.*, p. 162.
72 *Official Records of the Rebellion*, Ser. I, Vol. XXIX, Pt. II, p. 873.
73 Freeman, *R. E. Lee*, III, 211.   74 Sandburg, *op. cit.*, IV, 24.
75 Milton, *The Age of Hate*, p. 128.   76 Leech, *op. cit.*, p. 347.
77 Hendricks, *Lincoln's War Cabinet*, p. 454.   78 Flower, *James Parton*, p. 67.
79 Sandburg, *op. cit.*, II, 203.   80 Butler, *Correspondence*, V, 277.
81 B. F. Butler, "Vice-Presidential Politics in '64," *North American Review*, New York (October, 1885), CXLI, 332.
82 Sandburg, *op. cit.*, II, 471.   83 *Ibid.*, III, 100.
84 Helen Nicolay, *Lincoln's Secretary* (New York, 1949), p. 209.
85 Macartney, *op. cit.*, p. 64.   86 West, *The Second Admiral*, p. 271.
87 West, *Gideon Welles*, p. 292.   88 Butler, *Correspondence*, V, 139.
89 Sandburg, *op. cit.*, III, 87.
90 Butler, "Vice-Presidential Politics in '64," *North American Review*, New York (October, 1885), CXLI, p. 333.
91 Blaine, *Twenty Years of Congress*, I, 517.
92 Nicolay and Hay, *op. cit.*, IX, 72.   93 Blaine, *op. cit.*, I, 522.
94 Milton, *The Age of Hate*, p. 123.   95 New York *Herald*, Jan. 12, 1893.
96 *Butler's Book*, p. 754.   97 Dix, *Memoirs of John Adams Dix*, II, 85.
98 *Butler's Book*, p. 755.   99 Dowdey, *op. cit.*, p. 370.
100 Badeau, *Military History of Ulysses S. Grant*, III, 171.
101 August Belmont, *A Few Letters and Speeches of the Late Civil War* (New York, 1870), p. 113.
102 *Butler's Book*, p. 756.   103 *Ibid.*, p. 758.   104 *Ibid.*, p. 761.
105 *Ibid.*   106 *Ibid.*   107 *Ibid.*, p. 760.   108 Sandburg, *op. cit.*, III, 562.
109 *Butler's Book*, p. 770. Butler, although not a New Yorker, apparently had read somewhere that state's 1846 constitution, Article II, Section 2 of which denies suffrage to anyone betting upon an election.
110 *Ibid.*, p. 771.   111 *Ibid.*, p. 773.   112 Butler, *Correspondence*, V, 353.
113 George Meade, *The Life and Letters of George Gordon Meade* (New York, 1913), II, 229.
114 Butler, *Correspondence*, V, 364.
115 Hoar, *Autobiography of Seventy Years*, I, 335.
116 Rhodes, *History of the United States*, V, 310.

[117] Sandburg, *op. cit.*, III, 66.
[118] Storey, *The Record of Benjamin F. Butler*, p. 29.   [119] *Ibid.*, p. 31.
[120] *Ibid.*, p. 33.   [121] *Ibid.*, p. 34.   [122] *Ibid.*, p. 39.
[123] Butler, *Correspondence*, III, 407.   [124] *Ibid.*, IV, 23.
[125] *Ibid.*, III, 579.   [126] Storey, *op. cit.*, p. 37.   [127] *Ibid.*, p. 45.
[128] *Ibid.*, p. 47.   [129] *Ibid.*, p. 48.   [130] Boston *Traveller*, Oct. 26, 1868.
[131] Robinson Scrapbook, III, 181.   [132] Rhodes, *op. cit.*, V, 302.
[133] *Ibid.*, V, 303.   [134] Welles, *Diary*, I, 536.
[135] West, *The Second Admiral*, p. 271.   [136] Butler, *Correspondence*, III, 339.
[137] Welles, *op. cit.*, I, 544.   [138] *Ibid.*, II, 56.   [139] Storey, *op. cit.*, p. 15.
[140] *Ibid.*, p. 16.   [141] *Ibid.*, p. 18.   [142] Rhodes, *op. cit.*, V, 303.
[143] Bradford, *Damaged Souls*, p. 231.
[144] Charles Minor Blackford, *Letters From Lee's Army* (New York, 1947), p. 252.

CHAPTER XII

[1] Bland, *Life of Benjamin F. Butler*, p. 158.   [2] *Butler's Book*, p. 278.
[3] Boston *Globe*, Jan. 11, 1893.
[4] Otto Eisenschiml and Ralph Newman, *The American Iliad* (Indianapolis, 1947), p. 595.
[5] Bland, *op. cit.*, p. 158.   [6] Hoar, *Autobiography of Seventy Years*, I, 336.
[7] West, *The Second Admiral*, p. 274.   [8] Welles, *Diary*, II, 209.
[9] W. T. Sherman, *Memoirs*, II, 205.   [10] Welles, *op. cit.*, II, 216.
[11] Benson J. Lossing, *Pictorial History of the Civil War* (Hartford, 1868), III, 476.
[12] Grant, *Personal Memoirs*, II, 388.   [13] *Ibid.*, II, 604.
[14] Porter, *The Naval History of the Civil War*, p. 684.
[15] *Butler's Book*, p. 819.
[16] Badeau, *Military History of Ulysses S. Grant*, III, 324.
[17] B. H. Liddell Hart, *Sherman*, p. 357.   [18] West, *op. cit.*, p. 271.
[19] Porter, *op. cit.*, p. 693.   [20] West, *op. cit.*, p. 276.
[21] Hoar, *op. cit.*, I, 336.   [22] West, *op. cit.*, p. 279.
[23] Lossing, *op. cit.*, III, 477.   [24] Porter, *op. cit.*, p. 693.
[25] McMaster, *A History of the People of the United States During Lincoln's Administration*, p. 569.
[26] West, *op. cit.*, p. 278.   [27] *Ibid.*, p. 280.
[28] Lossing, *op. cit.*, III, 478.   [29] Porter, *op. cit.*, p. 696.
[30] West, *op. cit.*, p. 280.   [31] *Ibid.*, p. 283.   [32] Grant, *op. cit.*, II, 393.
[33] Lossing, *op. cit.*, III, 480.   [34] West, *op. cit.*, p. 283.
[35] Porter, *op. cit.*, p. 700.   [36] West, *op. cit.*, p. 283.
[37] Grant, *op. cit.*, II, 394.   [38] West, *Gideon Welles*, p. 303.
[39] Welles, *op. cit.*, II, 210.   [40] Porter, *op. cit.*, p. 710.
[41] *Ibid.*, p. 706.   [42] Hoar, *op. cit.*, I, 338.   [43] *Butler's Book*, p. 810.
[44] Sandburg, *Abraham Lincoln: The War Years*, IV, 24.
[45] Welles, *op. cit.*, II, 213.   [46] Hoar, *op. cit.*, I, 336.
[47] West, *The Second Admiral*, p. 284.   [48] *Butler's Book*, p. 827.
[49] Sandburg, *op. cit.*, IV, 23. Grant's apprehension about leaving the Massachusetts general in command may be seen from his letters. Thus Grant wrote to Stanton about an impending expedition, "I cannot go myself, so long as General Butler would be left in command" (Butler, *Correspondence*, V, 456). On one occasion the lieutenant general wrote to Butler, "Only expecting to be absent three (3) days, I will not relinquish command" (*ibid.*, V, 3). But the very next day

Butler wrote to his wife and said, "Grant has gone to Washington, and that leaves me in command of the army, which command he has turned over to me" (*ibid.*, V, 6).

50 *Butler's Book,* p. 829.   51 Welles, *op. cit.,* II, 215.

52 *Butler's Book,* p. 852.   53 West, *The Second Admiral,* p. 284.

54 *Butler's Book,* p. 827.   55 *Ibid.,* p. 888.

56 Gordon, *A War Diary,* p. 372.   57 Butler, *Correspondence,* V, 473.

58 *Ibid.,* V, 480.

59 Lloyd Lewis, *Sherman, Fighting Prophet* (New York, 1932), p. 478.

60 Meade, *Life and Letters,* II, 256.   61 Sandburg, *op. cit.,* IV, 26.

62 *Ibid.,* IV, 24.   63 Welles, *op. cit.,* II, 223.   64 *Ibid.,* II, 226.

65 McCormick, *Ulysses S. Grant,* p. 263.   66 Porter, *op. cit.,* p. 711.

67 *Official Records of the Rebellion,* Ser. I, Vol. XLVI, Pt. II, p. 20.

68 Welles, *op. cit.,* II, 226.   69 W. T. Sherman, *op. cit.,* II, 242.

70 *Butler's Book,* p. 807.   71 *Ibid.,* p. 806.

72 Butler, *Correspondence,* V, 468.   73 West, *The Second Admiral,* p. 291.

74 *Report of the Joint Committee on the Conduct of the War* (Washington, 1865), II, 27.

75 *Ibid.,* II, 31.   76 *Ibid.,* II, 46.

77 T. Harry Williams, *Lincoln and the Radicals,* p. 366.

78 Butler, *Correspondence,* V, 503.

79 Rhodes, *History of the United States,* V, 311.   80 *Butler's Book,* p. 904.

81 *Ibid.,* p. 907.

CHAPTER XIII

1 Rhodes, *History of the United States,* V, 154 n.

2 *Butler's Book,* p. 908.

3 Noah Brooks, *Washington in Lincoln's Time* (New York, 1896), p. 251.

4 Claude Bowers, *The Tragic Era* (Boston, 1929), p. 6.

5 T. Harry Williams, *Lincoln and the Radicals,* p. 371.

6 Milton, *The Age of Hate,* p. 168.   7 Bowers, *op. cit.,* p. 7.

8 Samuel Wilkenson to B. F. Butler, Butler Manuscript, April 23, 1865.

9 Milton, *op. cit.,* p. 169. The Republican party had taken the guise of a Union party in 1864, and it was the moderates in this group that had won Johnson his Vice Presidential nomination. But the Radical Republicans took over party domination in 1865 (Randall, *Lincoln the President,* II, 215).

10 Randall, *Constitutional Problems Under Lincoln,* p. 101.

11 B. F. Butler to Andrew Johnson, Butler Manuscript, April 25, 1865.

12 Welles, *Diary,* II, 367.

13 George W. Julian, *Political Recollections, 1840 to 1872* (Chicago, 1884), p. 257.

14 Orville Hickman Browning, *Diary* (Springfield, Ill., 1933), II, 65.

15 Lew Wallace, *An Autobiography,* II, 857.

16 Welles, *op. cit.,* II, 493.   17 *Ibid.,* II, 469.

18 5 Wallace 342 (1866).

19 Charles Warren, *The Supreme Court in United States History* (Boston, 1922), III, 148.

20 *Ex parte Milligan,* 71 U.S. 2 (1866).   21 Butler, *Correspondence,* V, 617.

22 Bowers, *op. cit.,* p. 158. Once Johnson had assumed the Presidency, his early vindictive expressions gave way to a reconstruction policy that was essentially the same as Lincoln's, including early restoration (Randall, *The Civil War and Reconstruction,* p. 707).

23 Randall, *The Civil War and Reconstruction*, p. 722.

24 Bowers, *op. cit.*, p. 126.

25 Ellis Paxson Oberholtzer, *A History of the United States Since the Civil War* (New York, 1917–1937), I, 395.

26 Blaine, *Twenty Years of Congress*, II, 232.

27 David Miller De Witt, *The Impeachment and Trial of Andrew Johnson* (New York, 1903), p. 128.

28 Bowers, *op. cit.*, p. 143.   29 Welles, *op. cit.*, II, 619.

30 *Butler's Book*, p. 919.   31 Oberholtzer, *op. cit.*, II, 93.

32 *Butler's Book*, p. 920.   33 Blaine, *op. cit.*, II, 289.

34 Donald Barr Chidsey, *The Gentleman from New York: A Life of Roscoe Conkling* (New Haven, 1935), p. 62.

35 DeWitt, *op. cit.*, p. 208.   36 Bowers, *op. cit.*, p. 164.

37 Oberholtzer, *op. cit.*, II, 67.   38 DeWitt, *op. cit.*, p. 147.

39 Eisenschiml, *Why Was Lincoln Murdered?* p. 382.

40 *Ibid.*, p. 138.   41 Bowers, *op. cit.*, p. 7.

42 Butler, *Correspondence*, V, 642.

43 Robert Selph Henry, *The Story of Reconstruction* (Indianapolis, 1938), p. 390.

44 *Ibid.*, p. 168.   45 Philadelphia *Evening Herald*, Jan. 3, 1868.

46 DeWitt, *op. cit.*, p. 222.   47 Bowers, *op. cit.*, p. 159.

48 Milton, *op. cit.*, p. 416.

49 George Templeton Strong, *Diary* (New York, 1952), IV, 114.

50 Samuel W. McCall, *Thaddeus Stevens* (Boston, 1909), p. 282.

51 Rhodes, *op. cit.*, VI, 116.

52 Georges Clemenceau, *American Reconstruction, 1865–1870* (New York, 1928), p. 151.

53 Oberholtzer, *op. cit.*, II, 122.   54 Julian, *op. cit.*, p. 313.

55 Randall, *The Civil War and Reconstruction*, p. 770.

56 Welles, *op. cit.*, III, 12.   57 Bowers, *op. cit.*, p. 184.   58 *Ibid.*

59 *Butler's Book*, p. 928.

60 Henry Luther Stoddard, *Horace Greeley* (New York, 1946), p. 260.

61 Milton, *op. cit.*, p. 520. The Managers of the Impeachment were Representatives Bingham, Butler, Logan, Boutwell, Stevens, Williams, and Wilson.

62 *Butler's Book*, p. 926.   63 Henry, *op. cit.*, p. 305.

64 *Butler's Book*, p. 97.   65 *Ibid.*, p. 632.

66 Albert Bushnell Hart, *Salmon Portland Chase* (Boston, 1899), p. 358.

67 *Ibid.*, p. 361.   68 Welles, *op. cit.*, III, 354.   69 *Butler's Book*, p. 929.

70 Milton, *op. cit.*, p. 531.   71 *Ibid.*, p. 549.   72 *Ibid.*, p. 545.

73 Frederick Trevor Hill, *Decisive Battles of the Law* (New York, 1907), p. 148.

74 Milton, *op. cit.*, p. 546.   75 DeWitt, *op. cit.*, p. 408.

76 Bowers, *op. cit.*, p. 184.

77 A. G. Riddle, *The Life of Benjamin F. Wade* (Cleveland, 1886), p. 283.

78 Randall, *The Civil War and Reconstruction*, p. 774.

79 Milton, *op. cit.*, p. 547.   80 DeWitt, *op. cit.*, p. 409.   81 *Ibid.*, p. 416.

82 *Nation*, April 2, 1868.

83 David J. Brewer, ed., *The World's Best Orations* (Chicago, 1923), III, 18.

84 Edwin M. Stanton to B. F. Butler, Butler Manuscript, April 1, 1868.

85 Milton, *op. cit.*, p. 545.   86 Welles, *op. cit.*, III, 321.

87 West, *Gideon Welles*, p. 334.   88 Bowers, *op. cit.*, p. 186.

89 Henry, *op. cit.*, p. 305.   90 Rhodes, *op. cit.*, VI, 135.

91 Lloyd Paul Stryker, *Andrew Johnson, A Study in Courage* (New York, 1936), p. 655.

[92] McCall, *op. cit.*, p. 339.   [93] Clemenceau, *op. cit.*, p. 172.
[94] McCall, *op. cit.*, p. 337.   [95] Milton, *op. cit.*, p. 566.
[96] Oberholtzer, *op. cit.*, II, 113.   [97] DeWitt, *op. cit.*, p. 515.
[98] Welles, *op. cit.*, III, 362.
[99] Edmund G. Ross, *History of the Impeachment of Andrew Johnson* (Santa Fe, N.M., 1896), p. 153.
[100] Welles, *op. cit.*, III, 336.
[101] Hoar, *Autobiography of Seventy Years*, I, 343.
[102] Randall, *The Civil War and Reconstruction*, p. 777.
[103] John Sherman, *Recollections of Forty Years* (Chicago, 1895), I, 428.
[104] Milton, *op. cit.*, p. 618.   [105] *Ibid.*   [106] Rhodes, *op. cit.*, VI, 151.
[107] *Ibid.*, VI, 152.   [108] Bowers, *op. cit.*, p. 236.

CHAPTER XIV.

[1] Butler, *Correspondence*, V, 677.   [2] *Ibid.*, V, 684.
[3] Secretary of the Commonwealth of Massachusetts to B. F. Butler, Butler Manuscript, May 26, 1866.
[4] Butler, *Correspondence*, V, 681.   [5] Cowley, *A History of Lowell*, p. 210.
[6] Blaine, *Twenty Years of Congress*, II, 289.   [7] *Independent*, March 14, 1867.
[8] Poore, *Reminiscences of Sixty Years in the National Metropolis*, II, 210.
[9] *Nation*, Oct. 10, 1868.   [10] *Butler's Book*, p. 921.
[11] Robinson Scrapbook, III, 195.
[12] Clemenceau, *American Reconstruction, 1865–1870*, p. 263.
[13] E. W. Evans to B. F. Butler, Butler Manuscript, Aug. 24, 1866.
[14] John I. Davenport, *The Election Frauds of New York City and Their Prevention* (New York, 1881), I, 84.
[15] *Ibid.*, I, 87.
[16] Letters in Butler Manuscript, June 7–14, 1867.
[17] Anthony Henry Frogmorton to B. F. Butler, Butler Manuscript, May 29, 1865.
[18] Sidney B. De Kay to B. F. Butler, Butler Manuscript, April 26, 1866.
[19] B. F. Butler to Otis F. Childs, Butler Manuscript, Oct. 2, 1868.
[20] Welles, *Diary*, II, 492.   [21] Fuess, *The Life of Caleb Cushing*, II, 295.
[22] *Nation*, Sept. 3, 1868.   [23] Boston *Traveller*, Oct. 26, 1868.
[24] See William Dana Orcutt, "Ben Butler and the 'Stolen Spoons,'" *North American Review*, New York (January, 1918), CCVII, 66.
[25] Speech at Ladd and Whitney Monument, Lowell, Butler Manuscript, June 17, 1865.
[26] Dunning, *Reconstruction Political and Economic, 1865–1877*, p. 68.
[27] *Butler's Book*, p. 960.
[28] E. Merton Coulter, *The South During Reconstruction, 1865–1877* (Baton Rouge, 1947), p. 115.
[29] *Butler's Book*, p. 909.   [30] *Ibid.*, p. 916.   [31] *Ibid.*, p. 917.
[32] Welles, *op. cit.*, II, 365.   [33] *Ibid.*, II, 368.
[34] La Salle Pickett, *What Happened to Me* (New York, 1917), p. 201.
[35] La Salle Pickett, *Pickett and His Men* (Atlanta, 1899), p. 302.
[36] Howard K. Beale, *The Critical Year* (New York, 1930), p. 372.
[37] Stanley F. Horn, *The Invisible Empire* (Boston, 1939), p. 151.
[38] *Butler's Book*, p. 908.   [39] Henry, *The Story of Reconstruction*, p. 326.
[40] Mrs. Roger A. Pryor, *My Day, Reminiscences of a Long Life* (New York, 1909), p. 41.
[41] Roger A. Pryor to B. F. Butler, Butler Manuscript, April 3, 1876.
[42] Adelbert Ames to B. F. Butler, Butler Manuscript, April 2, 1876.

⁴³ Bowers, *The Tragic Era*, p. 457. ⁴⁴ Henry, *op. cit.*, p. 394.
⁴⁵ Bowers, *op. cit.*, p. 302.
⁴⁶ Benjamin F. Butler, *Ku-Klux Outrages in the South. The Work of the Democratic Party* (Washington, 1871), p. 20.
⁴⁷ *Ibid.*, p. 24. ⁴⁸ Strong, *Diary*, IV, 352.
⁴⁹ David Macrae, *The Americans at Home* (Edinburgh, 1870), I, 156.
⁵⁰ *Ibid.* ⁵¹ *Ibid.*, I, 159.

CHAPTER XV

¹ Bowers, *The Tragic Era*, p. 168. ² *Ibid.*, p. 224.
³ George Suckley to B. F. Butler, Butler Manuscript, Jan. 29, 1866.
⁴ *Appleton's Cyclopedia of American Biography*, V, 738.
⁵ La Salle Pickett, "The Wartime Story of General Pickett," *Cosmopolitan Magazine*, New York (July, 1914), LVI, 196.
⁶ B. F. Butler to U. S. Grant, Butler Manuscript, Jan. 29, 1866.
⁷ William B. Hesseltine, *Ulysses S. Grant, Politician* (New York, 1935), p. 66.
⁸ B. F. Butler to James Parton, Butler Manuscript, Feb. 19, 1867.
⁹ B. F. Butler to Mrs. James Parton, Butler Manuscript, Feb. 10, 1868.
¹⁰ *Dictionary of American Biography*, XX, 218. ¹¹ Hesseltine, *op. cit.*, 117.
¹² George Wilkes to B. F. Butler, Butler Manuscript, April 12, 1868.
¹³ B. F. Butler to George Wilkes, Butler Manuscript, May 2, 1868.
¹⁴ U. S. Grant to George Wilkes, Butler Manuscript, June 19, 1868.
¹⁵ B. F. Butler to A. G. Upham, Butler Manuscript, July 4, 1868.
¹⁶ Boston *Traveller*, Oct. 26, 1868. Although Butler long had hesitated as to his decision, he plunged wholeheartedly into the fray once his mind was made up as to where expediency demanded that he should go (Louis Taylor Merrill, *General Benjamin F. Butler and the Campaign of 1868*, doctoral dissertation, University of Chicago [Chicago, 1939], p. 216).
¹⁷ B. F. Butler to E. J. Sherman, Butler Manuscript, Dec. 25, 1868.
¹⁸ B. F. Butler to Grant Club of Hartford, Butler Manuscript, Jan. 31, 1868.
¹⁹ Mrs. John A. Logan, *Reminiscences of a Soldier's Wife* (New York, 1913), p. 233.
²⁰ Edward Stanwood, *A History of Presidential Elections* (Boston, 1888), p. 273.
²¹ *Butler's Book*, p. 853. ²² Blaine, *Twenty Years of Congress*, II, 449.
²³ Welles, *Diary*, III, 564. ²⁴ *Butler's Book*, p. 855.
²⁵ Logan, *op. cit.*, p. 267. ²⁶ Lewis, *Sherman*, p. 606.
²⁷ Rhodes, *History of the United States*, VI, 389.
²⁸ Hoar, *Autobiography of Seventy Years*, II, 2.
²⁹ Oberholtzer, *A History of the United States*, II, 314.
³⁰ Schurz, *Reminiscences*, III, 332.
³¹ Bland, *Life of Benjamin F. Butler*, p. 160.
³² Badeau, *Military History of Ulysses S. Grant*, II, 247.
³³ Grant, *Personal Memoirs*, II, 152. ³⁴ Hoar, *op. cit.*, I, 362.
³⁵ Milton, *The Age of Hate*, p. 375. ³⁶ Hoar, *op. cit.*, II, 269.
³⁷ B. F. Butler to Charles Sumner, Butler Manuscript, July 3, 1869.
³⁸ *Butler's Book*, p. 867.
³⁹ Matthew Josephson, *The Politicos, 1865–1896* (New York, 1938), p. 173.
⁴⁰ Thomas C. Cochran and William Miller, *The Age of Enterprise: A Social History of Industrial America* (New York, 1942), p. 159.
⁴¹ Allan Nevins, *Hamilton Fish: The Inner History of the Grant Administration* (New York, 1936), p. 184.

[42] George Francis Dawson, *Life and Services of John A. Logan* (Chicago, 1887), p. 184.

[43] Hesseltine, *op. cit.*, p. 223.   [44] Nevins, *op. cit.*, p. 217.   [45] *Ibid.*, p. 174.

[46] Oberholtzer, *op. cit.*, III, 72.

[47] Russell H. Conwell, *Hon. Benjamin F. Butler. An Address Delivered Before the Aurora Club of Boston, Mass.* (Boston, 1874), p. 13.

[48] Nevins, *op. cit.*, p. 470.

[49] Charles Francis Adams, *Charles Francis Adams* (Boston, 1900), p. 388.

[50] B. F. Butler, *The Right of America to Present Her Claims Against Britain for Damages Without Menace* (Washington, D.C., 1872), p. 8.

[51] Randall, *The Civil War and Reconstruction*, p. 842.

[52] Hoar, *op. cit.*, II, 269.   [53] *Butler's Book*, p. 966.

[54] Oberholtzer, *op. cit.*, I, 541.

[55] Frank A. Golder, "The Purchase of Alaska," *American Historical Review,* Washington (April, 1921), XXV, 423.

[56] Strong, *Diary*, IV, 204.   [57] Nevins, *op. cit.*, p. 258.

[58] Carl Russell Fish, *American Diplomacy* (New York, 1923), p. 362.

[59] Nevins, *op. cit.*, p. 259.   [60] Hesseltine, *op. cit.*, p. 203.

[61] Nevins, *op. cit.*, p. 369.

[62] Andrew Dickson White, *Autobiography* (London, 1905), I, 487.

[63] Rhodes, *op. cit.*, VI, 193.

[64] David Saville Muzzey, *James G. Blaine* (New York, 1934), p. 54.

[65] Bland, *op. cit.*, p. 163.   [66] *Ibid.*, p. 172.   [67] Hoar, *op. cit.*, I, 354.

[68] Welles, *op. cit.*, III, 506.   [69] *Nation*, Sept. 3, 1868.

[70] Charles H. Coleman, *The Election of 1868: The Democratic Effort to Regain Control* (New York, 1933), p. 38.

[71] Theodore J. Grayson, *Leaders and Periods of American Finance* (New York, 1932), p. 275.

[72] Paul Studenski and Herman E. Krooss, *Financial History of the United States* (New York, 1952), p. 183.

[73] *Harper's Weekly,* May 16, 1874.   [74] Hesseltine, *op. cit.*, p. 333.

[75] Studenski and Krooss, *op. cit.*, p. 183.   [76] *Ibid.*, p. 184.

[77] Drake De Kay to B. F. Butler, Butler Manuscript, April 7, 1876.

[78] Louis R. Ehrich, *The Question of Silver* (New York, 1896), p. 23.

[79] J. Laurence Laughlin, *The History of Bimetallism in the United States* (New York, 1896), p. 188.

[80] *Harper's Weekly,* March 16, 1878.

[81] F. W. Taussig, *The Silver Situation in the United States* (New York, 1900), p. 2.

[82] *Ibid.*, p. 5.   [83] *Harper's Weekly,* March 9, 1878.

[84] *Ibid.*, March 23, 1878.

[85] J. B. Crawford, *The Crédit Mobilier of America, Its Origin and History* (Boston, 1880), p. 97.

[86] Oberholtzer, *Jay Cooke*, II, 179.

[87] B. F. Butler, *Speech Delivered in the House of Representatives*, Feb. 27, 1873 (Washington, 1873), p. 3.

[88] *Ibid.*, p. 8.   [89] *Ibid.*, p. 9.   [90] Robinson Scrapbook, III, 203.

[91] Bowers, *op. cit.*, p. 403.

[92] Robert Granville Caldwell, *James A. Garfield, Party Chieftain* (New York, 1931), p. 232.

[93] Logan, *op. cit.*, p. 280.   [94] West, *The Second Admiral*, p. 327.

[95] *Ibid.*, p. 331.

CHAPTER XVI

[1] Robinson Scrapbook, III, 221.
[2] George Lowell Austin, *The Life and Times of Wendell Phillips* (Boston, 1884), p. 270.
[3] *Ibid.*, p. 271.   [4] Robinson Scrapbook, III, 187.   [5] *Ibid.*, III, 199.
[6] Austin, *op. cit.*, p. 271.   [7] Strong, *Diary*, IV, 388.
[8] New York *Tribune*, Jan. 12, 1893.   [9] Nevins, *Hamilton Fish*, p. 465.
[10] Josephson, *The Politicos*, p. 125.
[11] Charles Edward Russell, *Blaine of Maine* (New York, 1931), p. 193.
[12] Josephson, *op. cit.*, p. 111 n.
[13] Emanie Sachs, *"The Terrible Siren," Victoria Woodhull* (New York, 1928), p. 77.
[14] G. S. Darewin, *A Synopsis of the Lives of Victoria C. Woodhull and Tennessee Claflin* (London, 18   ), p. 17.
[15] Rheta Childe Dorr, *Susan B. Anthony, The Woman Who Changed the Mind of a Nation* (New York, 1928), p. 234.
[16] Sachs, *op. cit.*, p. 80.
[17] Elizabeth Cady Stanton and others, *History of Woman Suffrage* (New York, 1882), II, 482.
[18] Harper, *The Life and Work of Susan B. Anthony*, I, 382 n.
[19] Robinson Scrapbook, III, 193.
[20] Harper, *op. cit.*, I, 429.   [21] *Dictionary of American Biography*, XX, 494.
[22] Sachs, *op. cit.*, p. 201.
[23] B. F. Butler to Brotherhood of Locomotive Engineers, Butler Manuscript, Feb. 3, 1872.
[24] William A. Richardson to B. F. Butler, Butler Manuscript, Jan. 5, 1872.
[25] Barnes, *Memoir of Thurlow Weed*, II, 501.
[26] Boston *Weekly Journal*, Jan. 13, 1893.
[27] Milton, *The Age of Hate*, p. 431.   [28] *Ibid.*, p. 430.
[29] Hoar, *Autobiography of Seventy Years*, I, 334.
[30] Rollo Ogden, *Life and Letters of Edwin Laurence Godkin* (New York, 1907), II, 93.
[31] Edward Winslow Martin, *Behind the Scenes in Washington* (Washington, 1873), p. 206.
[32] Bland, *Life of Benjamin F. Butler*, p. 179.
[33] H. J. Eckenrode and P. W. Wight, *Rutherford B. Hayes* (New York, 1930), p. 116.
[34] Hoar, *op. cit.*, I, 355.   [35] *Butler's Book*, p. 925.
[36] Oberholtzer, *A History of the United States*, III, 72.
[37] Rhodes, *History of the United States*, VII, 20.
[38] Storey, *The Record of Benjamin F. Butler*, p. 62.
[39] W. S. Robinson, *The Salary Grab* (Boston, 1873), p. 18.
[40] Oberholtzer, *op. cit.*, III, 74.
[41] James Parton to B. F. Butler, Butler Manuscript, Nov. 12, 1882.
[42] Robinson Scrapbook, III, 241.   [43] W. S. Robinson, *op. cit.*, p. 76.
[44] Oberholtzer, *op. cit.*, III, 130.
[45] Fred E. Haynes, *Third Party Movements Since the Civil War* (Iowa City, 1916), p. 102.
[46] Hesseltine, *Grant*, p. 323.   [47] Strong, *op. cit.*, IV, 485.
[48] *Harper's Weekly*, April 11, 1874.
[49] Denis Tilden Lynch, *"Boss" Tweed* (New York, 1927), p. 350.

[50] Albert Bigelow Paine, *Th. Nast: His Period and His Pictures* (New York, 1904), p. 92.

[51] Edward P. Mitchell, *Memoirs of an Editor* (New York, 1924), p. 104.

[52] Helen Todd, *A Man Named Grant* (Boston, 1940), p. 230.

[53] *Butler's Book*, p. 80.   [54] Conwell, *Hon. Benjamin F. Butler*, p. 8.

[55] Samuel S. Cox, *Three Decades of Federal Legislation* (Providence, 1886), p. 425.

[56] Storey, *op. cit.*, p. 65.   [57] Oberholtzer, *Jay Cooke*, II, 499.

[58] Storey, *op. cit.*, p. 67.   [59] *Ibid.*, p. 70.   [60] Hoar, *op. cit.*, I, 344.

[61] Storey, *op. cit.*, p. 74.   [62] *Ibid.*, p. 76.

[63] New York *Tribune*, Jan. 12, 1893.   [64] *Butler's Book*, p. 1010.

[65] New York *Tribune*, Jan. 12, 1893.   [66] New York *Times*, Jan. 12, 1893.

[67] Oberholtzer, *A History of the United States*, III, 179.

[68] Storey, *op. cit.*, p. 52.   [69] Bowers, *The Tragic Era*, p. 422.

[70] New York *Tribune*, April 8, 1874.   [71] Storey, *op. cit.*, p. 54.

[72] New York *Tribune*, April 8, 1874.

[73] Oberholtzer, *A History of the United States*, III, 134.

[74] Storey, *op. cit.*, p. 52.   [75] *Ibid.*, p. 57.

[76] New York *Tribune*, April 8, 1874.   [77] Bowers, *op. cit.*, p. 422.

[78] New York *World*, March 31, 1874.   [79] Rhodes, *op. cit.*, VII, 23.

[80] George S. Boutwell, *Reminiscences of Sixty Years in Public Affairs* (New York, 1903), II, 283.

[81] Oberholtzer, *A History of the United States*, III, 140.

[82] *Butler's Book*, p. 925.   [83] Hesseltine, *op. cit.*, p. 357.

[84] Cox, *op. cit.*, p. 596.   [85] Muzzey, *James G. Blaine*, p. 74.

[86] Josephson, *op. cit.*, p. 96.   [87] Hayes, *Diary and Letters*, III, 269.

[88] Conwell, *op. cit.*, p. 4.   [89] *Harper's Weekly*, Feb. 27, 1875.

[90] Macrae, *The Americans at Home*, I, 157.

[91] Medical certificate of Sarah Butler's death, signed by Arthur Folsom, Butler Manuscript, April 8, 1876.

[92] George S. Boutwell to B. F. Butler, Butler Manuscript, April 8, 1876.

[93] *Butler's Book*, p. 926.

[94] Roscoe Conkling to B. F. Butler, Butler Manuscript, Nov. 2, 1876.

[95] St. Joseph (Mo.) *Herald*, Nov. 12, 1876.   [96] Hayes, *op. cit.*, III, 638.

[97] Blaine, *Twenty Years of Congress*, II, 589.   [98] Hoar, *op. cit.*, I, 363.

[99] Edward Mitchell, *op. cit.*, p. 301.

[100] Roy Meredith, *Mr. Lincoln's Camera Man, Mathew B. Brady* (New York, 1946), p. 220.

[101] Thomas A. Edison, "The Phonograph and Its Future," *North American Review*, New York (May–June, 1878), CCLXII, 527. As Edison was a client of Butler's, the general might have seen the article before its publication.

[102] Thomas A. Edison to B. F. Butler, Butler Manuscript, Feb. 19, 1878.

[103] Frank Lewis Dyer and Thomas Commerford Martin, *Edison, His Life and Inventions* (New York, 1910), I, 217.

[104] Hoar, *op. cit.*, I, 358.   [105] Hayes, *op. cit.*, III, 508.

[106] Oberholtzer, *A History of the United States*, III, 187.

[107] Eckenrode, *op. cit.*, p. 123.   [108] *Butler's Book*, p. 976.

[109] Oberholtzer, *A History of the United States*, IV, 38.

[110] *Harper's Weekly*, Oct. 19, 1878.

[111] Allan Nevins, *Abram S. Hewitt* (New York, 1935), p. 289.

[112] Bland, *op. cit.*, p. 189.   [113] Boston *Weekly Journal*, Jan. 13, 1893.

[114] Storey, *op. cit.*, p. 5.

[115] Oberholtzer, *A History of the United States*, IV, 378.

[116] Schurz, *Reminiscences*, III, 393.

[117] Boston *Weekly Journal*, Jan. 13, 1893.

[118] Oberholtzer, *A History of the United States*, III, 343.

[119] *Harper's Weekly*, Oct. 26, 1878.   [120] *Harper's Weekly*, Jan. 18, 1879.

[121] Boston *Weekly Journal*, Jan. 13, 1893.

[122] *Harper's Weekly*, Nov. 22, 1879.

[123] M. P. Curran, *Life of Patrick A. Collins* (Norwood, Mass., 1906), p. 93.

[124] Clemenceau, *American Reconstruction*, p. 268.

[125] *Butler's Book*, p. 967.   [126] *Ibid.*, p. 79.

[127] George Scoville to B. F. Butler, Butler Manuscript, Oct. 15, 1881.

[128] H. H. Alexander, *The Life of Guiteau and the Official History of the Most Exciting Case on Record* (Detroit, 1882), p. 70. Actually the missing letter is part of the Butler Manuscript today; see Note 127.

CHAPTER XVII

[1] Boston *Weekly Journal*, Jan. 13, 1893.

[2] James Parton to B. F. Butler, Butler Manuscript, Nov. 12, 1882.

[3] Clara Barton to B. F. Butler, Butler Manuscript, Nov. 10, 1882.

[4] Percy H. Epler, *The Life of Clara Barton* (New York, 1932), p. 90.

[5] *Ibid.*, p. 240.   [6] *Dictionary of American Biography*, III, 359.

[7] Hart, *Commonwealth History of Massachusetts*, IV, 605.

[8] *Butler's Book*, p. 969.   [9] Hoar, *Autobiography of Seventy Years*, I, 346.

[10] *Ibid.*, I, 347.   [11] Bradford, *Damaged Souls*, p. 246.

[12] *Exercises at the Centennial Celebration on the Founding of Phillips Exeter Academy*, p. 59.

[13] *Ibid.*, p. 62.   [14] Henry James, *Charles W. Eliot* (Boston, 1930), II, 106.

[15] Boston *Globe*, Jan. 11, 1893.   [16] *Butler's Book*, p. 976.

[17] *Dictionary of American Biography*, III, 359.   [18] Hoar, *op. cit.*, I, 361.

[19] Thomas B. Reed, *Modern Eloquence* (Philadelphia, 1900), I, 174.

[20] Edward Sandford Martin, *The Life of Joseph Hodges Choate* (New York), 1920, I, 362.

[21] *Harper's Weekly*, June 9, 1883.   [22] Albany *Evening Post*, June 21, 1883.

[23] B. F. Butler to Blanche Butler Ames, Butler Manuscript, June 29, 1883.

[24] *Butler's Book*, p. 81.   [25] Lowell *Sun*, Sept. 7, 1918.

[26] *Butler's Book*, p. 867.   [27] *Ibid.*, p. 974.   [28] *Ibid.*, p. 965.

[29] Boston *Globe*, Jan. 12, 1893.   [30] Hoar, *op. cit.*, II, 219.

[31] Reed, *op. cit.*, I, 110.   [32] *Dictionary of American Biography*, III, 359.

[33] *Butler's Book*, p. 972.   [34] Curran, *Life of Patrick A. Collins*, p. 95.

[35] Hoar, *op. cit.*, I, 356.   [36] *Butler's Book*, p. 981.

CHAPTER XVIII

[1] New York *Times*, Jan. 12, 1893.   [2] Reed, *Modern Eloquence*, I, 179.

[3] Stanwood, *A History of Presidential Elections*, p. 375.

[4] Allan Nevins, *Grover Cleveland* (New York, 1932), p. 112.

[5] B. F. Butler to H. G. Hinkley, Butler Manuscript, Oct. 19, 1882.

[6] The platform: greenbacks should be issued "in sufficient quantities to supply the actual demands of trade." It was demanded that greenbacks be substituted for national bank notes (Harrison Cook Thomas, *The Return of the Democratic Party to Power in 1884* [New York, 1919], p. 138).

[7] Muzzey, *James G. Blaine*, p. 294.

[8] Haynes, *Third Party Movements Since the Civil War,* p. 149. Of the sometime Democrat, Republican, Democrat, Greenbacker, Anti-Monopolist it was said: "This surely was boxing the political compass thoroughly; but it did not imply any peculiar volatility on Butler's part. Throughout all he was rigidly consistent with his own character" (Harry Pratt Judson, "American Politics: A Study of Four Careers," *Review of Reviews,* New York [March, 1893], VII, 159).

[9] Muzzey, *op. cit.,* p. 280.   [10] *Ibid.,* p. 293.   [11] Nevins, *op. cit.,* p. 151.

[12] Edward Stanwood, *A History of the Presidency* (Boston, 1898), p. 393.

[13] Denis Tilden Lynch, *Grover Cleveland* (New York, 1932), p. 200.

[14] Thomas, *op. cit.,* p. 101.   [15] *Ibid.,* p. 185.   [16] Muzzey, *op. cit.,* p. 295 n.

[17] Lynch, *op. cit.,* p. 203.   [18] Haynes, *op. cit.,* p. 149.

[19] Muzzey, *op. cit.,* p. 294. It was not until August that Butler got around to accepting the Greenback and Anti-Monopoly nominations that had been offered him in May. To these parties he denounced the Democratic program as a mere vote catcher, while the Republicans were pointed out as the party of privilege and monopoly. He warned the workers that "those who ape the British aristocracy" were trying to get control of the government and labor could expect nothing from either of the old parties (Thomas, *op. cit.,* p. 209).

[20] Thomas, *loc. cit.*   [21] Muzzey, *op. cit.,* p. 305.

[22] New York *Post,* Jan. 11, 1893.   [23] Curran, *Life of Patrick A. Collins,* p. 92.

[24] Muzzey, *op. cit.,* p. 304.   [25] *Harper's Weekly,* Aug. 23, 1884.

[26] Oberholtzer, *A History of the United States,* IV, 200 n.

[27] Lynch, *op. cit.,* p. 257. H. J. Clark declared that the main claim of Butler for labor support was the fact that "all the snobs and all the dilettantes hate him, and Harvard College won't make him a doctor of laws" (Thomas, *op. cit.,* p. 139).

[28] *Letters of Grover Cleveland,* ed. Allan Nevins (Boston, 1933), p. 42.

[29] *Ibid.,* p. 40.   [30] Chidsey, *The Gentleman From New York,* p. 373.

[31] *Harper's Weekly,* Oct. 11, 1884.   [32] *Ibid.,* Sept. 13, 1884.

[33] Henry George, *Complete Works* (New York, 1900), X, 449.

[34] New York *World,* Oct. 20, 1884.   [35] *Harper's Weekly,* Nov. 11, 1884.

[36] Samuel Gompers, *Seventy Years of Life and Labor* (New York, 1925), II, 78.

[37] *Harper's Weekly,* Sept. 6, 1884.

[38] Frank M. O'Brien, *The Story of the* Sun (New York, 1928), p. 192.

[39] Harry W. Baehr, Jr., *The New York* Tribune *Since the Civil War* (New York, 1936), p. 234.

[40] Stanwood, *A History of the Presidency,* p. 409.

[41] Muzzey, *op. cit.,* p. 57.

[42] Commons, *History of Labor in the United States,* II, 440.

[43] Charles Edward Russell, *Blaine of Maine,* p. 402.

[44] New York *Tribune,* Jan. 12, 1893.   [45] New York *Times,* Jan. 12, 1893.

[46] R. T. Owen to B. F. Butler, Butler Manuscript, Nov. 8, 1882.

[47] West, *The Second Admiral,* p. 341.   [48] *Ibid.,* p. 344.   [49] *Ibid.*

[50] *Ibid.,* p. 342.   [51] *Butler's Book,* p. 15.

[52] Macartney, *Lincoln and His Generals,* p. 66.

[53] New York *World,* Jan. 12, 1893.   [54] Boston *Weekly Journal,* Jan. 13, 1893.

[55] *Butler's Book,* p. 463.   [56] *Ibid.,* p. 871.   [57] *Ibid.,* p. 860.

[58] *Ibid.,* p. 741.   [59] *Ibid.,* p. 812.   [60] *Ibid.,* p. 807.   [61] *Ibid.,* p. 1010.

[62] *Ibid.,* p. 752.   [63] *Ibid.,* p. 264.   [64] *Ibid.,* p. 865.

[65] Richard Nelson Current, *Old Thad Stevens* (Madison, Wis., 1942), p. 32.

[66] *Butler's Book,* p. 568.   [67] Hoar, *Autobiography of Seventy Years,* I, 329.

[68] *Butler's Book,* p. 39.   [69] Letter now owned by the author.

[70] New York *Tribune,* Jan. 12, 1893.   [71] New York *Times,* Jan. 12, 1893.

72 *Butler's Book,* p. 991.

73 Wendell Phillips to B. F. Butler, Butler Manuscript, April 21, 1882.

74 Bland, *Life of Benjamin F. Butler,* p. 16.

75 B. F. Butler to Mr. Steine, Butler Manuscript, Oct. 15, 1881.

76 Roger A. Pryor to B. F. Butler, Butler Manuscript, Dec. 27, 1881.

77 O. D. Barrett to B. F. Butler, Butler Manuscript, Nov. 22, 1882.

78 *Juilliard* v. *Greenman,* 110 U.S. 421 (1884).

79 *Butler* v. *National Home for Disabled Volunteer Soldiers,* 144 U.S. 64 (1892).

80 William E. Chandler, *Address Before the Grafton and Coos Bar Association* (Concord, N.H., 1888), p. 13.

81 Bland, *op. cit.,* p. 15.   82 *Butler's Book,* p. 994.

83 Boston *Globe,* Jan. 11, 1893.   84 *Ibid.,* Jan. 12, 1893.

85 New York *Tribune,* Jan. 12, 1893.

86 Henry Irving Dodge, "Forty Years on Twenty-Third Street," *Valentine's Manual of Old New York* (New York, 1924), p. 92.

87 New York *Post,* Jan. 11, 1893.   88 New York *Times,* Jan. 12, 1893.

89 New York *Tribune,* Jan. 12, 1893.

90 Boston *Weekly Journal,* Jan. 13, 1893.   91 New York *Post,* Jan. 11, 1893.

92 Boston *Weekly Journal,* Jan. 13, 1893.   93 New York *Post,* Jan. 11, 1893.

94 New York *Tribune,* Jan. 12, 1893.   95 Boston *Globe,* Jan. 12, 1893.

96 New York *Post,* Jan. 11, 1893.   97 *Ibid.,* Jan. 17, 1893.

98 Boston *Weekly Journal,* Jan. 13, 1893.   99 New York *Post,* Jan. 12, 1893.

100 New York *Herald,* Jan. 16, 1893.   101 New York *Times,* Jan. 16, 1893.

102 Boston *Weekly Journal,* Jan. 20, 1893.   103 *Ibid.*

104 *Ibid.,* Jan. 13, 1893.   105 New York *Times,* Jan. 16, 1893.

106 New York *Herald,* Jan. 12, 1893.

CHAPTER XIX

1 Welles, *Diary,* I, 209; I, 373.

2 Browning, *Diary,* II, 65; Parton, *General Butler in New Orleans,* p. 291.

3 *Butler's Book,* p. 13.   4 *Ibid.,* p. 77.

5 Chandler, *Address Before the Grafton and Coos Bar Association,* p. 14.

6 Boston *Globe,* Jan. 12, 1893.

7 Clemenceau, *American Reconstruction,* p. 168.

8 Gorham, *Life . . . of Edwin M. Stanton,* I, 314.

9 *Butler's Book,* p. 741.   10 *Ibid.,* p. 998.

11 Boston *Globe,* Jan. 12, 1893.

12 Plympton, *The Patriotic Service of . . . Butler,* p. 29.

13 New York *World,* Jan. 12, 1893.

14 Hart, *Commonwealth History of Massachusetts,* IV, 66.

15 Nicolay and Hay, *Abraham Lincoln,* V, 276.

16 DeWitt, *The Impeachment and Trial of Andrew Johnson,* p. 208.

17 Strong, *Diary,* IV, 114.

18 Blaine, *Twenty Years of Congress,* II, 289.   19 Parton, *op. cit.,* p. 412.

20 DeWitt, *op. cit.,* p. 422.

21 Orcutt, "Ben Butler and the 'Stolen Spoons,'" *North American Review,* New York (January, 1918), CCVII, 66.

22 Oberholtzer, *A History of the United States,* II, 93.

23 Charles Edward Russell, *Blaine of Maine,* p. 193.

24 James, *Charles W. Eliot,* II, 106.

25 Pierrepont, *A Review of General Butler's Defense,* p. 11.

[26] *Ibid.*, p. 21. "I thank Heaven for one thing, nothing more; I am a man that God made, not the newspapers" (B. F. Butler, *Speech Delivered in the House of Representatives February 27, 1873*, p. 14).

[27] Nevins, *Ordeal of the Union*, I, 157.   [28] *Butler's Book*, p. 822.

[29] *Ibid.*, p. 973. His wife doubtless recognized those words from her Shakespearean days (*The Merchant of Venice*), and on one occasion she wrote to her spouse: "So, so, 'sufferance is the badge of all your tribe,' is it? You make me smile. It is the one quality you most heartily abjure,—patience and sufferance will never be guests of yours. If pressed in they will get cheap entertainment and speedily be shown the door" (Butler, *Correspondence*, V, 363).

[30] Robinson Scrapbook, III, 205.

[31] Thomas Beer, *Hanna* (New York, 1929), p. 65.

[32] Sachs, *"The Terrible Siren," Victoria Woodhull*, p. 75.

[33] Badeau, *Military History of Ulysses S. Grant*, II, 259.

[34] Cowley, *A History of Lowell*, p. 174.

[35] New York *World*, Jan. 12, 1893.

[36] Major Otis B. Gunn, speech before the Farragut Post, G.A.R., Kansas City, Mo., Butler Manuscript, Feb. 9, 1893.

[37] James Harrison Wilson, *The Life of Charles A. Dana* (New York, 1907), II, 483. Not all of the general's contemporaries were so charitable. When Judge E. Rockwood Hoar was asked if he intended going to Butler's funeral, he replied, "No, but I am in favor of it" (Seitz, *The "Also Rans,"* p. 319).

[38] DeWitt, *op. cit.*, p. 423.   [39] Boston *Weekly Journal*, Jan. 13, 1893.

[40] Butler, *Correspondence*, III, 64.   [41] Parton, *op. cit.*, p. 36.

[42] DeWitt, *op. cit.*, p. 408.

[43] Lorenzo Sears, *Wendell Phillips, Orator and Agitator* (New York, 1909), p. 295.

[44] *Butler's Book*, p. 33.   [45] *Ibid.*, p. 80.   [46] *Ibid.*

[47] New York *Tribune*, Jan. 12, 1893.

[48] *Dictionary of American Biography*, III, 358.

[49] Adam Gurowski to B. F. Butler, Butler Manuscript, Jan. 3, 1863.

[50] DeWitt, *op. cit.*, p. 208.   [51] Schurz, *Reminiscences*, II, 226.

BIBLIOGRAPHY

MANUSCRIPT SOURCES

The Library of Congress in Washington possesses the Benjamin F. Butler Manuscript, consisting of letters, documents, commissions, newspaper clippings, and related material. These papers are arranged chronologically in 277 manuscript boxes. Apparently Butler never threw away anything: the boxes contain letters from his youth, a voluminous collection of deeds and other legal papers that he drew up since the earliest days of his legal practice, trunk checks, advertising material, letters of transmittal relating to seeds. The most extreme form of minutiae may appear next to a holograph letter of Abraham Lincoln.

The Boston Public Library has an eight-volume scrapbook prepared by William Stevens Robinson, journalist, pamphleteer, parliamentary lawyer, and clerk of the Massachusetts House of Representatives for many years. The scrapbooks contain letters to Robinson, personal souvenirs of him, and clippings from newspapers relating to the political history of Massachusetts, including Butler's gubernatorial campaigns and his governorship. This material has been pasted in ledgers, and for the purpose of citation the chronological number of each book is given together with the ledger page to which the cited material has been pasted. These books are sometimes referred to as the Butler Scrapbooks, but the Robinson Scrapbooks is a more accurate title and is the one employed here.

GOVERNMENT PUBLICATIONS

The *Official Records of the War of the Rebellion* was published by the Government Printing Office in Washington between 1880 and 1901. This work consists of 128 volumes. It is comprised primarily of dispatches and orders of the commanders and other officers in the field.

Use has been made of the published reports of United States and Massachusetts cases in which Butler participated.

NEWSPAPERS

Substantial reference was made to contemporary newspapers, as mentioned in footnotes in the text. National weeklies likewise were utilized, as indicated in the footnotes.

BOOKS AND ARTICLES

Abbott, John S. C., "Heroic Deeds of Heroic Men," *Harper's New Monthly Magazine,* New York (April, 1865), XXX, 575.

Adams, Charles Francis, *Charles Francis Adams.* Boston, 1900.

———, *An Autobiography.* Boston, 1916.

———, *Studies Military and Diplomatic, 1775–1865.* New York, 1911.

Adams, Henry, *The Education of Henry Adams.* Boston, 1918.

Alexander, H. H., *The Life of Guiteau and the Official History of the Most Exciting Case on Record.* Detroit, 1882.

Ambler, Charles H., *Francis H. Pierpont, Union War Governor of Virginia and Father of West Virginia.* Chapel Hill, N.C., 1937.

Ames, Blanche Butler, *The Butler Ancestry of Gen. Benjamin Franklin Butler in America.* Lowell, 1895.

[Anonymous], *Life and Public Services of Major-General Butler.* Philadelphia, 1864.

Appleton, Nathan, *Introduction of the Power Loom and Origin of Lowell.* Lowell, 1858.

Asbury, Herbert, *The French Quarter.* New York, 1936.

Austin, George Lowell, *The Life and Times of Wendell Phillips.* Boston, 1884.

Badeau, Adam, *Military History of Ulysses S. Grant.* New York, 1885, 3 vols.

Baehr, Harry W., Jr., *The New York* Tribune *Since the Civil War.* New York, 1936.

Bancroft, Frederic, *The Life of William H. Seward.* New York, 1900, 2 vols.

Barnes, Thurlow Weed, *Memoir of Thurlow Weed.* Boston, 1884, 2 vols.

Bates, Edward, *The Diary of, 1859–1866.* Washington, 1933.

Beale, Howard K., *The Critical Year.* New York, 1930.

Beer, Thomas, *Hanna.* New York, 1929.

Bell, Charles H., *History of the Town of Exeter.* Exeter, N.H., 1888.

Belmont, August, *A Few Letters and Speeches of the Late Civil War.* New York, 1870.

Bigelow, John, *Retrospections of an Active Life.* New York, 1909, 5 vols.

Bill, Alfred Hoyt, *The Beleaguered City.* New York, 1946.

Billington, Ray Allen, *The Protestant Crusade, 1800–1860.* New York, 1938.

Blackford, Charles Minor, *Letters From Lee's Army.* New York, 1947.

Blaine, James G., *Twenty Years of Congress.* Norwich, Conn., 1884, 2 vols.

Bland, T. A., *Life of Benjamin F. Butler.* Boston, 1879.

Boutwell, George S., *Reminiscences of Sixty Years in Public Affairs.* New York, 1902, 2 vols.

Bowen, Catherine Drinker. *Yankee From Olympus.* Boston, 1944.

Bowers, Claude, *The Tragic Era.* Boston, 1929.

Bradford, Gamaliel, *Damaged Souls.* Boston, 1923.

———, *Wives.* New York, 1925.

Brewer, David J., and others, eds., *The World's Best Orations.* Chicago, 1923, 10 vols.

Brooks, Noah, *Washington in Lincoln's Time.* New York, 1896.

Browne, A. G., Jr., *Sketch of the Official Life of John A. Andrew.* New York, 1868.

Browning, Orville Hickman, *The Diary of.* Springfield, Ill., 1933, 2 vols.

Buchanan, Lamont, *A Pictorial History of the Confederacy.* New York, 1951.

Burrage, Henry S., "The Beginnings of Waterville College, Now Colby University," *Collections and Proceedings of the Maine Historical Society.* Portland, Me., 1893, IV, 124.

Butler, Benjamin F., *Butler's Book: Autobiography and Personal Reminiscences.* Boston, 1892.

Butler, Benjamin F., *Ku-Klux Outrages in the South: The Work of the Democratic Party.* Washington, 1871.

———, *Official Documents Relating to a "Chaplain's Campaign (Not) With General Butler" but in New York.* Lowell, 1865.

———, *Private and Official Correspondence of, During the Period of the Civil War,* ed. Jessie Ames Marshall. Norwood, Mass., 1917, 5 vols.

———, *The Right of America to Present Her Claims Against Britain for Damages Without Menace.* Washington, 1872.

———, *Speech Delivered in the House of Representatives, February 27, 1873.* Washington, 1873.

———, *The Treaty of Washington.* Boston, 1871.

———, "Vice-Presidential Politics in '64," *North American Review,* New York (October, 1885), CXLI, 330.

Caldwell, Robert Granville, *James A. Garfield, Party Chieftain.* New York, 1931.

Carr, Joseph B., "Operations of 1861 About Fort Monroe," *Battles and Leaders of the Civil War,* ed. Robert Underwood Johnson and Clarence Clough Buel. New York, 1884–1888, 4 vols.

Cash, W. J., *The Mind of the South.* New York, 1941.

Caskey, Willie Malvin, *Secession and Restoration of Louisiana.* Baton Rouge, 1938.

Chandler, William E., *Address Before the Grafton and Coos Bar Association, January 6, 1888.* Concord, N.H., 1888.

Chesnut, Mary Boykin, *A Diary From Dixie.* New York, 1906.

Chidsey, Donald Barr, *The Gentleman From New York: A Life of Roscoe Conkling.* New Haven, 1935.

Clemenceau, Georges, *American Reconstruction, 1865–1870.* New York, 1928.

Cleveland, Grover, Letters of, 1850–1908, ed. Allan Nevins. Boston, 1933.

Cochran, Thomas C., and William Miller, *The Age of Enterprise: A Social History of Industrial America.* New York, 1942.

Cogswell, Elliott C., *History of Nottingham, Deerfield, and Northwood.* Manchester, N.H., 1878.

Cole, Arthur Charles, *The Irrepressible Conflict, 1850–1865.* New York, 1934.

Coleman, Charles H., *The Election of 1868: The Democratic Effort to Regain Control.* New York, 1933.

Commons, John R., and others, *History of Labour in the United States.* New York, 1918, 4 vols.

Conwell, Russell H., *Hon. Benjamin F. Butler. An Address Delivered Before the Aurora Club of Boston, Mass., July 31, 1874.* Boston, 1874.

Coolidge, John, *Mill and Mansion: A Study of Architecture and Society in Lowell, Massachusetts, 1820–1865.* New York, 1942.

Coulter, E. Merton, *The Confederate States of America.* Baton Rouge, 1950.

———, *The South During Reconstruction, 1865–1877.* Baton Rouge, 1947.

Cowley, Charles, *A Hand Book of Business in Lowell.* 1856.

———, *A History of Lowell.* Boston, 1868.

Cox, Samuel S., *Three Decades of Federal Legislation.* Providence, 1886.

Craven, Avery, *The Coming of the Civil War.* New York, 1950.

Crawford, J. B., *The Crédit Mobilier of America, Its Origin and History.* Boston, 1880.

Crippen, Leo F., *Simon Cameron.* Oxford, Ohio, 1906.

Curran, M. P., *Life of Patrick A. Collins.* Norwood, Mass., 1906.

Current, Richard Nelson, *Old Thad Stevens.* Madison, Wis., 1942.

Dabney, Thomas Ewing, "The Butler Regime in Louisiana," *Louisiana Historical Quarterly,* Baton Rouge (April, 1944), XVII, 487.

Dana, Charles A., *The Life of Ulysses S. Grant.* Springfield, Mass., 1868.

Darewin, G. S., *A Synopsis of the Lives of Victoria C. Woodhull and Tennessee Claflin.* London, 18 .

Davenport, John I., *The Election Frauds of New York City and Their Prevention.* New York, 1881, 2 vols.

Davidson, Marshall B., *Life in America.* Boston, 1951, 2 vols.

Davis, Jefferson, *The Rise and Fall of the Confederate Government.* New York, 1912, 2 vols.

Davis, William T., *History of the Judiciary of Massachusetts.* Boston, 1900.

Dawson, George Francis, *Life and Services of John A. Logan.* Chicago, 1887.

Desmond, Humphrey J., *The Know Nothing Party.* Washington, 1904.

DeWitt, David Miller, *The Impeachment and Trial of Andrew Johnson.* New York, 1903.

Dictionary of American Biography, ed. Allen Johnson. New York, 1928, 20 vols.

Dix, Morgan, *Memoirs of John Adams Dix.* New York, 1883, 2 vols.

Dodge, Henry Irving, "Forty Years on Twenty-third Street," *Valentine's Manual of Old New York, 1924.* New York, 1924.

John Dooley, Confederate Soldier, His War Journal. Washington, 1945.

Dorr, Rheta Childe, *Susan B. Anthony, The Woman Who Changed the Mind of a Nation.* New York, 1928.

Dowdey, Clifford, *Experiment in Rebellion.* Garden City, N.Y., 1946.

Du Bois, W. E. Burghardt, *Black Reconstruction.* New York, 1935.

Dumond, Dwight Lowell, *The Secession Movement, 1860–1861.* New York, 1931.

Dunning, William Archibald, *Reconstruction Political and Economic, 1865–1877.* New York, 1907.

Dyer, Frank Lewis, and Thomas Commerford Martin, *Edison, His Life and Inventions.* New York, 1910, 2 vols.

Eckenrode, H. J., and P. W. Wight, *Rutherford B. Hayes*. New York, 1930.

Edison, Thomas A., "The Phonograph and Its Future," *North American Review*, New York (May–June, 1878), CCLXII, 527.

Ehrich, Louis R., *The Question of Silver*. New York, 1896.

Eisenschiml, Otto, *In the Shadow of Lincoln's Death*. New York, 1940.

——, *Why Was Lincoln Murdered?* New York, 1939.

——, and Ralph Newman, *The American Iliad*. Indianapolis, 1947.

Epler, Percy H., *The Life of Clara Barton*. New York, 1932.

Exercises at the Centennial Celebration on the Founding of Phillips Exeter Academy, New Hampshire, June 20 and 21, 1883. Exeter, 1884.

Ficklen, John Rose, "History of Reconstruction in Louisiana," *Johns Hopkins University Studies in Historical and Political Science*, Baltimore, 1940, XXVIII, 9.

Field, Maunsell B., *Memoirs of Many Men*. New York, 1874.

Fish, Carl Russell, *American Diplomacy*. New York, 1923.

Fiske, John, *The Mississippi Valley in the Civil War*. Boston, 1900.

Flick, Alexander Clarence, *Samuel Jones Tilden*. New York, 1939.

Flower, Milton E., *James Parton: The Father of Modern Biography*. Durham, N.C., 1951.

Freeman, Douglas Southall, *R. E. Lee*. New York, 1935, 4 vols.

——, *Lee's Lieutenants*. New York, 1942–1944, 3 vols.

Fuess, Claude M., *The Life of Caleb Cushing*. New York, 1923, 2 vols.

Fuller, J. F. C., *The Generalship of Ulysses S. Grant*. London, 1929.

The Gatling Gun. Official Reports of Trials, Description, General Directions, Targets, &c. Hartford, 1878.

George, Henry, *Complete Works*. New York, 1900, 10 vols.

Golder, Frank A., "The Purchase of Alaska," *American Historical Review*, Washington (April, 1921), XXV, 411.

Gompers, Samuel, *Seventy Years of Life and Labor*. New York, 1925, 2 vols.

Gordon, George H., *A War Diary of Events in the War of the Great Rebellion, 1863–1865*. Boston, 1882.

Gorham, George C., *Life and Public Services of Edwin M. Stanton*. Boston, 1899, 2 vols.

Grant, Ulysses S., *Personal Memoirs*. New York, 1886, 2 vols.

Grayson, Theodore J., *Leaders and Periods of American Finance*. New York, 1932.

Greeley, Horace, *The American Conflict*. Hartford, Conn., 1864.

Gurowski, Adam, *Diary*. New York, 1864, 2 vols.

Harper, Ida Husted, *The Life and Work of Susan B. Anthony*. Indianapolis, 1898, 3 vols.

Harrington, Fred Harvey, *Fighting Politician, Major General N. P. Banks*. Philadelphia, 1948.

Harris, Wilmer C., *Public Life of Zachariah Chandler, 1851–1875*. Lansing, Mich., 1917.

Hart, Albert Bushnell, *Salmon Portland Chase*. Boston, 1899.

Hart, Albert Bushnell, ed., *Commonwealth History of Massachusetts*. New York, 1900, 5 vols.

Hay, Clara, ed., *Letters of John Hay and Extracts From His Diary*. Washington, 1908, 3 vols.

Haydon, F. Stansbury, *Aeronautics in the Union and Confederate Armies*. Baltimore, 1941.

Hayes, Rutherford Birchard, *Diary and Letters*. Columbus, Ohio, 1922, 5 vols.

Haynes, Fred E., *Third Party Movements Since the Civil War*. Iowa City, Ia., 1916.

Hendricks, Burton J., *Lincoln's War Cabinet*. Boston, 1946.

Henry, Robert Selph, *The Story of the Confederacy*. Indianapolis, 1931.

————, *The Story of Reconstruction*. Indianapolis, 1938.

Hesseltine, William B., *Ulysses S. Grant, Politician*. New York, 1935.

————, *Lincoln and the War Governors*. New York, 1948.

Hill, Frederick Trevor, *Decisive Battles of the Law*. New York, 1907.

Hoar, George F., *Autobiography of Seventy Years*. New York, 1905, 2 vols.

Horn, Stanley F., *The Invisible Empire*. Boston, 1939.

Howe, Henry Warren, *Passages From the Life of*. Lowell, Mass., 1899.

Hudson, Henry Newman, *A Chaplain's Campaign with Gen. Butler*. New York, 1865.

Irwin, Richard B., "Military Operations in Louisiana in 1862," *Battles and Leaders of the Civil War*, ed. Robert Underwood Johnson and Clarence Clough Buel. New York, 1884–1888, 4 vols.

James, Henry, *Charles W. Eliot*. Boston, 1930, 2 vols.

Johnston, David E., *The Story of a Confederate Boy in the Civil War*. Portland, Ore., 1914.

Jones, J. B., *A Rebel War Clerk's Diary*. Philadelphia, 1866, 2 vols.

Jordan, Donaldson, and Edwin J. Pratt, *Europe and the American Civil War*. Boston, 1931.

Josephson, Matthew, *The Politicos*. New York, 1938.

Judson, Harry Pratt, "American Politics: A Study of Four Careers," *Review of Reviews*, New York (March, 1893), VII, 159.

Julian, George W., *Political Recollections, 1840 to 1872*. Chicago, 1884.

Kautz, Albert, "Incidents of the Occupation of New Orleans," *Century Illustrated Monthly Magazine*, New York (July, 1886), XXXII, 455.

Kendall, John Smith, *History of New Orleans*. Chicago, 1922, 3 vols.

Keyes, E. D., *Fifty Years' Observation of Men and Events, Civil and Military*. New York, 1884.

Kibler, Lillian Adele, *Benjamin F. Perry, South Carolina Unionist*. Durham, N.C., 1946.

Kohler, Max J., "The Board of Delegates of American Israelites," *Publications of the American Jewish Historical Society*, XXIX, New York, 1925.

Laughlin, J. Laurence, *The History of Bimetallism in the United States*. New York, 1896.

Leech, Margaret, *Reveille in Washington*. New York, 1941.

Lewis, Lloyd, *Sherman, Fighting Prophet*. New York, 1932.

Liddell Hart, B. H., *Sherman: Soldier, Realist, American*. New York, 1929.

Logan, Mrs. John A., *Reminiscences of a Soldier's Wife*. New York, 1913.

Lonn, Ella, *Desertion During the Civil War*. New York, 1928.
———, *Foreigners in the Confederacy*. Chapel Hill, N.C., 1940.
Lossing, Benson J., *Pictorial History of the Civil War*. Hartford, 1868, 3 vols.
Lothrop, Thornton Kirkland, *William Henry Seward*. Boston, 1898.
Lynch, Denis Tilden, *"Boss" Tweed*. New York, 1927.
———, *Grover Cleveland*. New York, 1932.
Macartney, Clarence Edward, *Lincoln and His Generals*. Philadelphia, 1925.
McCall, Samuel W., *Thaddeus Stevens*. Boston, 1909.
McClellan, George B., *McClellan's Own Story*. New York, 1887.
McCormick, Robert R., *Ulysses S. Grant, The Great Soldier of America*. New York, 1934.
McFee, William, *The Law of the Sea*. Philadelphia, 1950.
McLaughlin, Andrew C., *A Constitutional History of the United States*. New York, 1935.
[McLaughlin, James Fairfax], *The American Cyclops*. Baltimore, 1868.
McMaster, John Bach, *A History of the People of the United States During Lincoln's Administration*. New York, 1927.
Macrae, David, *The Americans at Home*. Edinburgh, 1870, 2 vols.
Mahan, Alfred T., *Admiral Farragut*. New York, 1905.
Martin, Edward Sandford, *The Life of Joseph Hodges Choate*. New York, 1920, 2 vols.
Martin, Edward Winslow, *Behind the Scenes in Washington*. Washington, 1873.
Meade, George, *The Life and Letters of George Gordon Meade*. New York, 1913, 2 vols.
Meredith, Roy, *Mr. Lincoln's Camera Man, Mathew B. Brady*. New York, 1946.
Merrill, Louis Taylor, *General Benjamin F. Butler and the Campaign of 1868*, doctoral dissertation. University of Chicago, 1939.
———, "General Butler in Washington," *Columbia Historical Society Records*, Columbia, S.C. (1938), XXXIX, 71.
Miles, Henry A., *Lowell, As It Was and As It Is*. Lowell, 1845.
Milton, George Fort, *The Age of Hate*. New York, 1930.
———, *Conflict*. New York, 1941.
Mitchell, Edward P., *Memoirs of an Editor*. New York, 1924.
Mitchell, Stewart, *Horatio Seymour of New York*. Cambridge, Mass., 1938.
Muzzey, David Saville, *James G. Blaine*. New York, 1934.
Nevins, Allan, *Hamilton Fish: The Inner History of the Grant Administration*. New York, 1936.
———, *Grover Cleveland*. New York, 1932.
———, *Abram S. Hewitt*. New York, 1935.
———, *Ordeal of the Union*. New York, 1947, 2 vols.
Nichols, Roy Franklin, *The Disruption of American Democracy*. New York, 1948.
Nicolay, Helen, *Lincoln's Secretary*. New York, 1949.
Nicolay, John G., and John Hay, *Abraham Lincoln: A History*. New York, 1890, 10 vols.

Oberholtzer, Ellis Paxson, *Jay Cooke, Financier of the Civil War*. Philadelphia, 1907, 2 vols.

———, *A History of the United States Since the Civil War*. New York, 1917–1937, 5 vols.

O'Brien, Frank M., *The Story of the Sun*. New York, 1928.

Ogden, Rollo, *Life and Letters of Edwin Laurence Godkin*. New York, 1907, 2 vols.

Orcutt, William Dana, "Ben Butler and the 'Stolen Spoons,'" *North American Review*, New York (January, 1918), CCVII, 66.

Owsley, Frank Lawrence, *King Cotton Diplomacy*. Chicago, 1931.

Paine, Albert Bigelow, *Th. Nast: His Period and His Pictures*. New York, 1904.

Parker, Margaret Terrell, *Lowell: A Study of Industrial Development*. New York, 1940.

Parton, James, *General Butler in New Orleans*. New York, 1864.

Pickett, George E. (letters of), *The Heart of a Soldier*. New York, 1913.

Pickett, La Salle, *Pickett and His Men*. Atlanta, 1899.

———, "The Wartime Story of General Pickett," *Cosmopolitan Magazine*, New York (July, 1914), LVI, 196.

———, *What Happened to Me*. New York, 1917.

Pierrepont, Edwards, *A Review of General Butler's Defense, Before the House of Representatives in Relation to the New Orleans Gold*. New York, 1865.

Plympton, Noah A., *The Patriotic Service of Gen. Benjamin F. Butler*. Boston, 1896.

Pomeroy, M. M., *Life and Public Services of Benjamin F. Butler*. New York, 1868.

Poore, Ben: Perley, *Reminiscences of Sixty Years in the National Metropolis*. Philadelphia, 1886, 2 vols.

Porter, David D., *The Naval History of the Civil War*. New York, 1886.

Pratt, Fletcher, *Ordeal by Fire*. New York, 1935.

Pryor, Mrs. Roger A., *My Day, Reminiscences of a Long Life*. New York, 1909.

[Puffer, A. F.], "Our General," *Atlantic Monthly*, Boston (July, 1863), XII, 104.

Randall, J. G., *The Civil War and Reconstruction*. Boston, 1937.

———, *Constitutional Problems Under Lincoln*. New York, 1926.

———, *Lincoln the President*. New York, 1945, 1952, 3 vols.

Reed, Thomas B., *Modern Eloquence*. Philadelphia, 1900, 15 vols.

Report of the Joint Committee on the Conduct of the War. Washington, 1865, 3 vols.

Rhodes, James Ford, *History of the United States from the Compromise of 1850 to the Final Restoration of Home Rule in the South*. New York, 1902–1919, 8 vols.

Riddle, A. G., *The Life of Benjamin F. Wade*. Cleveland, 1886.

Robinson, Harriet H., *Loom and Spindle, or, Life Among the Early Mill Girls*. New York, 1898.

Robinson, W. S., *The Salary Grab*. Boston, 1873.

Ross, Edmund G., *History of the Impeachment of Andrew Johnson*. Santa Fe, N.M., 1896.

Russell, Charles Edward, *Blaine of Maine*. New York, 1931.

Russell, William Howard, *My Diary North and South*. Boston, 1863.

Sachs, Emanie, *"The Terrible Siren," Victoria Woodhull*. New York, 1928.

Sandburg, Carl, *Abraham Lincoln: The War Years*. New York, 1939, 4 vols.

Schurz, Carl, *Reminiscences*. New York, 1907, 3 vols.

Sears, Lorenzo, *Wendell Phillips, Orator and Agitator*. New York, 1909.

Seitz, Don C., *The "Also Rans."* New York, 1928.

————, *The Dreadful Decade*. Indianapolis, 1926.

Shannon, Fred Albert, *The Organization and Administration of the Union Army, 1861–1865*. Cleveland, 1928, 2 vols.

Sherman, John, *John Sherman's Recollections of Forty Years*. Chicago, 1895, 2 vols.

Sherman, W. T., *Memoirs*. New York, 1891, 2 vols.

Smith, Edward Conrad, *The Borderland in the Civil War*. New York, 1927.

Smith, William Ernest, *The Francis Preston Blair Family in Politics*. New York, 1933, 2 vols.

Smith, William Farrar, *From Chattanooga to Petersburg Under Generals Grant and Butler*. Boston, 1893.

Southwood, Marion, *"Beauty and Booty," The Watchword of New Orleans*. New York, 1867.

Stanton, Elizabeth Cady, and others, *History of Woman Suffrage*. New York, 1882, 4 vols.

Stanwood, Edward, *A History of the Presidency*. Boston, 1898.

————, *A History of Presidential Elections*. Boston, 1888.

Steiner, Bernard C., *Life of Reverdy Johnson*. Baltimore, 1914.

Stoddard, Henry Luther, *Horace Greeley*. New York, 1946.

[Stoddard, William Osborn], *The Volcano Under the City*. New York, 1887.

[Storey, Moorfield], *The Record of Benjamin F. Butler*. Boston, 1883.

Strong, George Templeton, *The Diary of*. New York, 1952, 4 vols.

Stryker, Lloyd Paul, *Andrew Johnson, A Study in Courage*. New York, 1936.

Studenski, Paul, and Herman B. Krooss, *Financial History of the United States*. New York, 1952.

Taussig, F. W., *The Silver Situation in the United States*. New York, 1900.

Thomas, Harrison Cook, *The Return of the Democratic Party to Power in 1884*. New York, 1919 (Columbia University Studies in History, Economics, and Public Law).

Todd, Helen, *A Man Named Grant*. Boston, 1940.

Townsend, George Alfred, *Rustics in Rebellion*. Chapel Hill, N.C., 1950.

Van Deusen, Glyndon G., *Thurlow Weed*. Boston, 1947.

Wallace, Lew, *An Autobiography*. New York, 1906, 2 vols.

Wallace, Sarah Agnes, and Frances Elma Gillespie, *The Journal of Benjamin Moran, 1857–1865*. Chicago, 1942, 2 vols.

Ware, Caroline F., *The Early New England Cotton Manufacture*. Boston, 1931.

Warren, Charles, *The Supreme Court in United States History*. Boston, 1922, 3 vols.

Watson, William, *Life in the Confederate Army.* New York, 1888.

Welles, Gideon, *Diary.* Boston, 1911, 3 vols.

West, Richard S., Jr., *Gideon Welles: Lincoln's Navy Department.* Indianapolis, 1943.

————, *The Second Admiral.* New York, 1937.

Whipple, Wayne, *The Story-Life of Lincoln.* N.p., 1908.

White, Andrew Dickson, *Autobiography.* London, 1905, 2 vols.

Whittemore, Edwin Carey, *Colby College, 1820–1925.* Waterville, Me., 1927.

Williams, Kenneth P., *Lincoln Finds a General.* New York, 1949, 1952, 3 vols.

Williams, T. Harry, *Lincoln and His Generals.* New York, 1952.

————, *Lincoln and the Radicals.* Madison, Wis., 1941.

Williams, Thomas, "Letters of General Thomas Williams, 1862," *American Historical Review,* Washington (January, 1909), XIV, 22.

Wilson, James Harrison, *The Life of Charles A. Dana.* New York, 1907, 2 vols.

————, *The Life of John A. Rawlins.* New York, 1916.

Wolf, Simon, *The Presidents I Have Known From 1860–1918.* Washington, 1918.

Woodward, W. E., *Meet General Grant.* New York, 1928.

Young, John Russell, *Around the World with General Grant.* New York, 1879, 2 vols.

INDEX

DATE DUE

25